TRAVELER'S GUIDE TO
Jewish Germany

To the memory of Marvin Lowenthal,
whose 1933 book, *A World Passed By,*
inspired us to seek out the past in the present

We are grateful to the Ronald S. Lauder Foundation
for its assistance with this book.

German title:
Reiseführer durch das jüdische Deutschland
© by Roman Kovar Verlag, Eichenau, Germany

Published in German by Roman Kovar Verlag
Published by arrangement in English in the rest of the world by
Pelican Publishing Company, Inc.

ISBN: 1-56554-254-1

Printed in Hong Kong

Published by Pelican Publishing Company, Inc.
1101 Monroe Street, Gretna, Louisiana 70053

TRAVELER'S GUIDE TO
Jewish Germany

Billie Ann Lopez
Peter Hirsch

PELICAN PUBLISHING COMPANY
Gretna 1998

CONTENTS

FOREWORD

No country in the world, outside of Israel itself, contains more Jewish historical sites of importance and significance than Germany today. The stones of ancient synagogues, mikvoth, and cemeteries eloquently bear witness to the life and culture of German Jewish communities for a thousand years or more. These monuments have not only withstood the turbulent passage of centuries, but even survived the concentrated efforts of the Third Reich to erase them from Germany's historical slate.

Many Jewish customs, rituals and traditions, ways of dressing, family names, even the Yiddish language and the Talmudic teaching still practiced today trace their origins back to the Jewish communities of Germany. Thus German history is Jewish history for large parts of the centuries preceding the Holocaust. Some of the most revered voices in European Jewish history, Gershom ben Judah, Rashi, Meir of Rothenburg, Moses Mendelssohn, Samson Raphael Hirsch, Leopold Zunz, and Martin Buber, to name a very few, were first heard here.

A curious cause emerges for the existence of a thousand years of continuous Jewish settlement in Germany. Germany was not a state with a strong central power until the late 19th century. Instead it was made up of small princely and city territories which were often bitterly opposed or even at war with each other. The German King and Roman Emperor held only nominal power over the German states during most of the eight centuries that the "Holy Roman Empire of the German Nation" existed, from 962 to 1806.

Centralized states like England, France, Portugal and Spain expelled their entire Jewish populations at some point in their histories, thereby destroying community life as well as the sites in which their traditions and rites were practiced. In Germany, when the tide turned against the Jews in one area, they were often able to seek refuge in an adjoining area until the situation reversed itself and they were once again invited back to pay the high taxes that allowed them to enjoy the new protections and guarantees of safety, often meaningless, being offered in exchange. It was not until the Nazis came to power that Germany far surpassed the barbarities of other nations and earlier times.

Because of the systematic murder or expulsion of half a million German Jews and the massive destruction of Jewish property and institutions during the Nazi regime, it is widely believed that few sites of historical significance could have survived those years. However, that is not the case.

The Nazis and their supporters did burn almost all the synagogues and other Jewish community buildings in the larger cities and towns throughout the country on "Reichskristallnacht", November 9-10, 1938. However, many hundreds of smaller towns and villages did not destroy their synagogues because either they had been sold to Christians before or the lack of proper fire brigades meant a risk of burning down neighboring buildings or the whole village. During the war, many of these synagogue buildings were converted to homes, businesses, barns, garages, or storehouses. After the war, and throughout the 1950s and 1960s as Germany rebuilt, many of these former synagogues were torn down. However, towards the end of the 1970s and on to the present, quite a number of these small towns and villages have raised public and private funds to restore their old synagogues and other Jewish historical sites of importance for use as both memorials and community centers.

Consequently, excavations, restorations, and rediscoveries in recent years have made it possible for visitors to view a thousand years of German Jewish history and culture through hundreds of surviving Jewish historical sites in Germany. In addition, new Jewish museums have been established in Augsburg, Berlin, and Frankfurt and many major museums now have Judaica on permanent display. Even many small local museums have dug into their attics and basements to come up with exhibits of Judaica for their particular communities or areas.

Although archeological finds indicate that Jews accompanied the Romans to what is now Germany some 2,000 years ago, evidence of continuous Jewish settlement begins in the Middle Ages. This Guide has been written to aid visitors interested in exploring German Jewish history and culture over the last thousand years.

Visitors seeking to explore Jewish Germany will find themselves traveling primarily outside of the large population centers because most of what survives will be found in the smaller towns and villages. We have personally visited the vast majority of these sites; only a very few were included without a personal visit in the interest of completeness. The Guide provides specific addresses, opening hours, and instructions for obtaining access wherever possible. However, particularly in rural areas, addresses are often meaningless or non-existent. In those cases the Guide provides detailed instructions as to what roads to use and where to turn.

A WORD OF CAUTION to users of this Guide. Interest in German Jewish history and culture is on the increase throughout the world and is reflected in the growing numbers of visitors to the few better known Jewish historical sites in Germany. However, many, if not most, sites included in this Guide are visited only occasionally. Consequently, opening hours are not always reliable. Sometimes persistence and ingenuity will help; sometimes not. This situation is, of course, frustrating when you've made a special trip to see a synagogue, mikveh, or cemetery and find you can't get in. Try to keep your travel schedule flexible. We have found local people and authorities extremely friendly and helpful in almost all instances; we hope you will have the same experience.

Work on this guide started in 1984 when we stumbled upon the wonderful ritual bath in Speyer. We started writing an article on this 12th century mikveh, then much to our surprise found out that there were a lot more surviving structures. First we wrote a guide to the former Federal Republic of Germany. After re-unification we expanded the guide to include the former German Democratic Republic.

Most of the information contained in our guide was collected though correspondence with city administrations, tourist offices or Jewish community centers. In addition we received information from many private persons or organizations who try to keep the Jewish heritage in Germany alive. We would like to take this opportunity to thank all the many people who have helped us with our work.

We would like to acknowledge the great efforts of many Germans who over the years have invested much of their time and money to maintain or restore a Jewish historical site in Germany. It requires no special effort to set a fire or knock over a gravestone; these activities of a tiny minority on the lunatic fringe make the headlines, while the patient work of thousands of people to keep the memory of Jewish life in Germany alive mostly goes unnoticed.

No guide can ever be complete. If you find mistakes, gaps or out of date information in this guide, please let us know so we can improve the next edition. You can reach us through our publisher. Thank you in advance.

We would also like to thank Irmgard Burmeister, Emmi Rosdolsky and Poldi Schnabl for their valuable aid in getting this guide written. Furthermore, our thanks go to the Ronald S. Lauder Foundation for its interest and its contribution towards the publication of this guide.

How to Get Around in Germany.

Germany has an excellent network of public transport by air, rail or road, both long range, medium range and local within most cities of some size. However, service intervals in rural areas may be long, making visits to small towns or villages by public transport not practical for those with limited time.

If you want to visit the larger cities (or, if you have enough time, even the small towns and villages) mentioned in our guide by public transport, the people to see are either German travel agents (Reisebüro) in big cities or German Rail (DB or Deutsche Bundesbahn) representatives in the general area that you wish to visit. They will have all the rail and bus schedules for their areas at hand and can help you to plan a route, provide the times of departure and arrival, tickets and reservations and provide you with the necessary documentation.

Trains and buses are usually well-run in Germany. Your hotel staff might be able to provide information, but often they will not have the necessary schedules if your destination is off the beaten track.

Renting a car is probably the most practical way for visiting many of the places listed in our guide. The familiar international car rental companies have offices in most large or medium-sized towns in Germany. Smaller, local companies might be able to offer you a better price. However, some of these companies have no offices outside their general area. If you want to return the car at a different location, make sure you can do that without a surcharge.

Every city, town or village listed in our guide comes with a set of specifications. These consist of the nearest "point of reference", the direction from this point of reference, the distance from it, the map sketch where you can find the site, major road(s) through or near the location and, if appropriate, a nearby landmark.

We use eleven major cities as points of reference. From north to south and west to east, these are: Hamburg, Berlin, Hannover, Köln (Cologne), Kassel, Erfurt, Dresden, Frankfurt, Nürnberg (Nuremberg), Stuttgart, München (Munich). By the way, we only use the German spelling for city names. In the back of the book you will find eleven maps for the regions around these points of reference.

The direction from these points of reference is approximate and given as north, northwest, west, southwest, and so on.

The distance given is in kilometers and is the approximate distance by major roads, not "as the crow flies". We realize that kilometers probably make it more complicated for you, but since all maps, road signs and other information will be in kilometers, this is really the only practical way. If you need to know miles, divide kilometers by 1.6 (or divide them by 8 and multiply the result by 5). On German highways, there is a 100 kilometer/hour speed limit; depending on conditions, you can expect to cover between 50 and 70 kilometers an hour on average. On motorways, there is no speed limit at the time of writing; however, a maximum speed of 130 kilometers/hour is recommended.

Roads mentioned in our guide as going near or through the location are either A for Autobahn (motorway) or B for Bundesstrasse (highway).

On most maps, motorways are represented as double red lines. The motorway number is given in a blue sign the shape of a barrel lying on its side both on the maps and the motorway signs. In our guide, motorway numbers are always given with a leading A (for Autobahn), for example A6.

Highways are usually represented by single, medium-wide red lines on maps. The highway number is given in a rectangular yellow sign both on maps and on highway signs. Regional roads (Landes- or Bezirksstrassen) are not numbered on most maps and represented by single, thin, red, yellow or white lines.

You will need a good map of Germany if you travel by car. Most rented cars come with maps. Make sure it is indexed, reasonably recent and has sufficient detail. Most maps with scales of 1:1,000,000 or so will not show some of the villages you may want to visit. The car rental company should be able to provide you with a road atlas with a scale of 1:500,000 or better, and an index. Motorway stations offer free maps with reasonable detail, but without an index.

We recommend that you also get a good general travel guide to Germany. The country is extremely rich in cultural heritage and natural sights, and a good guide will make your trip much more interesting. Most guides also provide a lot of information on German ways of life and customs.

Throughout our guide, we have treated the letters ä, ö, and ü (called Umlaut in German) like a, o and u wherever we provide alphabetical order listings. However, this usage is far from universal in German. Often, ä, ö and ü are treated like ae, oe and ue, respectively. If you can't find one of our place names in an index and the name contains an Umlaut, look it up as if the Umlaut were two letters; for example, Muenchen and Munchen would be far apart in an index of any size.

Once You Get There - Finding Your Way Around in Cities or Villages.

Our guide provides you with addresses. Here are our suggestions for finding the address once you have made it into town:

Large cities and many smaller cities in tourist areas have tourist offices that give away maps (free or at a low price) and also can help you find addresses on these maps. The tourist offices are usually in the center, either in or near city hall or the main train station.

Most cities and towns display maps on billboards at strategic locations. These maps are usually signposted with a white "i" (for information) on a blue, square sign. They may be located where the highway enters the city, or at the local tourist office, at city hall or the train station. Most of these maps are also indexed. Locate where you are and where your destination is; then make a rough sketch of the streets leading from one to the other. Don't forget to add street names to your sketch.

If the village is too small to have a map, and if there is more than one street, you will have to ask directions. Generally speaking, we have found people very willing to help. To make the asking easier, we have provided the most frequent questions in German on the next page. However, have paper and pencil ready when the answer comes and get your informant to draw a little map and provide street names (unless your German is good, of course). Don't forget, you will have to go to city hall in many cases to get the key.

In what used to be the German Democratic Republic, street names are still undergoing some changes. Be prepared to be directed to a street with a name different from what you asked for.

Where is the former synagogue, please?

Bitte, wo ist die alte Synagoge?

Where is the Jewish cemetery, please?

Bitte, wo ist der Judenfriedhof?

Where is the local museum, please?.

Bitte, wo ist das Heimatmuseum?

Where is city hall, please?

Bitte, wo ist das Rathaus?

I am looking for a street. (Have street name ready, either on a separate piece of paper or point it out in the guide).

Bitte, ich suche eine Strasse.

Proper Etiquette.

Synagogues and cemeteries are revered places for Jews. There are only a few basic rules, but try and keep them.

Dress should be moderate. Shorts, low-cut T-shirts, or bare chests are inappropriate (as they would be in churches or Christian cemeteries).

Men should always cover their heads in consecrated synagogues and cemeteries. Synagogues will sometimes provide skull caps for their visitors, but be prepared and bring your own hat or cap.

Everything that grows in a cemetery is considered the property of the dead and for their exclusive use. Please don't pick any flowers, even wild flowers, or break any twigs. Don't remove stones or fragments. Stones on top of a gravestone or a grave are a sign that the grave has been visited, a sign of respect and love like flowers in a Christian cemetery. Please don't remove them.

Some more Orthodox Jews object to photography and videography. If you take pictures in a synagogue or cemetery and somebody accosts you, stop immediately and put away your equipment. Be sensitive to the religious principle involved.

We have put this advice together from our experience in investigating the Jewish past in Germany for many years. Needless to say, there may be ideas for doing this that never occurred to us, and we may have omitted important facts simply because they seemed too obvious to us. Please let us know through our publishers if you have any comments.

CHRONOLOGY OF MAJOR HISTORICAL EVENTS IN GERMAN JEWISH LIFE AND CULTURE.

The history of the Jews in Germany started far from Central Europe and at a time when Germany did not yet exist. However, the events in Judaea almost 2,000 years ago have had an important influence on the history of Jews in Germany up to the present day.

70 Common Era - The defeat of the peoples of Judaea by the Romans and the destruction of the Temple in Jerusalem marks the beginning of almost 2,000 years of exile. The Jewish survivors are expelled by the victorious Romans and dispersed throughout the Roman empire, then comprising large parts of Western and Southern Europe, North Africa, and the Near East. Even Judaea, their country, is named Palestine after their old enemies, the Philistines. After the loss of their homeland, the Torah becomes the Jews' portable fatherland. In exile, the Talmud takes shape, adapting the Torah to a life without a Temple, without a geographical or political center.

During the remaining centuries of the Roman empire, Jews serve their Roman rulers in a variety of capacities such as merchants, soldiers, and slaves; eventually they are granted citizenship. Despite their citizenship, however, they must pay a special Jewish tax proclaimed by emperor Vespasian (70-79 C.E.). This special tax establishes one of the precedents whereby the emperors ruling the Holy Roman Empire more than a thousand years later justify their claim of ownership of all Jews and the special tax they levy on them.

306-337 - Constantine the Great makes the Roman empire Christian. Thereafter, Jews enjoy less religious tolerance and freedom than they had under most of Constantine's pagan predecessors.

Soon Jews are prohibited from serving in the army or holding public office. They are also prohibited from owning Christian slaves; pagan slaves who let themselves be baptized have to be set free. Since agriculture was impossible without slaves then, and most other occupations were also closed to Jews, commerce and trade become more and more important as primary occupations for Jews.

All these restrictions are included in the body of Roman law and will serve future rulers, who claimed to be the successors of the Roman emperors, as precedents to distinguish between the rights and the obligations of their Jewish and Christian subjects. However, the part of the Roman law giving citizenship to the Jews was conveniently forgotten.

The young Christian church which was still fighting for dominance—and sometimes for its survival—had an ambivalent attitude towards the Jews. On the one hand, the Jews were considered condemned because they refused to recognize the teachings of

Jesus and had caused him to be crucified; on the other hand, the holy books of the Jews were the foundation for the Christian bible and it was believed that the prophets had predicted the coming of the Messiah and Christianity. The church fathers were inclined to protect the Jews so they could serve as witnesses that the prophecies of the Old Testament were the truth and not Christian inventions. Jews were to be allowed to live wherever Christians lived to bear witness to those truths.

321 - The first written document pertaining to Jews in what is now Germany is a decree issued by the Roman emperor Constantine the Great revoking an earlier decree which had exempted the Jews of Colonia Agrippina, known as Köln today, from serving on the curia, or city council. Service on the curia entailed collecting taxes for the imperial treasury. Since any tax deficits had to be made up from the members' own pockets, exemption from this service was highly valued. Losing the exemption was probably very costly for the Jews of Colonia. (See Köln.)

395 - The Roman empire is split into an Eastern and a Western part, with Byzantium and Rome as their respective capitals. The west and south of what is now Germany becomes a province of the Western Roman empire.

4th or 5th Century - A clay lamp and lead seals with menorah patterns from the ancient city of Trier, then a capital of the Roman empire, provide the first archaeological evidence of Jews in Germany. (See Trier.)

476 - The Western Roman empire ceases to exist under the onslaught of Teutonic tribes. Western and Central European settlements are destroyed in constant raids by various tribes and all civilization and historical continuity perishes.

768-814 - Charlemagne, king of the Franks, becomes the ruler of large parts of Western Europe. He is crowned Roman Emperor by Pope Leo III in 800 C.E., thereby reviving the Western empire. His main imperial residence is in Aachen, although he spends most of his life engaged in army campaigns. (See Aachen.)

8th and 9th Century - A huge shift in population occurs when the Islamic Arabs invade large parts of the Byzantine empire where many Jews had previously settled. Subsequently, these Jews move west and north to the revived Western Roman empire. However, the rulers of this new empire require their vassals to swear a Christian oath of allegiance before allotting them land. Because of their religion, Jews can not swear such an oath; thus agriculture continues to be closed to Jews, which forces most of the immigrants to live in the newly forming cities. But here, too, problems soon arise. As the cities develop, the Christian artisan guilds become more and more powerful and to keep down competition, they refuse admittance to Jews.

16

With most other means of earning a living cut off due to their religion, many Jews in Western and Central Europe become merchants, utilizing their contacts in the network of Jewish communities still existing throughout the former Roman empire; the common language and the common Talmudic laws as well as the skills of reading and writing which were rare outside the Jewish communities certainly aid in their success. Furthermore, trade routes are partly Christian, partly Muslim; Jews can be mediators between the hostile camps. They primarily trade in luxury goods from the East, such as rugs, jewels, perfumes, spices, medicines, silk and other textiles. Because such commerce requires money, a scarce commodity in the barter system of those days, many Jews also become moneylenders, an occupation denied Christians by the church due to the religious laws against charging interest on loans.

900 - Jews first documented in Mainz.
960 - Jews first documented in Worms.
981 - Jews first documented in Regensburg.

11th century - Rabbis and community leaders from Speyer, Worms and Mainz form a federation known as Shum (the cities' first letters in Hebrew make up the name) to discuss religious and community issues and resolve disputes. The Shum becomes a decisive influence on Jewish communities throughout the Rhineland and far beyond, thus unifying community life. Its influence is well established by the end of the 11th century and continues on into the 14th century, ending only with the Black Death persecutions in 1348-50.

960-1040 - Gershom ben Judah (born in Metz, France, but lives most of his life in Mainz), known as the "Light of the Exile", is one of the first of the great German rabbis. Not only is his influence felt in the structuring of community and family life, but he is also influential in directing the study of the Talmud in Western Europe, thereby unifying the religious learning of the German Jewish communities into a specific Jewish culture. It is thought that amongst Gershom's many contributions were the establishment of rules governing divorce, abolishment of polygamy, privacy of correspondence, majority rule in communal affairs safeguarded by the right of the individual to interrupt service in the synagogue to be heard, prohibiting Jews from renting houses from Christians who had unjustly evicted another Jew, and forbidding insults to Jews who returned to Judaism after becoming Christians. Legend lends poignancy to the latter as his son Eliezer was forced to convert to Christianity during the expulsion of Jews from Mainz in 1012 and died before he could return to Judaism; Gershom nevertheless performed the rites of mourning for him. (See Mainz.)

1034 - A synagogue is built in Worms. Until it was destroyed by the Nazis in 1938, it had long been the oldest synagogue in continuous use in Europe. (See Worms.).

1040-1105 - Solomon ben Isaac, better known as Rashi, was born in Troyes, France and studied in Worms from 1055 to 1065. Some of Rashi's teachers had been students of Gershom. Rashi later writes commentaries on the Bible and the Talmud which are still studied today. The clearness of his religious teachings and writings have been highly revered by German Jews throughout the centuries. (See Worms.)

1084 - The bishop of Speyer invites Jews seeking refuge from persecution in Mainz to settle in Speyer stating that by doing so he is "increasing the honor of the town a thousand fold". His is the earliest written guarantee of rights and protections. In 1090, these guarantees are confirmed and expanded by emperor Henry IV. Similar guarantees are regularly granted (and just as regularly denied or ignored) by the emperors, bishops and princes in the centuries that follow. (See Speyer.)

1096 - The First Crusade starts in France, then moves on through the German Rhineland and down the Danube on its way to Jerusalem. Many kinds of groups participate in the crusade: religious fanatics, impoverished noblemen seeking to leave the hopelessness of their lives behind them and find new riches in the orient, farmers looking for land, and outcasts looking for another chance. As the crusade gains momentum, every non-Christian becomes the enemy. Although the French Jews contribute to the crusade with a special tax and make payments to individual leaders, the crusaders ransack, plunder, and massacre them without mercy. The survivors send messages warning their brethren in the Rhineland, who fail to heed the warnings answering "we will hold a fast and help you however we can, but we have nothing to fear". And then the crusaders and their camp followers are upon them as well and the tragedies of Rouen and Metz are repeated throughout the Rhineland and along the Danube.

The First Crusade not only establishes a precedent for violence against Jews and reduces their social status, but it also undermines the economic base of Jewish life. Before the First Crusade, Jews in the German lands were occupied primarily in international trade with the East. Moneylending was a secondary interest. Jews were respected and valued by the ruling powers both for the taxes they paid and the luxury goods only they could supply. As the routes of commerce to the Middle East pass from Muslim into Christian hands, the mediating role of the Jewish merchant becomes redundant and moneylending becomes the only feasible way of making a living for many Jews who are denied alternative occupations by the city guilds. The repercussions of this period last on into the 20th century.

1103 - The Jews are included in the Reichslandfrieden, the general peace law, by Henry IV. They are now under the emperor's personal protection like monks, priests and women. However, this law prohibits them from bearing arms, a doubtful privilege to survive for almost 700 years.

1146 - The Second Crusade is less zealous and fewer massacres are committed, in part due to imperial protection. The Würzburg community is the only major casualty. Five more crusades follow but none match the slaughter of Jews in Germany that characterized the First Crusade.

1157 - Jews are declared Kammerknechte or Serfs of the Imperial Chamber, which makes them the personal property of the emperor. There are no immediate changes due to the new legal position.

1179 - The Third Lateran Council prohibits Jews from having Christian servants or living amongst Christians. Until the Counter-Reformation in the 16th century, however, the latter edict is only enforced occasionally. At the same time, the council also protects Jews from forced baptism.

1182 - The Jews of France are expropriated and expelled.

1215 - The Fourth Lateran Council prescribes special dress for Jews and the pointed hat and yellow badge become common. In addition, the clergy is directed to restrict its business dealings with Jews. A further difficulty for the Jews is a moratorium on the interest on all debts owed to Jews by Christians who participate in the crusades. The Holy Office, the inquisition, is founded.

1235 - The first blood libel in Germany occurs in Fulda and is later followed by numerous similar charges of host desecrations and ritual murders in communities throughout the German lands. (See Schlüchtern.) These charges often lead to massacres, expulsions, property confiscations, and other acts of violence against Jews.

A blood libel accuses Jews of having used the blood of Christian children slaughtered for that purpose for the matzoth, the unleavened bread eaten at Pessach (Passover), or for other ritual purposes. The often repeated accusation of host desecration charges that the killing of Jesus is repeated in the destruction of consecrated hosts. From the beginning, papal and secular authorities have disproved these libels; however, the last ritual murder trial in Central Europe was held less than 100 years ago.

1236 - Using old Roman laws as a precedent, Jews are once more declared "Serfs of the Imperial Chamber" (Kammerknechte) by emperor Friedrich II. While providing some degree of imperial protection, this reduces Jews to the status of personal property of the emperor. When no emperor is elected from 1254 to 1273, a period known as the interregnum, local princes assume the rights to the Jews and their taxes.

19

1273-91 - Emperor Rudolph I of Habsburg seeks to re-establish the imperial right to Jewish taxes previously claimed by numerous princes by proclaiming once again that Jews are "Serfs of the Chamber" and that the emperor alone has the right to tax them.

1286 - Meir ben Baruch of Rothenburg (1215-1293), known as the "Light of the Exile" as was Gershom ben Judah before him, disputes the imperial claim and attempts to leave the empire to settle in the Promised Land with thousands of followers. Unfortunately, Rabbi Meir is captured in Upper Italy and held for ransom until his death in 1293. (Even then his corpse is held captive until 1307, when Alexander ben Salomon Wimpfen pays a large sum of money on the sole condition that he be buried beside Rabbi Meir.) During his captivity, Rabbi Meir forbids to be ransomed as this would mean a recognition of Jewish serfdom. (See Rothenburg and Worms.)

Before and during his imprisonment, Rabbi Meir serves his people as a highly respected teacher, scholar, and supreme judge in ritual, legal, and community affairs throughout Germany for almost 50 years. His surviving opinions and decisions, numbering around a thousand, continue to influence community life for many generations.

1290 - After a century of repression and persecution, the last Jews are expelled from England.

1298 - A Franconian knight named Rindfleisch, from Röttingen, leads a mob against Jewish communities in Franconia and Bavaria after a host desecration accusation. In less than six months, more than 140 communities are destroyed.

1306 - Almost all French Jews are expelled after the French king is convinced that all Jews are the property of the Roman emperor.

1337 - Many Jewish communities in Bavaria are destroyed after a host desecration accusation in Deggendorf.

1336-1338 - A tavern keeper straps a piece of leather to his arm and calls himself King Armleder. Assisted by a nobleman, he leads an army of destitute farmers through Alsace and along the Mosel and Rhine, killing Jews wherever he finds them. In 1339, an imperial army finally catches him and he is beheaded, not for killing Jews but for the damage he did to the emperor's property. 120 Jewish communities are destroyed before Armleder loses his head.

1342 - The Jewish poll tax (Opferpfennig) is introduced by emperor Ludwig IV and collected on Christmas Day. The precedent for this tax is the Temple tax paid by the Jews to the Roman emperors after the destruction of the Second Temple in 70 CE. This tax, ostensibly to be used to protect Jews, applies to all Jews over the age of 12. They have to pay one Gulden for every 20 they possess.

1348-50 - The Black Death persecutions are caused by the terror of a plague epidemic that kills a third of Europe. As we know today, the plague was caused by rat fleas spread throughout Europe by a new species of rats introduced from Asia. However, when the epidemic rages in 1348-50, it is believed that the Jews are poisoning the wells and springs, thereby causing the plague. This claim is supported by confessions under torture of some Jews. When the Black Death finally subsides, 300 Jewish communities have been destroyed in Germany alone.

1356 - In the Golden Bull, a constitution of the empire, Charles IV ceded his rights to the Jews to the German princes together with his rights to minerals and metals found underground. The Golden Bull further splintered the German territories and sealed the weakness of the central power in Germany for centuries to come.

1394 - French Jews are expelled again. For almost 400 years, very few Jews will be able to live in France.

1424 - Jews expelled from Köln.

1439 - Jews expelled from Augsburg.

1440 - Probable date for European invention of movable type. The invention of the printing press and the ensuing availability of printed information plays a major role in bringing an end to the Middle Ages.

1473 - Jews expelled from Mainz.
1492 - Jews expelled from Spain.
1496 - Forced baptism or expulsion from Portugal.

Recovery is slow following these massacres and expulsions. The situation for the surviving Jews in Germany is substantially altered. Before, Jews could still find refuge in an adjoining town or state until they were allowed to return to the city that had expelled them a few weeks, months or even years later. Now, their new position is much more precarious. Jews have become superfluous, their know-how and their connections have been taken over by Christians. Often their admittance is subject to high taxes or "protection contributions" (Schutzgelder) and is restricted to a specified time period like three or five years, after which time they must reapply and pay new fees. Their numbers are also limited. They are no longer allowed to buy land or houses and are forced to live in special ghettos, known as the Judengasse or Judenhof, with walls and gates that further restrict their movements and limit contact with their Christian neighbors. Also, by now moneylending is practically the only profession that is officially open to Jews in the cities, forcing many to live in rural areas as small-scale moneylenders and peddlers. The money necessary for the taxes and fees drives up interest rates, creating new hatred against the Jews.

These events also initiate a new shift of the European Jewry - from west to east this time, from Spain to the

Turkish lands and Palestine, and from France and Germany to Poland. Yiddish, the language of the Eastern European Jews, stems from this time, being a German dialect with Hebrew and Slavic words added over the years. Ladino, the old form of Spanish spoken by the Jews of Southern Europe, also originates from that period.

1499 - Jews expelled from Nürnberg.

1510-1520 - The influential Dominican order of monks makes efforts to have all Jewish religious books confiscated, believing that once their books have been destroyed, Jews will convert to Christianity. Johannes Reuchlin, a Christian and humanist, had spent many years studying Hebrew and Jewish religious texts. When asked his opinion by emperor Maximilian, Reuchlin suggested that instead of burning the books, two chairs of Hebrew be endowed at every German university for their study. Johannes Pfefferkorn, a converted Jew allied with the Dominicans, charges that Reuchlin has been bribed by the Jews and a long and costly trial ensues. Although Reuchlin eventually loses, the books are saved. The anonymous pamphlets supporting him, especially the satirical "Letters of obscure men", destroy the Dominican influence and weaken the Catholic church.

1519 - Jews are expelled from Regensburg shortly after Maximilian I, their protector, dies.

1523 - Martin Luther (1483-1546) publishes a widely read book defending and praising the Jews; however, when they refuse to convert to his new doctrines, he turns against them and in 1543 publishes "Of the Jews and their Lies", which retells centuries of anti-Jewish myths, praises their persecution, equates Jews with the devil, and advises measures against them that seem to be prophecies of actions taken 400 years later.

Luther's quest for reform within the all-powerful Catholic church eventually leads to a division of the Church which culminates in the Thirty Years' War between Catholics and Protestants, 72 years after his death.

ca. 1520-1554 - Josel von Rosheim, an Alsatian Jew, takes up the struggle against the dangers threatening the Jewish communities of the empire. By constant appeals to emperors and princes, he somehow manages again and again to avert the persecution or expulsion of Jews. During a trip to the Palatinate he dies. There is no successor for his self-created office of protector of the Jews.

1551 - Jews expelled from Bavaria.

For the Jews, conditions in modern times soon evolve into further religious repression. Now that two Christian churches exist, each jealously guards its spheres of influence against any dissidents, Christian or Jewish.

1555 - Pope Paul IV decrees that the

22

medieval principles set out in the Third Lateran Council in 1179, which "prohibited true believers even from lodging amongst the infidels", be enforced. The systematic ghettoization of Jewish life, already visible in many cities, begins again in earnest. Walls are built and gates are kept locked at night as well as on Sundays and most Christian holidays.

End of 16th century - A group of wealthy Portuguese Marranos (newly converted Christians) are allowed to settle in Hamburg, even after it is discovered they are still secretly practicing Judaism, because of their important business and commerce connections. Throughout the coming century, more and more Marranos seeking refuge from the inquisition in Spain and Portugal settle in northern Europe, particularly in the Netherlands, Danish territories, and in the Hanseatic cities of northern Germany where they can return to Judaism. They introduce capital and expertise in international trade and develop new industries. (For much the same reasons, Marranos also were the first Jewish settlers in the Americas.)

1618-1648 - The Thirty Years' War between Catholics and Protestants ravages Germany, destroying cities and villages, the streets of the burghers, the farmers' fields, and the Judengassen alike. With its conclusion, Christian religious fervor seems spent. Tolerance for opposing beliefs and attitudes now becomes a distinct possibility in the newly forming modern world.

A major result of this religious war, which destroyed Central Europe and lacked a true victor, is the shift of political power from the once all-powerful Church to the secular rulers of Europe. Commerce and banking are greatly valued, and the Jews, by virtue of being forced into those two occupations, have over the centuries gained a degree of expertise that makes their participation an asset to the new secular rulers. By now investment and management of resources can be seen to have distinct advantages over the gamble entailed in fighting for the spoils in expensive wars.

From the middle of the 17th century and on until the end of the 18th century, the Court Jew becomes an important figure at the courts of the numerous German secular rulers, serving as a financial advisor to the ruler and providing him with credit or cash, collecting taxes, and acting as his agent in supplying his armies with provisions and equipment. At the same time, the Court Jews are able to secure protection for existing Jewish communities, get permission to form new ones, obtain positions for other Jews in the court, have some of the more oppressive restrictions abolished, and build synagogues. Although the position of a Court Jew is rarely secure, their continued presence reflects their usefulness to the secular rulers as well as increased tolerance and helps pave the way to eventual emancipation. Israel Aaron in Berlin, Leffmann Behrends in Hannover, Alexander David in

Braunschweig, Joseph Suess Oppen-heimer (who became very powerful but fell from favor in 1738 and was hanged) in Württemberg, to name a very few, all play important roles in development of their communities (see Braunschweig, Baiersdorf, Bayreuth.)

1648/49 - The Chmelniecki massa-cres in Poland lead many Jews to seek refuge in the west again—in the Ger-man lands.

1649 - Jews expelled from Hamburg.

1670/71 - Jews are expelled from Vienna and the hereditary lands of the Habsburgs; 50 wealthy Viennese families are allowed to settle in Berlin and Brandenburg.

1646-1724 - Glückel of Hameln, whose diary provides a unique view into the German Jewish world of the late 17th and early 18th centuries, was born in Hamburg. She married at 14, gave birth to 12 children, was widowed at 44 and took over her hus-band's business while caring for her remaining 8 unmarried children, remarried at 54, was bankrupted at 56, widowed again at 66, and died at 78. She began a journal of her life in 1690 for the benefit of her children, revealing in detail the daily life of her family, friends, and neighbors by describing births, marriages, illnesses, and deaths as well as her business activities and the larger events of her time. (See Hamburg.)

Her report also tells us about the Messianic movement of her time, the belief that the arrival of the Messiah was imminent and that the Jews would soon be released from exile, their sufferings and humiliations, and be led to the Promised Land. When Shabbatai Zevi, a religious fanatic born in Smyrna in 1626, was declared Messiah by Nathan of Gaza in 1665 and prophesied the return of the Jews to the Promised Land the following year (the year of change according to the Kabbala), many Jews follow his call, sell their property and get ready for the big journey eastwards. When it became known that Shabbatai Zevi had converted to Islam and accepted a minor official position in the court of the Sultan in Istanbul, there was some disappointment, but the belief in the Messiah was not weakened: suffering and hopelessness were too great to be born without this belief. More than a hundred years later, Jacob Frank and his daughter Eva were able to build on this belief and use it for their pur-poses (see Offenbach). The constant disappointments in Messianism lead many Jews away from their traditional religion and brought support for the enlightenment movement.

Mid-18th Century - The Enlighten-ment is a period of great intellectual activity directed against religious prejudice and repressive conventions and traditions through the force of reason. Gotthold Ephraim Lessing, a Christian playwright and philosopher, and Moses Mendelssohn, a Jewish philosopher, are important leaders of this movement in Germany and through their discussions and writings

24

do much to pave the way for eventual emancipation of the Jews.

1729-86 - Moses Mendelssohn, considered the first modern Jewish thinker of the German Enlightenment and spiritual leader of German Jewry, seeks to remove the barriers separating Jews from German society and culture. In addition to his voluminous writing, he was also a successful businessman and managed a silk factory later in life. By translating the Torah into German and publishing the German text (in Hebrew letters initially) along with the Hebrew original and commentaries, he makes it possible for Jews to learn to read and write in German and for others to do the same in Hebrew. Mendelssohn believed that access to the German language and culture would not necessarily endanger the preservation of a Jewish identity. However, his efforts to pave the way for better understanding and appreciation between the two peoples eventually lead to large scale conversion and almost brought about the self-dissolution of German Jewry. His friend G. E. Lessing gave him a lasting memorial in his play "Nathan der Weise". (See Berlin and Dessau.)

1778 - David Friedländer founded the first Jewish Free School which uses German instead of Hebrew as the language of instruction.

1781 - The pamphlet "Über die bürgerliche Verbesserung der Juden" ("About the civic improvement of the Jews") by Ch. W. Dohm, a highly-placed Prussian civil servant, is published in Berlin. His ideas about the emancipation of the Jews influenced the Prussian and German lawmakers throughout the 19th century.

1791 - The French Revolution brings civic emancipation not only to French Jews but also, temporarily, to Jewish communities in Germany when Napoleon invades and reorganizes the country.

1797-1856 - Heinrich Heine, one of the great poets in the German language, is born a Jew but converts in 1825 in response to the growing movement for assimilation. Although he never formally returns to Judaism he is recorded as saying "I make no secret of my Judaism, to which I have not returned because I never left it". (See Düsseldorf and Hamburg.)

1806 - The Holy Roman Empire that has ruled the German lands with varying degrees of authority since the coronation of Charlemagne in 800 comes to an end. Faced with Napoleon's victory, the Habsburg emperor Francis II abolished the Holy Roman Empire, thus thwarting Napoleon's efforts to succeed him. Before doing that, he founded the hereditary Austrian empire, of which he became emperor Francis I.

1812 - Prussian decree of emancipation for Jews. However, in the following years the new-found liberties were taken away again, one after the other.

1818 - Leopold Zunz (1794-1886)

25

publishes his pamphlet "Etwas über die rabbinische Literatur" (An Essay on Rabbinical Literature) introducing a preliminary program for the study of Jewish history and its literature, later refined as the "Wissenschaft vom Judentum" (Science of Judaism). These studies are published in many journals which stimulate further discussions between Jewish and Christian intellectuals and help raise Jewish self-esteem. Later on, the Jüdisch-theologisches Seminar is established in Breslau (1854). This is the first institution devoted to the Science of Judaism and leads to the founding of similar organizations throughout Germany and abroad. (See Berlin.)

1819 - Hep! Hep! is the rallying cry during the anti-Jewish riots that break out in many parts of Germany partly due to the social and economic rise of Jews and the economic threat Jewish emancipation is perceived to pose to many Christians.

1836 - Samson Raphael Hirsch (1808-1888) publishes his "Nineteen Letters on Judaism" and "Essays on Israel's Duties in the Diaspora" which concern the "relationship of Judaism to world culture". Rabbi Hirsch is the foremost spiritual leader of German Orthodoxy in the 19th century. (See Frankfurt.)

1848 - Within weeks of the Paris revolution in February, German revolutionaries, seeking more liberal rule and a constitution providing for full civic and political rights for all, rebel as well. The Basic Laws of the German People, as set out by the parliament in Frankfurt, also extends equal rights to Jews. The National Assembly, led by its president Eduard Simson, a baptized Jew, offers the imperial crown to the Prussian king Friedrich Wilhelm IV, who declines the crown as being "molded from the dirt of the revolution". The revolution is eventually suppressed by the military and is followed by more repression.

Second half of the 19th Century - Jewish life in Germany changes dramatically. Germany becomes a modern state. Rural Jewish communities dissolve when emigration to the USA or moving to larger cities becomes possible. The stormy success of Jews in reaching top positions of industry, banking, finance, politics, art and science is accompanied by ever new and ever more scientific theories of racial anti-Semitism. More and more Jews from Eastern Europe come to Germany during this time, partly fleeing from pogroms and partly to seek a better life. They form an Orthodox lower social class which is alien to the assimilated Reform German Jews.

1871 - After emerging as the most powerful state in Germany, Prussia defeats Denmark (in 1864), Austria (1866), and France. As a result, the German princes offer the King of Prussia the crown of the new German empire; the new (second) Reich comes into existence. Eduard Simson becomes president of the German parliament.

26

On April 14, the Constitution of the German Empire, which includes civic and political rights for Jews, is ratified. The emancipation, while extensive, does not allow Jews to serve in the civil service, as officers in the Army, or as full professors in the universities. (These latter restrictions are finally removed by the Weimar Republic following WWI.)

1860-1904 - Theodor Herzl (born in Budapest) is considered the founder of modern Zionism. In 1896, under the influence of his disappointment for integration in Christian society without having to give up his Jewish identity, he publishes a pamphlet called "Der Judenstaat", which proposes establishing a self-governing Jewish state as the only means of safeguarding Judaism from both the threats of increasing assimilation and anti-Semitism. His pamphlet and lectures are received with great enthusiasm throughout Europe and lead to the first Zionist International Congress held in Basel, Switzerland, in 1897.

1878-1965 - Martin Buber (born in Vienna) is the editor of Die Welt, a weekly Zionist newspaper, in 1901. Later he is one of the founders of Jüdischer Verlag in Berlin, which is one of the major publishers of Jewish literature in German. He is one of the leading Zionist thinkers and leaders in Germany prior to his emigration to Palestine in 1938. (See Heppenheim.)

1914-1918 - 100,000 Jews serve in the German army during WWI; 12,000 are killed. The German empire, the Second Reich, ends after 47 years, together with the Austrian, Russian, and Turkish empires.

1919 - The Weimar Constitution is formally adopted by the National Assembly for the new German Republic after being drafted by Hugo Preuss, a Jew. Many Jews hold important positions in the new government, including Walter Rathenau, who was assassinated in 1922 after becoming foreign minister. However, in spite of the Jews' full equality under the new constitution and their assimilation into German culture, anti-Semitism steadily increases throughout the Republic.

1933 - The Nazi rise to power, aided by the worsening economic crisis, culminates with the appointment of Adolf Hitler as chancellor. This Nazi triumph unleashes violent anti-Semitic attacks and demonstrations. In late 1934, after the death of Hindenburg, Hitler also becomes president, assuming the new titles of Führer and Reichskanzler; the Third Reich is founded. It will last less than 11 years, although the Nazis call it "the thousand-years Reich".

1935 - The infamous Nürnberg Laws depriving Jews of civil laws virtually make anti-Semitism a part of every aspect of German public life and culture.

March 1938 - Annexation of Austria.

November 9-10, 1938 - "Reichskristallnacht" (Night of the Broken Glass). Triggered by the assassination of a German diplomat in Paris by a Jew whose family had been deported to Poland, a carefully orchestrated wave of anti-Semitic violence sweeps across Germany and Austria, heavily damaging or destroying hundreds of synagogues, Jewish homes, businesses, schools, and cemeteries. Thousands of Jews are arrested and sent to concentration camps. Many are tortured and killed.

1939-1945 - WWII and the Holocaust. After Jews are blamed for most of Germany's economic problems, isolated and persecuted in many ways, Heydrich's plan for the Final Solution of the Jewish Question is adopted in 1941, leading to the organized murder of the Jews of Europe in German camps (see Berlin). An estimated 160,000 to 180,000 German Jews are murdered or die from the abuse and persecution suffered at the hands of the Nazis together with six million fellow Jews, mostly from Eastern Europe. The survivors of the annihilation camps live in DP camps after the war before they emigrate.

May 14, 1948 - The establishment of an independent Jewish state, Israel, brings to an end nearly 2,000 years of exile.

With the end of the war, most surviving German Jews emigrate to other countries, thus bringing almost to a close Jewish Germany's thousand year history. In recent years, however, West Germany's Jewish population has been increasing through immigration from Israel and other countries in part due to Germany's favorable economic and social climate, while the Jewish population of the German Democratic Republic dwindled and almost disappeared. Unfortunately, anti-Semitic incidents still occur. However, the vast majority of the German population have approved of the extended efforts of its government to face its past. Throughout the 1970s and 1980s, individuals and groups have raised public and private funds to set up memorials and special exhibitions covering their community's Jewish histories and many of the surviving synagogues and cemeteries damaged or destroyed during the years of the Third Reich have been restored or rebuilt. Where a resident Jewish community no longer exists, these former synagogues serve as memorials and community centers.

The Talmud says that the doors of return are always open. It may well be that the doors of these restored synagogues and cemeteries are such doors of return.

After unification, German rightists gained strength and growing discrimination against foreigners as well as the reemergence of Nazi slogans now cause concern. Further development, especially in the former German Democratic Republic, must be watched carefully.

AACHEN

lies about 70 km west of Köln between the A 4 and the A 44, close to the border between Belgium and Germany (map 4).

* 1957 synagogue
* Memorials
* International Museum of Journalism
* 18th century cemetery

The first mention of Jews in Aachen sounds like a legend: In 797 C.E. Isaac the Jew, serving as guide and interpreter, accompanied two Frankish noblemen sent by Charlemagne, king of the Franks, to visit the Caliph Harun al-Rashid in Baghdad. Charlemagne was the ruler of large parts of Western Europe then and became Roman emperor in 800. Not only was Isaac the sole survivor reporting back to Charlemagne some four years later, he also succeeded in bringing the Caliph's gift, an elephant named Abulabaz, to Charlemagne. Just how Isaac managed to get this elephant from Baghdad to Aachen isn't known, but do it he did.

Although court records indicate the presence of a few Jews amongst Charlemagne's entourage, Jews did not really settle in Aachen until about 820. However, Jews lived here in Aachen almost continuously (except for a ten year break after a 1629 expulsion) from the dawn of the First until the last years of the "Third Reich". 700 Aachen Jews emigrated, almost 1,000 were killed in Nazi camps.

Today, little remains to tell of Aachen's long Jewish history. The Judengasse (Jews' street) may date back to the 9th century. However, today nothing but the name remains. A memorial to Aachen's old synagogue, built in 1862 and destroyed by the Nazis during "Reichskristallnacht" in November 1938, may be seen on Synagogenplatz. A new synagogue and community center were built in 1957 at nearby Oppenhoffallee 50. In 1995 the small community moved to a synagogue on Synagogenplatz in the center of Aachen again.

A memorial to Paul Julius Reuter, born in Kassel as Israel Beer Josaphat, the founder of the Reuters' News Agency, can be seen at Pontstrasse 117. Mr. Reuter started his news service here in 1849, using carrier pigeons to transmit news quickly, an early pioneer of the Information Age. Down the street at Pontstrasse 13 is the International Museum of Journalism with a collection of over 100,000 publications, including early Jewish newspapers in several languages. The museum can be visited on Tuesday-Friday 9:30-1 and 2:30-5 and on Saturday 9:30-1. It is closed Sunday and Monday.

The Jewish cemetery, from 1820, is located on Lütticherstrasse 39 and has a memorial tablet for the Jewish victims of the Nazis. The oldest stone in this cemetery stands near the street wall and dates back to 1820, the year the cemetery was founded. The old part of the cemetery has tall old trees shading rows of gray tombstones of equal height which are set close together in the old-fashioned style of the period. Only the newer part has family graves, marble grave borders, and figural ornamentation. The cemetery has a guard house and can be visited during daylight hours, except on the Sabbath and on Jewish holidays.

AFFALTRACH

is a small village incorporated in Obersulm, about 50 km northeast of Stuttgart, between the A 6 and highway 39 (map 8, 9, 10).

* Former synagogue from 1851
* Cemetery from 1706

Jews began living here in the 17th century. The community reached its peak in 1858, with more than 200 members, but then declined due to emigration and the move to larger cities. Four of the 19 Jews living here in 1933 were killed in Nazi camps. Large windows in a 19th century mixture of neo-Gothic and neo-Romanesque styles, with panes of blue and red glass, add their beauty to the carefully restored light rose colored brick building of the synagogue complex.

The former synagogue, built in 1851, stands only a few paces from the village church and is of almost equal size, a sign of a prosperous and confident community. Inside, the richly ornamented wooden women's gallery looks down on the Torah ark niche (now empty) from three sides, still supported by the original wooden columns. A former mikveh in the basement of the adjoining school is visible through small windows. The synagogue complex originally

The former synagogue of Affaltrach is located very close to the village church. There is a ritual bath in the basement of the former Jewish school.

30

included the prayer room itself, a school, the mikveh mentioned above, the teacher's apartment, and a guest room. After the complex was devastated in the "Reichskristallnacht" in November 1938, it was used as a storeroom and refugee shelter.

It has recently been restored as a museum memorial and community center by a local "Association for the Maintenance of the Affaltrach Synagogue". The synagogue museum complex is open from February to November Wednesdays and Sundays 3-5. At other times, the key may be obtained either at the Rathaus (city hall) or at the Protestant vicarage nearby. A few ritual objects in the museum collection demonstrate the religious life of the community, and posters and pictures deal with the history of the Jews in the Heilbronn area. The former synagogue is located in the center of the village at Untere Gasse and Pfarrgasse. It is signposted on both ends of town.

The cemetery of Affaltrach, established in 1706, is located on the Salzberg outside of town. To get there, follow Salzbergstrasse, turn right at Johanniterstrasse and go up the hill, keeping the hill to your right, for about 600 meters. The cemetery is directly beside the road across from a large orchard. The cemetery is locked (key at city hall or Protestant vicarage), but you can see into the cemetery through the barred gate. There is a sword-shaped memorial to Jewish soldiers killed in WWI directly opposite the gate. The cemetery also has a small taharah house.

AHRWEILER

(part of Bad Neuenahr-Ahrweiler) is a small town about 60 km south of Köln, off the A 61 and on highway 267 (map 4, 8).

* Former synagogue from 1894
* Cemetery from 1867

Written records indicate there was a Jewish community in Ahrweiler as early as 1248. Like so many other communities, it was destroyed in the Black Plague persecutions in 1348. Its successor community was wiped out in local wars around 1400. Another community dispersed around 1700. After that, no Jewish community was formed in Ahrweiler until 1850, although a few Jewish families lived here in the beginning of the 19th century. After 1900 the community declined because of a movement to larger cities; in the 1930's, the rise of the Nazi party caused many Ahrweiler Jews to emigrate. Fourteen Jews were deported from Ahrweiler in 1942, one Jewish woman married to a Gentile went into hiding and was the only Ahrweiler Jew to survive the Nazi years.

In 1894, the small Jewish community built a synagogue in a mixture of neo-Romanesque and Moorish (or neo-Oriental) styles from local volcanic rock. It was devastated by the Nazis during "Reichskristallnacht" in 1938 and the building later had to be sold to a restaurant owner. In 1945, US military officers ordered the city to restore the synagogue for use by Jewish GI's and the sole surviving

Ahrweiler Jew. For a short time services were held in the synagogue. However, since no new Jewish community was formed in Ahrweiler, the synagogue was eventually sold again and used as a storehouse for fertilizer. After many difficulties, the building was bought by a group of citizens for use as a memorial and documentation center in 1981 and eventually restored. The former synagogue is located on Altenbaustrasse 12a, opposite the Ahrgau Museum. The key is available from a Protestant minister, H. Warnecke, at Burgstrasse 56. Mr. Warnecke played an important part in saving the synagogue and has written a brochure about the history of the Jewish community and the synagogue of Ahrweiler.

The small Jewish cemetery, from 1867, is located on Schützenstrasse. The key is available from the family living across the street from the main entrance.

The former synagogue of Alsenz is part of a private home today.

ALSENZ

is a small farming village about 90 km southwest of Frankfurt, on highway 48 about 15 km south of Bad Kreuznach (map 8).

* Former synagogue from 1776
* Cemetery from the early 18th century

The former synagogue, built in 1776 in a Baroque style, is located behind Kirchberg 1. In 1932, it was sold to Christians by the dissolving Jewish community and has had numerous owners since then. The present owner recently renovated the building and is using it as a private gallery. There is no commemorative tablet.

The law tablets adorn the gable of the former Ahrweiler synagogue again.

32

The former synagogue is quite beautiful with tall narrow windows and still contains the ark niche although the ark itself is in the Speyer Historical Museum of the Palatinate. Remnants of 18th century decorative scroll painting can be seen over the ark niche. The ceiling is dark blue, with a pattern of stars. Outside over the door you can still see the outlines of an inscription in Hebrew "This is the gate of the Lord, into which the righteous shall enter" which one of the previous owners unsuccessfully attempted to efface with a chisel during the Nazi years.

The cemetery, most probably established in the early 18th century, lies on the side of a very steep hill above the village just beyond the intersection of Berg-Strasse and Am Goldgraben. The cemetery is terraced and most of the gravestones are white. All are standing. However, the older stones are badly weather-beaten and many of the inscriptions are no longer legible.

The unsuccessful efforts of a former owner to remove the inscription over the door of the Alsenz synagogue can still be seen.

ALSFELD

lies about 100 km northeast of Frankfurt, or 90 km south of Kassel, in the Schwalm valley on the A 5 (map 5, 6, 8).

* Small museum collection of Judaica
* Memorial tablet for synagogue
* Cemetery from the mid-19th century

The Regionalmuseum of Alsfeld has a small collection of Judaica including the Torah and mantle from the Alsfeld synagogue that was destroyed in 1938. The museum is located on Rittergasse 3-5. Opening hours: Monday-Friday 9-12:30 and 2-4:30; Saturday 9-12 and 1-4; and Sunday 10-12 and 2-4:30. There is also a street named Am Judenbad (At the Jewish Bath), but no mikveh survives. On Lutherstrasse there is a small commemorative tablet to the Alsfeld synagogue, which was destroyed by the Nazis in the 1938 "Reichskristallnacht".

The Jewish cemetery, from the second half of the 19th century, is located at one end of the Christian cemetery on Reibertenröder Weg. The street entrance is locked. However, inside there is no wall or fence separating the Jewish cemetery from the Christian cemetery. The oldest stones are from the late 19th century.

ANDERNACH

lies between the Rhine and highway 9, about 80 km southeast of Köln (map 4, 8).

* Mikveh from 13th century
* Anti-Jewish depiction of a crucifixion from the early 14th century
* Cemetery from 1888

The first mention of Jews in Andernach was made by Benjamin of Tudela, the Jewish traveler, around 1170. As was the case for other Jewish communities in the Rhineland, the Andernach Jews were periodically killed or expelled; after a few years a new community would be admitted again. In 1287, for instance, the citi-

Pointed Gothic arches support the walls of the Andernach ritual bath.

zens of Andernach were forced by their ruler, the archbishop of Cologne, to rebuild the Jewish houses and "Jewish schools" (synagogues) they had destroyed in the wake of a ritual murder accusation; this, however, did not prevent the persecutions in 1337 (the Armleder pogrom) or in 1349, when the Black Plague was blamed on the Jews.

After all this carnage, the medieval Jewish community dissolved in 1450. A mountain, hill, street, and fortification tower bear the prefix "Juden", indicating the likelihood of a sizable Jewish community at one time. Today only the 13th century mikveh beneath the Old Town Hall survives from these times.

Slate was used to build the 13th century early Gothic mikveh in Andernach. The mikveh lies 13 meters (43 feet) below the Old Town Hall, close to where the medieval synagogue of the Andernach community once stood. The mikveh was used by the Jewish communities until the middle of the 15th century.

The mikveh resembles a sunken, four-cornered fortification tower. A staircase leads down in what could be described as its outer walls. Its once clean Gothic lines are somewhat altered by the clumsy addition of later partitions. The entrance is hidden behind a very low door in the lobby of the old city hall. The bath chamber has an arched ceiling, a feature not found in later mikvoth in Germany. The former mikveh may be visited during business hours Monday-Friday between 9-4. You can get the key at the new Rathaus (city hall) a block away on Läufstrasse.

A demeaning depiction of Jews and the Crucifixion can be seen in the Liebfrauen Church. It can be found on the north wall of the center aisle and is a few years younger than the mikveh. It shows one Jew holding a hammer and a second Jew holding a spear that pierces the side of Jesus, in direct contradiction to the relevant parts of the New Testament.

A new Jewish community was founded in the 1860's. Its small and well-kept cemetery, from 1888, is part of the city cemetery on Koblenzer Strasse.

The mikveh of Andernach is large and resembles a fortification tower built into the ground. After the Jews were expelled, it lay forgotten for centuries.

ANSBACH

lies on the Rezat river about 40 km west of Nürnberg, on highways 13 and 14 and close to the A 6 (map 8, 9, 10).

* Synagogue from the 18th century
* Cemetery from 1813

Jews began settling in Ansbach at the beginning of the 14th century. The community suffered severe losses during the Black Death persecutions in 1349 and was expelled for about 50 years in 1564. By the end of the 17th century and on into the early 18th century, the service of influential court Jews, particularly Marx Model and Elkanan Fränkel, at the court of the local margraves provided the community much more protection and stability than it had ever enjoyed before. However, this protection ended when the two men fell from favor. One of the oldest synagogues in Germany to survive "Reichskristallnacht" (November 9-10, 1938) almost undamaged is the 18th century Ansbach synagogue on Rosenbadstrasse 3. Its position near other buildings protected the synagogue that night from being destroyed. The SA did burn the Torah and ritual objects, however. The synagogue, built between 1744-46 by the Italian architect Leopoldo Retty, is used once a year nowadays, on November 9, for a memorial service attended by Catholics, Protestants and Jews from all over Bavaria.

In the entry hallway there is a memorial to Ansbach's Jews. The interior has two rows of three brass chandeliers each, complete with imperial eagles, reflecting the imperial protection the Ansbach Jews once claimed. The women's gallery is white with gold

The remarkable Baroque synagogue of Ansbach now serves as a place of worship once a year.

The Baroque furnishings of the synagogue are as old as the building itself.

trim and is supported by a single column. The octagonal bimah, with eight rose-colored spiraling columns like those framing the Torah ark, fills the center of the room. The room is lit by candles from a large single brass chandelier. Most of the furnishings are as old as the building.

Ansbach's Jewish cemetery was established in 1815. It was completely razed during the Nazi period. Some stones were returned when the cemetery was restored in 1946. A commemorative tablet to this destruction as well as to the desecrations that took place there in 1948 and 1950 stands in the center of the rear wall. Today, the cemetery is locked and protected by a stone wall. It is located off Rügländer Strasse behind the church on Uhlandstrasse and Josef-Fruth-Platz. The key to the synagogue and the cemetery may be obtained from the Amt für Kultur und Touristik at the Stadthaus (city hall) Monday-Friday 9:00-12:30 and 2:00-5:00 from November to April, and Monday-Friday 9:00-5:00 from May to October.

AROLSEN

is located 50 km west of Kassel, on highways 450 and 252 (map 4, 5, 6).

* International Tracing Service

Arolsen is home to the International Tracing Service run by the Red Cross and funded by the Federal Republic of Germany. The ITS collects, records, maintains and evaluates data on 14 million individuals who were persecuted or enslaved by the Third Reich.

This facility contains records on 45 million file cards which are kept in more than 20 kilometers of files and 141 kilometers of microfilm.

The organization has responded to millions of queries since it was established. The ITS still receives about 175,000 questions annually, primarily concerned with pension related information and assistance. The ITS is located on the corner of Grosse Allee/ Jahnstrasse. There is a rather peculiar memorial to the victims of Nazi persecutions by Alexander Zickendraht in the lobby.

The former synagogue, built about 1750, has been altered considerably and nothing remains to indicate its former use. It is located on Mannel-strasse 3. Jews from Arolsen were buried in nearby Helsen.

ASCHAFFENBURG

is located on the Main river about 50 km southeast of Frankfurt, on the A 3 (map 8, 9).

* Memorials
* Documentation center and exhibition in former rabbi's house
* Cemetery from 1719

As early as 1147 Jews were reported to be living in Aschaffenburg. During the Black Death years of the mid-14th century, they suffered greatly as did Jewish communities throughout Germany. Jews were allowed to return in 1359 and their numbers grew slowly over the following centuries. A new synagogue was built on what is now

Wolfsthalplatz in 1698, rebuilt in 1893, and destroyed by the SA during "Reichskristallnacht" in 1938. Today there are memorials to the Jewish victims of Aschaffenburg and to their destroyed synagogue in the small park on Wolfsthalplatz. The rabbi's house still stands next to the site of the destroyed synagogue. The house is now a documentation center and maintains an exhibition on Aschaffenburg's Jewish community. The exhibition consists mainly of large poster size photographs and texts covering Aschaffenburg's Jewish citizens and their fate, as well as a few ritual objects. The exhibition may be seen on Wednesday 10-12; Thursday 4-6; and on the first Sunday of the month 10-12. There is also a prayer room used by the small Aschaffenburg community.

Wolfsthalplatz was named to honor the memory of Otto Wolfsthal, an Aschaffenburg banker and philanthropist. He, his wife and five friends, all in their 60s and 70s, killed themselves the night before they were to be deported to Theresienstadt. Their graves and a memorial may be visited in the Schweinheim cemetery.

This cemetery, established in 1719, lies outside of town on the side of a large hill near Schweinheim overlooking Aschaffenburg. Eight other neighboring communities used this cemetery as well. It would have taken two hours or more to walk there from the town. The cemetery, with its old, tall trees, is locked (you can get the key from the Stadtgärtnerei on Grossostheimerstrasse 201) and surrounded by a high stone wall. You can see into the cemetery from outside the barred gate. The stones are mostly red sandstone and are in good condition. All graves are oriented towards the east.

To get there, follow Unterhainstrasse in a westerly direction until you come to a path marked with an "R" which leads off to the left near a small railroad bridge. (There is a high concrete wall on the right side of the street and a little group of trees with a red sandstone crucifix column in the fork of the path). Follow this narrow asphalt road for about two kilometers until it goes steeply uphill. The cemetery walls appear on the right.

A second cemetery was opened in the late 19th century and is located inside the city cemetery on Altstadtfriedhof near the center of town. It includes a memorial to the Jewish WWI dead, a guardhouse, and a taharah house. It is also locked but you may get the key in the chapel of the Christian cemetery.

ASCHENHAUSEN

is a small village about 100 km southwest of Erfurt, off highway 285 between Fladungen and Kaltennordheim, close to Kaltensundheim (map 5, 6, 8).

* Former synagogue from 1767
* Cemetery from the early 17th century

The local barons of Spesshardt admitted Jews to their village of Aschenhausen at the end of the 17th century.

The new community must have developed rapidly, as a large synagogue was built in 1767. This former synagogue is a tall imposing building with a half-frame construction and a pyramid roof. It lies in a prominent position on the main road of the village, a few paces away from city hall.

The ceiling of the former synagogue depicts an unusually expressionistic sky with sun, moon, clouds and constellations of stars instead of the more usual geometric pattern of golden stars. To the right and the left of the aron niche there are painted palm leaves, and a similar pattern could be seen on parts of the exterior wall prior to renovation. The women's gallery stretches around three sides of the high interior. The synagogue seems to be larger than the village church and also stands on higher ground. All this indicates a fairly rich and confident community. Jews still made up almost half the population of Aschenhausen in 1900. By 1932 the community had dwindled to twelve, and in 1938 only five Jews lived in Aschenhausen; they were all deported to Theresienstadt in 1943. The synagogue was sold to a farmer for use as a barn in 1937 or 1938 which saved it from destruction during the 1938 "Reichskristallnacht". Renovation was begun in 1990. The former synagogue can be visited by contacting Mr. Dittmar at Kirchstrasse 3.

The large Jewish cemetery dates from the beginning of the 18th century. It lies on a hill overlooking the village.

The former Aschenhausen synagogue before restoration...

Go past the church, turn right after the last houses of the village and follow the narrow path uphill. After about twenty meters, turn left towards the edge of the forest. The oldest remaining stone is from 1708. The cemetery also served the Kaltennordheim, Kaltensundheim and Oepfershausen communities.

The almost Expressionist ceiling has been restored, but the wall paintings have been replaced by white walls.

AUERBACH

is located about 60 km south of Frankfurt on highway 3 close to highway 47 and just off the A 5 (map 8).

* Former synagogue from 1779
* Cemetery from 1615 in nearby Alsbach

Jews probably began to settle in

...and after its rescue from years of neglect.

Auerbach early in the 17th century. The community grew slowly and could not afford a synagogue for a long time. The Auerbach Jews used the nearby Bensheim synagogue, even though Auerbach was a part of Hessen-Darmstadt and Bensheim was ruled by Kurmainz. A synagogue in Auersbach was built in 1779. The move from the Bensheim synagogue was accompanied by lawsuits, since the Bensheim Jews lost the Auerbach fees for the maintenance of their synagogue; even the prayer books of the Auerbach Jews were impounded for a while.

The Auerbach community declined from the middle of the 19th century on, as its younger members emigrated or moved to larger cities. By 1915, the community had become so small that it could no longer hold services for which ten Jewish men are required. The neighboring community of Zwingenberg was faced with a similar situation, so the two communities decided to use the newer Zwingenberg synagogue together. The Auerbach synagogue building was sold to a Christian in 1934 and was not damaged on "Reichskristallnacht". It was used as a machine repair shop until 1972 when the land was sold to the city. After the school building (which had a ritual bath) in front was torn down, the half-forgotten former synagogue emerged. It was renovated by the city in the 1980's.

The ceiling is painted in the same way as it was when the synagogue was first constructed: a light blue sky with small golden stars at regular intervals.

The two women's galleries could not be reconstructed completely, because no pre-1934 photographs or drawings exist. The upper gallery had been destroyed by changes in connection with the use of the synagogue as a workshop. Behind the lower gallery, a small genisah with 18th century prayer books was found. The niche for the ark is still there, but the ark itself is missing. The bimah was not reconstructed either. The building is used for religious and cultural purposes today. It lies in Bachgasse opposite number 19, a small distance back from the street behind a small park. The former synagogue is open to visitors every first Sunday in the month between 3 and 5. The key may be obtained from the Catholic priest of Auerbach, Pfarrer Storch at Diefenbachweg 5.

The small former synagogue of Auerbach lies at some distance from the street; the Jewish school once stood in front of it.

The Auerbach Jews were buried in nearby Alsbach as were the Jews of 28 other communities from the area. The cemetery was founded in 1615 and has about 2,000 stones today. Not surprisingly for a conservative rural community, the red sandstone stones are of equal height and unadorned. There are no family plots and the only ornaments are symbols for the tribe or the position of the deceased: the Cohen hands, the Levi pitcher, and the circumcision instruments of the mohel. As usual in the countryside, German inscriptions did not appear until the late 19th century.

AUGSBURG

is located about 70 km northwest of München, off the A 8 (map 10, 11).

* Synagogue from 1917 in the Art Nouveau style
* Jewish museum
* Former mid-19th century synagogue in Kriegshaber
* Cemeteries from 17th and 19th centuries

Although it is thought a Jewish community was present as early as the Roman period (about 200 C.E.), documents confirm the presence of Jews in 1212. Augsburg was a free and imperial city from 1276 until 1806 which meant it was directly associated with the Holy Roman Empire. It was governed by a city council, and only owed allegiance and taxes to the emperor and not to one of the German princes.

For the most part, the Jewish community prospered from the middle of the 13th century on into the middle of the 15th century sufficiently to have a community center, synagogue and cemetery, rabbinical court, mikveh, bakery, and a dance hall for weddings. Originally, the community belonged to the emperor and was protected by him. A seal from 1296 shows the imperial eagle wearing the pointed hat of the Jews, with Latin and Hebrew inscriptions around it. This seal can be seen in the city archives. Throughout this period, however, there was a continuous power struggle between the city, church, and imperial authorities for control over the Jewish community and its revenues resulting in some rather imaginative administration. Emperor Ludwig the Bavarian (1314-1347) actually rented out the rights to Jewish revenues to various municipalities.

In both the 1298 and 1336 crusades, the city protected the Jews from massacre. However, in 1348, the fury of the Black Death rioters overwhelmed the community, resulting in great slaughter. Readmitting Jews a year later, the city authorities continued to extort as much as they could from the Jewish coffers and then, having emptied the till, proceeded to expel the community in 1439. The following year, the community cemetery was dismantled by the city and its 13th and 14th century gravestones used to build a new city hall. Jews were not officially allowed back for more than a few years at a time until the early 19th century, almost 400 years later.

The Jewish bankers admitted in 1803 were invited to try and save the city from bankruptcy, but the financial situation was beyond repair. Augsburg became part of the young Bavarian kingdom in 1806 when the Holy Roman Empire finally ceased to exist. These bankers were then very active in helping the Wittelsbacher kings of Bavaria and at least two of the bankers, the Seligmann brothers, were made barons without having to become Christians. The community continued to grow throughout the 19th century, eventually outgrowing their 1858 synagogue on Wintergasse. In 1917 a new synagogue, built in a very successful mixture of Byzantine and Jugendstil (or Art Nouveau) style, was consecrated. At this time, about one percent of the population of about 100,000 was Jewish.

The Nazi persecutions started early in Augsburg with a desecration of the Jewish cemetery in 1924. During "Reichskristallnacht", the fire in the synagogue was put out by the fire brigade but the interior was largely destroyed and the Torah scrolls were desecrated. Of the approximately 1,000 Jews living in Augsburg in 1933, about 450 emigrated and another 100 moved to other German cities. Most of the remaining Jews were deported in 1942 and killed in the Nazi camps. About 25 Augsburg Jews returned to their city after 1945, mainly from Theresienstadt, and together with survivors from Eastern Europe formed the new community.

In 1985, the very impressive restored synagogue was consecrated again.

Restoration took about twenty years altogether, ten years for securing the financing and another ten years for the construction work. The large cupola, adorned with golden stars, resembles the cupolas in old Byzantine churches or Turkish mosques. The bimah stands in front of the ark; two griffins holding menorahs stand on each side. The cupola displays four hexagonal tablets with religious themes (the burnt offering; the palm tree as a symbol for the righteous; the three crowns of the Torah, the priest and the king with the fourth crown of the good name over them; and law tablets and the Torah). Six round tablets on the gallery railings depict the symbols of the tribes of Israel.

The Augsburg synagogue is probably the only surviving German Jugendstil synagogue. The synagogue complex houses a Jewish museum which contains a very rich collection of ritual and secular objects from the 17th to the 19th century such as Torah scrolls, Torah mantles, Torah shields, Torah pointers, rimonim and Torah crowns, mesusoth, sabbath and Chanukah lamps, seder plates, besamim boxes, circumcision implements, and wedding rings. Augsburg was a major gold and silver crafts center and many of the religious objects seen elsewhere in Germany were actually made here. There are two memorials to Jewish soldiers killed in WWI, one in the lobby of the synagogue and one in the courtyard.

The museum is open daily, except Saturday and Monday, from 10-3, Sunday from 10-5. The synagogue,

The splendid Art Nouveau synagogue of Augsburg was restored a few years ago. A remarkable Jewish museum is attached to the synagogue.

The small former synagogue of Kriegshaber, a suburb of Augsburg, was restored externally and may be used as a library in the future.

museum, and community center are located at Halderstrasse 8.

After being expelled from Augsburg in 1439, some Augsburg Jews settled in the nearby village of Kriegshaber which is now a suburb of Augsburg. A synagogue from the mid-19th century survived destruction in 1938 due to its proximity to other houses. It has been restored on the outside, the interior awaits restoration. It still has its ark niche in the east wall and a Star of David over the door. Supposedly the synagogue was connected to the surrounding Jewish houses by subterranean passages. Similar stories are told about other synagogues. The synagogue is located on Ulmer Strasse 228. Since the renovation has

not yet been completed, visits to the interior are not yet possible at the time of writing.

A large 17th century cemetery lies in the middle of a US military housing complex on Hooverstrasse 15 in Kriegshaber. The cemetery is locked. However, there is a guardhouse on the premises and you can ring the bell for entry.

A second cemetery was established in the 19th century at Haunstetterstrasse 64. This cemetery contains a memorial to Jewish soldiers killed in WWI and a memorial to the victims of the Nazis. The cemetery is locked. The key may be obtained at the Jewish Community Center on Halderstrasse.

BAIERSDORF

lies about 30 km north of Nürnberg, between the A 73 and the Regnitz river (map 9).

* Cemetery from the 14th century

All that remains of Baiersdorf's 600 year old Jewish community is its elaborate 14th century cemetery. The cemetery was used continuously until 1938, not only by Jews living in Baiersdorf, but also by those living in Bamberg, Bayreuth and other communities in the area. There is a memorial to the Jewish victims of the Nazis. The cemetery contains many impressive Cohanite and Levite stones ornamented in the Baroque style. Among the graves is that of Moses Hameln, son of Glückel of Hameln whose memoirs provide a vivid view of the German Jewish world of the 17th and 18th centuries. Moses Hameln's father-in-law, Samson Baiersdorf from Vienna, was one of the more famous court Jews and responsible for building Baiersdorf's synagogue in 1711. There is a memorial tablet to this synagogue, which was destroyed in 1938, on the side of a bank at Judengasse 14.

You may get the key to the cemetery at the Rathaus (city hall) on Waaggasse 2, Monday-Friday 8-12, Tuesday 4-5, and Thursday 2-6.

To get to the cemetery, turn off Hauptstrasse towards the city cemetery on Am Friedhof. Turn right at the city cemetery gate, go left through the wooden gate at the end of the alley and continue on. The Jewish cemetery is almost at the end of this narrow path.

BAMBERG

lies about 60 km north of Nürnberg on the A 73 (map 9).

* Marienkirche was a synagogue prior to 1349, parts of the original structure remain
* Synagogue and community center
* Memorials
* Cathedral has a statue of the Synagogue Defeated
* Historical Museum has a model of the 18th century Horb synagogue
* Cemetery from 1851

Jews began settling in Bamberg some time before 1096. During the First Crusade, the community was given the choice of baptism or massacre by the crusaders. Over the centuries that followed, the community was frequently attacked or expelled for

The medieval synagogue of the Bamberg Jews has had many uses in the course of the centuries.

The splendid Gothic statue of the Synagogue Defeated used to stand outside the cathedral...

... on this pillar later adorned with a mischievous devil pulling a Jew's ears.

varying periods of time. It suffered destruction during the Rindfleisch massacres of 1298 and the Black Plague pogroms of 1348. In the course of local hunger riots in 1699, the community was again threatened with massacre which was only averted when one of its members poured plums over the mob. This event was later commemorated in an annual "plum fast".

The medieval community had a synagogue, mikveh, dance hall for weddings, a hostel, and a Judengasse. The synagogue was converted into a church called Marienkirche (St. Mary's) following the Black Death massacres in 1348. After its use as a Catholic church and an athletic club, this former synagogue was converted into a Protestant church. It is located at Judenstrasse 1.

The new Bamberg synagogue and Jewish Community Center are located on Willy-Lessing-Strasse 7, where the synagogue destroyed in 1938 once stood. The street is named for the former president of the Jewish community who died from injuries he received in the 1938 "Reichskristallnacht" pogrom.

The Bamberg cathedral displays Gothic statues of the Synagogue Defeated and the Church Triumphant in its south nave. The Synagogue is shown blindfolded, with a broken staff and law tablets slipping from her fingers; the unknown sculptor - who also created the famous Bamberg horseman - seems to have treated her with more sympathy than he did the rather proud and stiff Church Triumphant. Outside on the north portal is a column on which a medieval Jew in a pointed hat can be seen with a devil pulling his ears perched above him. The Synagogue Defeated statue once stood on top of this column. In the past, when Judaism was still considered a threat to the -then - relatively young Christian religion, sculptures such as these were often found on cathedrals and churches throughout Germany. However, most have now been removed. The north portal also shows another familiar theme of Gothic Christian art: The twelve apostles, their feet resting on the shoulders of the twelve prophets. During the winter, the cathedral is open from 9-12 and 2-4, during the summer until 6.

The Historical Museum contains a model of a synagogue painted by Eliezer Sussmann ben Solomon, a Polish Jewish artist responsible for many of the brightly painted synagogues of Franconia in the 18th century. The original painted synagogue from Horb, a small village in the area, is on permanent loan to the Israel Museum in Jerusalem. The museum, in the Old Residence opposite the cathedral, is open daily from 9 to 5.

The cemetery, from 1851, borders the city cemetery on Siechenstrasse 102. The cemetery is locked but you can gain admission from the resident caretaker. There is a memorial to the victims of the Nazis as well as a taharah house and a guardhouse. Before this cemetery was opened, the Bamberg dead were buried in the cemeteries in Zeckendorf and Walsdorf.

There is a memorial to the victims of the Nazis at the Altes Rathaus on Untere Brücke and a memorial to the synagogue destroyed on "Reichskristallnacht" on Herzog-Max-Strasse/Urbanstrasse.

BAYREUTH

is located about 80 km northeast of Nürnberg, on the A 9 (map 9).

* Synagogue from 1760
* Cemetery from 1786

Jews settled in Bayreuth in the 13th century. Many were killed during the Black Death persecutions, but afterwards the community was granted more effective protection by the margrave of Bayreuth instead of the faraway emperor. The community members were able to travel freely and had the rare right to seek justice against Christians before a mixed tribunal made up of both Jewish and Christian judges until the 15th century. They were subject to periodic expulsions from the 15th to the 17th centuries but were always allowed to resettle after a short time.

In 1759, the court Jew and banker Moses Seckel bought a small palace which was converted into a synagogue and consecrated in 1760. Although the synagogue was ransacked in 1938, it was not destroyed. It has been restored and may be seen at Münzgasse 2. The Jewish community center is located next to the synagogue. Call the community center (0921) 65407 to arrange a visit.

A cemetery, from 1786, is located on Nürnberger Strasse 9. Before that date, burials took place in the nearby cemeteries in Baiersdorf, Burgkundstadt, and Aufsess. The cemetery includes a taharah house. The cemetery is locked, the key is available from the community center. Very little can be seen from the gate.

BEESKOW

is located about 80 km southeast of Berlin, on highways B 87 and B 246 (map 2).

* Former synagogue from 1860
* Cemetery from the first half of the 19th century

The first Jews came to Beeskow comparatively late at the end of the 18th century. The community was already dissolved in 1918. The synagogue from 1860, an imposing brick building located next to the old city wall at Brandstrasse 45, was sold by the last Jews of Beeskow and the new owner converted the building into a residence. Only the round windows in the gables remind one of the former use of the building.

The small cemetery on Kohlsdorfer Chaussee looks well-kept today; however, because of numerous desecrations practically none of the gravestones are in their original position.

BERGEN-BELSEN

a former concentration camp, lies on highway 3 about 60 km north of Hannover, in a bleak part of the Lüneburg heath (map 1, 3).

* Concentration Camp Memorial

The land here has little agricultural value and population is sparse. The German military has used it as a training area for a long time. In 1940, a POW camp was built here where about 50,000 Soviet POW's died from starvation and disease. In 1943, the camp was first used to hold Jews who were to be exchanged for Germans interned abroad. From 1944 on, however, it also received sick prisoners from other concentration camps. As the allies advanced, more and more prisoners from Auschwitz and other camps were transferred here. If they survived the death marches, they faced extreme overcrowding, epidemics, and starvation. This led to the death of about 35,000 prisoners, among them Anne Frank. 13,000 more died from the infectious diseases raging in the camp between April 15, 1945, the day the camp was liberated by British troops, and the end of June 1945.

Today, Bergen-Belsen stands as a memorial to all the victims of the Third Reich. The site includes memorials, mass graves, and a documentation center. The documentation center includes information concerning the POW camp, histories of survivors, and the trials against perpetrators. The site is visited by thousands of visitors each year, including students in the Lower Saxony schools whose visit is a mandatory part of their history curriculum. Many visitors go on to visit the 18th century synagogue in Celle, 25 km south from here. (See Celle). The memorial can be visited daily from 9 to 6.

BERKACH

is a small village south of Meiningen and east of Mellrichstadt, directly on the former border between the two Germanys, about 100 km southwest of Erfurt (map 5, 6, 8).

* Synagogue from 1854
* Mikveh from 1838
* Cemetery from 1846

Berkach was isolated for 40 years due to its location directly on the German-German border; the nearest border crossing was far, and a visit to Berkach was impossible for citizens of the German Democratic Republic without special permission.

The rural Jewish community of Berkach built a mikveh near the Grüne river in 1838. The small building was renovated in recent years. Driving into Berkach from the direction of Nordheim, you cross the Grüne creek over a small bridge. Turn right into Poststrasse immediately after crossing this bridge; along this street there are some farm buildings and barns on the left. To the right there are meadows along the creek. After about 150 meters there is a small stone building standing by itself next to the creek. This is the former mikveh of Berkach. There is a small stone tablet with the inscription "Samuel Isagk Darmas 1838" in Latin letters over the door;

The small former ritual bath of the Berkach Jews stands next to a creek and is fed by ground water. It was restored after having been used as a shed for decades.

the Darmas may stand for Parnas, the president of the community. Inside the door there is a mezuzah on the doorpost. Stone steps lead down about 2.2 meters to the simple bath fed by the ground water of the Grüne; next to the bath there is a well whose purpose is unknown. After 1945, the building was used as a garden shed and the bath and well were filled in. Renovation was started before 1990.

The synagogue from the middle of the 19th century is a large half-frame building. It stands on Mühlfelderstrasse, a side street to the south and opposite the church, and about 50 meters away from the main street leading through the village.

The synagogue still has its high arched windows. The women's gallery rests on twelve wooden columns and arches. After 1945 the building was used as a storehouse and as a blacksmith's workshop by the local farm cooperative. In 1990 restoration was started by the state of Thuringia. The synagogue was consecrated again on November 3, 1991. The key is available from city hall.

The Jewish cemetery lies away from the village, on a hill next to the former border fortifications. Go south on the main street in the direction of Behrungen. After a short distance, the street forms a right angle towards the left, and an agricultural road leads straight up the hill. This is the old road to Behrungen that was blocked by the border for 40 years. After about 500 meters you will see a group of trees surrounded by a fence on the left. The Orthodox cemetery with its orderly rows of single graves lies here. The key is available from town hall.

The former synagogue of Berkach had been used as a blacksmith workshop for many years.

Renovation of the Berkach synagogue was begun in 1990 and resulted in this stately building overlooking the village.

BERLIN (map 2).

* Five (former) synagogues
* Two museum collections of Judaica
* Documentation center - Topography of Terror
* Memorials
* Five cemeteries

In 1295, a decree forbidding wool merchants to buy wool yarn from Jews provides the first evidence that Jews were living in Berlin. Other early references concern the taxes they had to pay in order to marry, circumcise their sons, buy wine, ritually slaughter their cattle, or allow other Jews into their community. The Black Death persecutions in 1349-50 led to the death of many and the expulsion of all the survivors. However, the Jews must have been allowed to return soon afterwards as the next reference is from 1354, but the community was once again expelled and their property confiscated in 1446. The community was allowed to return again the following year and numbered 23 families by 1454.

A host desecration charge in 1510 left many dead and the rest of the community was expelled. In 1539, the German Diet found the dead innocent thanks to the work of Josel of Rosheim, the "Emperor of the Jews", and the humanist Philipp Melanchthon. Jews were once again allowed to settle - if they could afford it - until another "eternal" expulsion in 1571. Resettlement was denied until the expulsion of Jews from Austria in 1671 led the Prussian elector to accept 50 wealthy Jewish Viennese families into his domain; seven families settled in Berlin. Their presence was continually challenged by the Berlin merchants and guilds well into the 18th century, but the economic benefits of Jewish presence were considered essential by the council and the electors and later kings of Prussia, so that demands for their expulsion were regularly denied. However, the community was forced to accept a wide variety of restrictions governing their social and economic lives, and to pay the high taxes and other contributions demanded by the Prussian rulers. Difficult as these restrictions and high taxes were, the community continued to increase until 1730, when it was limited to only one hundred families, forcing many Jews into exile at least temporarily. But by 1737 there were again 234 Jewish families in Berlin, and this time their number was limited at 168; at the same time, ownership of houses by Jews was prohibited.

Throughout the 18th century and on into the 19th century, the community also faced internal friction and turmoil. With partial emancipation in the early years of the 19th century followed by full emancipation in 1860, a strong movement promoting assimilation threatened to depopulate the community; it is estimated that 50 per cent, perhaps more, of the Jews of Berlin became Christians during this period. At the same time a strong movement for reform and an equally strong conservative faction brought about splits resulting in the establishment of many religious groups

In 1988 the street facade, the remains of the cupola and the Moorish towers of the grand Oranien-burgerstrasse synagogue still showed the scars of destruction.

54

Since then the building has been restored with a lot of effort and today houses the Centrum Judaicum of Berlin.

among the Berlin Jews. During this time, Jews like Moses Mendelssohn, who translated the Torah into German, David Friedländer, and Isaac Daniel Itzig sought to eliminate the differences and misunderstandings existing between German Christians and German Jews by promoting understanding through education. In 1819 Leopold Zunz founded the important "Society for Jewish Culture and Learning", which gave the Jews consciousness of and pride in their past.

By the beginning of the 19th century, the Berlin Jewish community had become increasingly important as a religious center in Germany, and later with full emancipation their participation in industry, the arts, journalism, and politics made it increasingly important socially and politically throughout Germany. This increased importance, unfortunately, also made Berlin a center for anti-Semitism. The community grew rapidly following emancipation and numbered over 172,000 in 1933. About a third of Germany's Jews lived here at the onset of the Nazi years. It is estimated that 55,000 Berlin Jews suffered deportation and death at the hands of the Nazis. About 6,000 Jews survived in Berlin, most of them because of their marriages with Gentile partners, and some of them in hiding.

Today, Berlin again has the largest Jewish community in Germany. Of the more than 100 synagogues existing in Berlin before the Nazis took power, only a few have survived.

The oldest synagogue of the second Berlin Jewish community was built in 1714 and stood in Heidereutergasse. It was not damaged during the "Reichskristallnacht" pogrom since it had already been taken over by the German postal authorities. During the bombings of Berlin, the building was destroyed and the ruin was torn down after the war. Heidereutergasse does not exist today, only a parking lot between Spandauerstrasse and Rosenstrasse in Berlin Mitte.

The very grand Fasanenstrasse synagogue was built in 1912, gutted due to arson in 1938, further damaged during the 1945 fighting between the Wehrmacht and the Red Army besieging Berlin, and finally razed in 1957. A new synagogue and community center including a kosher restaurant, an adult education center and an important library have been

This memorial stands in front of Berlin's main synagogue on Fasanenstrasse.

built on the site. In front of the synagogue stand two columns and the doorway which were salvaged from the old synagogue. There is a memorial in the form of a Torah scroll which has an inscription from the second book of Moses: "There shall be one law for you and for the strangers who dwell in your midst". The synagogue and community center are located on Fasanenstrasse 79-80 in Charlottenburg.

Quite close by, at Joachimstaler Strasse 13 in Charlottenburg, is the synagogue of the Orthodox community. Its prayer room used to be the gym of a Jewish primary school which was founded in 1935 when Jewish children were expelled from German schools. Many Jewish organizations are housed in the same building. The only surviving synagogue in what used to be East Berlin is located on Rykestrasse 53 in the Prenzlauer Berg quarter. It was carefully and beautifully restored during the Communist rule and served a very small East Berlin community when Berlin was divided. The main synagogue was only used for festival service. There is a small prayer room for sabbath prayer opposite the entrance.

The neo-Romanesque synagogue was built in 1903-4, seated 2,000, and was used until 1940, at which time it was converted to a storehouse for the army. Due to its location in the middle of residential blocks it was not burned down in the 1938 "Reichskristallnacht". The synagogue is set back in the courtyard and has stars of David and law tablets in Hebrew over both entrance doors. The building in front is a former school.

The large synagogue on Rykestrasse served the small Jewish community of East Berlin.

The Fraenkelufer synagogue, of neo-classicist design, was built in 1916 and largely destroyed in 1938. The main synagogue was torn down after the war and the former youth synagogue was converted to an Orthodox synagogue. The complex includes a Jewish community center. It has been beautifully restored with a lovely apse on the west side and a row of columns on the south. It is located on Fraenkelufer 10-16 in Kreuzberg.

The Pestalozzistrasse synagogue was saved due to its physical attachment to neighboring buildings in 1938. It was built in 1911 and is located on Pestalozzistrasse 14 in Charlottenburg. For some time during the war, it served as a laundry for the dwindling Berlin community. In 1947 the building was renovated and now serves the Reform community.

The recently restored large and very grand Neue Synagoge, from 1866, stands at Oranienburgerstrasse 30 in Berlin Mitte. This synagogue was heavily damaged by the "Reichskristallnacht" pogrom in 1938 as well as by the bombing and fighting during WWII. The burnt-out and bullet-marked shell was a monument to the madness of the Holocaust and the war. The prayer room had first been destroyed by the SA and later bombed out; it was torn down in 1958. The top of the main cupola was gone but the rim remained as did the two accompanying Moorish towers. During GDR times there were plans to stabilize the facade and establish a Jewish museum; the opening was planned for 1996. After unification, things speeded up; in 1991, the street front was already restored. The building houses the Centrum Judaicum today.

The former East Berlin Jewish Community Center was located next door at Oranienburgerstrasse 28 in Berlin Mitte. Today parts of the Jewish central archive formerly stored in the Potsdam archives are housed in the Centrum Judaicum here as well as the community library and a coffeehouse.

The Beth Zion synagogue was probably founded around the turn of the century in the courtyard of Brunnenstrasse 33 in Berlin Mitte. The building was devastated in 1938, stood empty for almost 50 years and is an office building today. Outside the neo-Romanesque building can still be recognized as a former synagogue, but it has been thoroughly altered inside.

There was a very rich collection of Judaica on the ground floor of the Berlin Museum. It contained a wide variety of ritual objects from the 18th and 19th centuries including Torah shields, curtains and crowns, rimonim, silver and gold-plated sabbath and Chanukah lamps, as well as silver besamim boxes, kiddush cups, etrog boxes, lithographs by Thielmann with scenes from Berlin synagogues, a pitcher of the Chevra Kaddisha, collection boxes of Adass Yisroel, and a circumcision bench from 1720.

In addition there were photographs and models of Berlin's pre-1938 synagogues and documentation concerning the fate of Berlin's Jewish community. The museum is located on Lindenstrasse 14 in Kreuzberg. However, it will be closed until 1997 or 1998 since it is being enlarged. A separate Jewish museum is being built.

An annex of this museum collection is located on the second floor in the rear in the Gropius Bau Museum on Stresemannstrasse 110 in Kreuzberg. This museum exhibit contains documentation of Berlin's Jewish community life including letters of protection, portraits of famous and important German Jews along with biographical information, mementos, family chronicles and memorabilia, books, magazines, and leaflets written and published by Jews, paintings by Jewish artists, and documents concerning the community during the Nazi years. The museum also displays a collection of Judaica including Torah curtains, Chanukah and sabbath lamps, seder plates, Esther scrolls, etrog boxes, besamim boxes, mezuzahs, tefillin pouches, kiddush cups, astronomical instruments for calculating Jewish festivals, a chuppah, a Torah scroll, several mantles, shields, pointers, rimonim, crowns, and old gravestones found in the Spandau citadel which was built in the 16th century using the gravestones of the oldest of Berlin's many Jewish cemeteries. This museum is open Tuesday-Sunday 10-10.

Next to the Gropius Bau Museum is a documentation center called Topography of Terror. The center is located in the former basement of the SS, Gestapo, and RSHA (main office for security of the Reich) headquarters and documents their actions against the Jews and the opposition in Germany, Poland, the USSR, Hungary and other European countries. The buildings themselves were destroyed by bombs and fighting and razed in the 1950's. Since the site was next to the Berlin wall, no rebuilding took place. The documentation center is open Tuesday-Sunday 10-6.

There are many memorials throughout Berlin. Memorials have been established at the deportation centers at the former synagogue site on Levetzowstrasse 7-8 in Tiergarten, the Jewish hospital on Iranische Strasse 11a in Wedding, and the Putlitzstrasse (Tiergarten) and Grunewald (Wilmersdorf) train stations from where transports to the extermination camps departed. A memorial to the Jewish school is located on Siegmundshof 11 in Tiergarten, and to the destroyed synagogues on Westarpstrasse/Münchener Strasse in Schöneberg, Prinzenallee 87 in Wedding (the building is being used by Jehovah's Witnesses today), Lindenstrasse 48 in Kreuzberg, Prinzregentenstrasse 69 in Wilmersdorf, Franzensbaderstrasse 7 in Wilmersdorf and Lindenufer 12 in Spandau. There is also a commemorative tablet on Meinekestrasse 10 in Charlottenburg to the Jewish Agency which helped thousands of Jews emigrate. A Jewish home for the mentally retarded and its 180 inhabitants killed in German camps is commemorated in Smetanastrasse 53 in Weissensee. At Parkstrasse 22 in Weissensee there is a memorial to the home for the deaf and dumb and its 146 deported inmates. There is also a memorial in Wilhelm-Wolff-Strasse 30-38 in Pankow to the 150 children who had lived in a Jewish children's home here and were taken to Auschwitz and killed. The house is an old age home today. A tablet in Tucholskystrasse 9, Berlin Mitte, a residential building today, commemorates the Institute for the Science of Judaism founded by Leopold Zunz and later led by Leo Baeck.

On the corner of Grosse Hamburger Strasse 26 and Oranienburger Strasse, Berlin Mitte, there is a memorial to the first Jewish old age home in Berlin. In 1942, the Gestapo used the building for a transit camp. 55,000 members of the Jewish community were deported from this site to Auschwitz and Theresienstadt. There is a small memorial commemorating the home.

Next to it, at Grosse Hamburgerstrasse 27, Berlin Mitte, the former Talmud-Tora-School, from 1863, stood. This school was originally founded in 1778 as a Reform school with German language lessons and, from 1825, led by Leopold Zunz. There are plans to open a Jewish high school here. There is a portrait bust of Moses Mendelssohn on the facade.

Nearby, in Grosse Hamburgerstrasse 26, is an old cemetery from 1672 which is now a small park. It was used until 1827 and was destroyed by the Gestapo in 1943. Moses Mendelssohn is buried here. The stone bearing his name, however, is post-war and only marks the approximate location of his grave. There were several old gravestones in the rear wall, but they have been removed for renovation. There is a memorial to this oldest Jewish cemetery in Berlin as well as a beautiful memorial depict-

This memorial, on Grosse Hamburgerstrasse, was established in memory of the deported and murdered Jews of Berlin.

ing 13 Jewish men, women and children of different ages commemorating the victims of the Nazis.

The second oldest Jewish cemetery on Schönhauser Allee 23-25, in the Prenzlauer Berg quarter, from 1827, reflects the growing assimilation of the Berlin community. While the oldest stones are simple and unadorned, the stones from the second half of the 19th century resemble Christian gravestones of the same period. The older stones are oriented towards the East, while in later burials this tradition has been given up. Many well-known Berlin Jews are buried here, for example, Leopold Zunz and Abraham Geiger, founders of the "Teaching Institute for the Science of Judaism", the composer Giacomo Meyerbeer, the painter Max Liebermann, the publisher Leopold Ullstein as well as Gerson von Bleichröder, the banker of both chancellor Bismarck and emperor Wilhelm I. There is a memorial near the entrance. The cemetery is open Sunday-Thursday 8-4, Friday 8-2.

The Adass Yisroel Orthodox community cemetery on Wittlicher Strasse 2 in Weissensee was started in 1880. In front there is a memorial to the Adass Yisroel Jews killed by the Nazis as well as a gravestone to the destroyed and desecrated Torahs buried here. The cemetery was restored by the East German government and returned to the Orthodox community in 1986. The grave register was redone in 1986 as well. The newly founded Adass Yisroel community offers a guided tour every other Sunday. The cemetery is open

Monday-Thursday 8-4, Friday 8-2, and Sunday 10-4. There is a memorial plaque to the Adass Yisroel community center and rabbinical school on Tucholskystrasse 40, Berlin Mitte. This building has also been given back to Adass Yisroel.

The largest Jewish cemetery in Europe is the Weissensee Cemetery on Herbert-Baum-Strasse 45. There are over 115,000 graves in this cemetery which was established in 1880. The cemetery contains many elaborate gravestones and monuments to important Jewish families of the 19th and early 20th centuries. There is a memorial to the Jewish victims of the Nazi years in front of the entrance building, as well as to the graves of Herbert Baum and his young followers who formed a Jewish-communist

Crumbling plaster revealed Hebrew letters on some facades near the Weissensee cemetery.

61

resistance group against the Nazis and were executed or murdered in 1942. The cemetery was a very important institution for many Berlin Jews during the Nazi years: it provided work, agricultural training for prospective emigrants, a hiding place for Torahs, and later a hiding place for Jews trying to avoid deportation, thus becoming a true "house of life". It is open Sunday through Thursday from 8 until dusk (around 6 in summer, 5 in the late autumn and early spring months, and 4 in winter), Friday from 8 to 2.

The new Jewish cemetery of Berlin, the only one accessible for the Jewish community of West Berlin for many years, is located in a forest inside a large park on Heerstrasse 141 in Charlottenburg. The cemetery, from 1955, contains a few 14th and 15th century gravestones which were used in the construction of Spandau citadel in the 16th century. The cemetery includes a memorial to these old stones and a memorial to the Jewish victims of the Nazis. The cemetery is open Sunday-Thursday from 7 to 5 and Friday from 7 to 3. To get there, take the access road off the corner of Scholzplatz.

The Potsdam Central Archives contained the local archives of hundreds of Jewish communities, some of them reaching back to the 17th century. The "Central Archive of German Jews" was started in 1906 to save the documents of many small Jewish communities that had ceased to exist. During the Nazi years, when all Jewish organizations were prohibited, their archives were stored there as well and "protected" by a special Gestapo branch. The huge archive survived the war years undamaged and then was taken over by the East German government's central archives. During the GDR government, the Jewish archives were not available for research. Today, the larger part of the archives have been handed over to Israel, about a third of the documents have been moved to the Centrum Judaicum in Oranienburgerstrasse 28, Berlin Mitte.

On Am Grossen Wannsee 56-58 in Zehlendorf the villa where the barbaric decisions about the organization necessary for the "final solution of the Jewish question in Europe" were made in 1942 is still standing and is a memorial today. There is a commemorative tablet to the Jewish victims of Auschwitz, Sobibor, Bergen-Belsen and the many other concentration camps.

BINSWANGEN

is located about 100 km northwest of München, on regional highway 2033 between Wertingen and Dillingen (map 10, 11).

* Former synagogue from 1835
* Cemetery from 1663

Jews were probably living in Binswangen from 1348 on when the Augsburg Jews were expelled. However, the first mention of Jews dates from 1439 when it was reported that a Jew won a court case against Count Johann of Sultz who had banned peddling in his

The former synagogue of Binswangen with its Moorish style elements served as the storehouse of a construction company...

...before being restored in the 1990s for future use as a cultural center.

territory. The community was poor, occupied primarily in horse dealing and peddling. However, despite their poverty, records indicate the community was forced to pay a tax of about 500 Gulden a year, quite a fortune at the time, in 1632.

That same year, invading Swedes burned down eight houses owned by Jews. The community grew until the mid-19th century, when about one-third of Binswangen was Jewish; then emigration to the USA and moves to bigger cities with better possibilities led to a decline. It was very common for young Jews to flee the narrowness of the German village with its very limited possibilities then. At least seven Binswangen Jews were deported and killed during the Nazi years.

The former synagogue, built in 1835 on the pattern of the Ingenheim synagogue, was devastated but not destroyed in 1938 and subsequently sold to a construction company which used it as a storehouse. In 1987, the county bought the building and renovated it. After completion of the renovation, probably in 1996, the building will be used as a cultural center.

The former synagogue is a large two-story brick structure with a mortar finish. It has two rows of Moorish style windows. In 1988, the windows were still boarded up. There were remnants of decorative wall paintings on the outside walls. The ark niche was gone as well as the formerly stepped gabled walls. In 1994, the exterior was already restored to its former splendor, while work on the interior was in progress. The former synagogue is located on Judengasse 3.

Three formerly Jewish houses survive on Hauptstrasse 26, 27, and 33. They date from the second half of the 18th and early 19th century, respectively, and were built with the very prominent gabled facades traditional in the area.

The cemetery was established in 1663 and enlarged in 1761. In 1763 a protective wall was built for an enormous 1,100 Gulden. The cemetery was razed in 1940, the stones removed, and the wall torn down. After 1945, some stones, mostly 19th and early 20th century, were returned and the cemetery was restored. It is located about 600 meters outside of Binswangen, close to the road to Wertingen. Take a left where the forest begins and you can see the wall from the road. There is a memorial stone by the entrance. The cemetery is locked. The key is available at Binswangen city hall.

BOIZENBURG

is a small town about 50 km east of Hamburg, on highway 5 and the Elbe (map 1).

* Former synagogue from 1799
* Cemetery from the late 18th century

When Boizenburg was made a city in 1267, Jews were mentioned in the document. However, the Boizenburg community had to leave the province of Mecklenburg after the Sternberg host desecration trial in 1492, like all other Mecklenburg communities.

The former synagogue of Boizenburg overlooks a small river at the edge of town.

Jews did not settle in Boizenburg again until the end of the 18th century. The small community built a half-frame synagogue at Kleine Wallstrasse 7, a few meters from the market and the church at the edge of town. In 1864 the synagogue had to be restored and received a neo-Romanesque brick facade. As was the case with many other small town Jewish communities, the Boizenburg community declined in the second half of the 19th century. It sold its synagogue to the freemasons in 1892. After some years the former synagogue housed the local museum; after the war, a music school moved in. Since 1994 the building is owned by the freemasons again. There is a commemorative tablet to the community and its synagogue.

The small cemetery from the end of the 18th century lies on a low hill on Lauenburger Postweg at the edge of the old town. About 30 late 19th and early 20th century stones remain.

On Elbberg, west of Boizenburg, an auxiliary camp to the Neuengamme concentration camp was opened in 1944. About 400 Jewish women had to work for the German armaments industry here. In 1969 a memorial was unveiled.

BONN

the former capital of the Federal Republic of Germany, lies about 30 km south of Köln, between the A 565 and the Rhine (map 4, 8).

* Synagogue
* Memorials
* Cemeteries

With the exception of a few cemeteries and several memorials, nothing remains of Bonn's centuries of Jewish life. The community was martyred during the First Crusade in 1096, suffered severe persecutions during the Second Crusade of 1146 of which Ephraim ben Jacob of Bonn, who was 13 at the time, left a detailed account in the Bonn memor book. It was martyred again in 1288, and yet again in the Black Death persecutions in 1349. The Archbishop of Cologne, the overlord of Bonn, pardoned the perpetrators of this last sack and slaughter on condition that all debts owed to the Jewish victims by the burghers should be paid to him instead.

The Jews returned later that century and began once again to contribute heavily to the coffers of the various authorities. Their numbers were augmented in 1424 by the arrival of refugees fleeing persecution in Köln. After that, the community lived in relative peace until 1578 when Queen Elizabeth of England sent a Protestant army into Germany which plundered and pillaged, murdered and took hostages. The community had to raise large sums for ransom. Then came the Thirty Years' War in which Gentile and Jew suffered alike all over Europe. Historical accounts of this period indicate that the Jews in Bonn helped their Protestant neighbors by hiding their valuables in the ghetto when a Catholic army approached. Their aid went unappreciated, however, and new restrictions, regulations and penalties ensued following the end of the war. In 1716, the Jews had to move to a ghetto separated from the city by guarded gates.

The 18th century brought earthquakes and floods which caused great fear and suffering. However, as the century came to a close, the French Revolution secured equal rights for the Jews and tore down the gates of the ghetto. Thus, the community grew and prospered until the rise of the Third Reich. In 1933, 1,268 Jews lived in Bonn; all the synagogues were destroyed in 1938, and about 350 Bonn Jews were killed in the camps.

There are several Jewish cemeteries in the Bonn area, one of which was established around the middle of the 17th century. It is located in Schwarzrheindorf, a suburb of Bonn. To get there, follow Bergheimer Strasse north and turn left when it crosses a little creek. Leave your car at the sewage treatment plant and walk along the Rhine dike for about 500 meters. The cemetery is large, shaded by old trees and very picturesque with its many rows of old stones, showing local variations of the

The old Jewish cemetery of Schwarzrheindorf, overgrown with ivy, lies on the bank of the Rhine.

Baroque, Rococo, and Classicist styles in their ornamentation. There is a memorial to the victims of the Nazis at the head of the stairs. The older section is covered in thick ivy. The oldest gravestone is from 1656, and there is a group of Cohen graves close to the southwestern fence. The cemetery is unlocked.

The suburb of Endenich has a cemetery on Hainstrasse 78 which was established in the mid-19th century and is just down the road from the Christian cemetery. The key is available from Friedhofsverwaltung, Mr. Helfer, on Stationsweg in the Poppelsdorf cemetery. An old cemetery from 1730 on Ännchenstrasse, on the northern slope of the Godesburg hill in Bad Godesberg, is open as well as the 1895 cemetery on Am Burgfriedhof nearby. The cemetery on Römerstrasse/Augustusring is open Sunday-Friday between 10-5.

There are several memorials to the victims of the Nazi terror and to the destruction of the synagogues throughout the Bonn area. A new synagogue is located on Tempelstrasse (not the same street as the Tempelstrasse where the main synagogue stood until its destruction in the 1938 "Reichskristallnacht"), close to Adenauerallee.

BOPFINGEN

is located about 110 km east of Stuttgart, or about 100 km southwest of Nürnberg, on highway 29 (map 9). Two small villages, Oberdorf and Aufhausen, now part of Bopfingen, had old Jewish communities.

Aufhausen:
* Cemetery from the 17th century

Oberdorf:
* Former synagogue from 1812
* Cemetery from the early 19th century

Jews came to Aufhausen in the 16th century and prospered alongside the

The relatively well-preserved former synagogue of Oberdorf served as an electrician's storehouse for some years before its restoration as the town's cultural center.

67

Christian community. They were occupied primarily in the cattle, wine, grain, and tobacco trades as well as in peddling. By the mid-19th century, Jews made up 43% of Aufhausen's population. The local city hall housed both the Jewish and Catholic schools as well as the living quarters for the Jewish and the Catholic teachers. However, by 1933 the Jewish population, as in many other rural areas, had declined to five. Four of these were later killed in Nazi camps. Only one Aufhausen Jew managed to emigrate. The synagogue, on Lauchheimer Strasse 21, was built in 1823, partly destroyed in the 1938 "Reichskristallnacht", and later partly torn down. The rest was altered beyond recognition in 1950.

The cemetery, one of the largest in the province of Württemberg, was established in the 17th century and is located on Schenkensteinstrasse north of the Christian cemetery below Schenkenstein fortress. Some of the stones are quite old and all are standing. The stone used is rather soft and the inscriptions are badly weather-beaten. If locked, you can get the key at city hall.

Oberdorf is a few kilometers down the Bopfingen road from Aufhausen.

Jews settled in Oberdorf around 1510 and by the mid-19th century made up a third of the population. The synagogue, built in 1812, was damaged by arson in the 1938 "Reichskristallnacht", converted to a Catholic church in the 1950's, and then to a storehouse for an electrician until 1989. In 1988, the exterior was in very poor condition although the building looked structurally sound. The broken stained glass windows were half covered by pieces of scrap metal.

In 1989, the building was bought by the "Former Synagogue Oberdorf Association" and renovated. Ever since restoration the old building is showing some of its former pride and splendor. There are still two doors in the west wall, formerly one for the men and one for the women of the community. Above the doors are Hebrew inscriptions reading "How awesome is this place" and "This is the house of the Lord and this is the gate of heaven". The former synagogue, now a memorial and community center, is located on Lange Strasse 13 in the alley between the kindergarten and Lange Strasse 17. The key is available from the mayor's office in Bopfingen.

The mikveh and school, on Ipfstrasse 11, are now part of a private home. The Germanische Nationalmuseum in Nürnberg has a prayer shawl and two mesusoth from Oberdorf.

Oberdorf's cemetery, established in the early 19th century, is located up the hill on the corner of Karksteinstrasse and Brandströmweg. There are several different styles of stones with the oldest stones in the middle of the cemetery. There is a memorial to five Oberdorf Jewish soldiers killed in WWI at the entrance. In 1985, the city council erected a memorial to Oberdorf's Jewish citizens who were killed in Nazi camps. The memorial lists the names of 68 Oberdorf Jews in family groups.

BRAUNSCHWEIG

lies 60 km east of Hannover, on the A 2 and A 39 (map 3).

* 18th century former synagogue
* Jewish Museum
* Two 19th century cemeteries

Jews began settling in Braunschweig in the early 12th century. In 1137, the emperor transferred jurisdiction over the Jews to the duke who, along with the municipality, provided protection in return for Jewish revenues. Conditions were thus favorable enough to attract Jews from other areas of northern Germany until the Black Death persecutions in the mid-14th century killed at least half of the community and prevented further immigration. From then until the end of the 16th century, the situation for the Jews of Braunschweig was unstable. There was an accusation of a host desecration in 1510, followed by riots triggered by the writings of Martin Luther in 1543, and short-term expulsions in 1571 and 1590. However, by the beginning of the 17th century, conditions had stabilized sufficiently for the Jews to begin returning.

By the late 18th century, Duke Charles William Ferdinand was corresponding with Moses Mendelssohn, one of the great German-Jewish representatives of Enlightenment. The court Jew Israel Jacobson, who served the duke, founded a very progressive Jewish school in nearby Seesen in 1801. This school enjoyed the duke's patronage. A second similar school was opened in Wolfenbüttel in 1807. The 19th century brought emancipation, in stages and with a few relapses, while the 20th century brought terror and death to hundreds of Braunschweig Jews and exile for the rest.

Alexander David (1687-1765), court Jew of Braunschweig, is known as the father of Jewish museums. Not only did Alexander David fund and build the community synagogue in the early 18th century, he became the earliest known collector of Jewish religious and secular objects. His collection encompassed all sorts of Judaica such as menorahs, besamim boxes, embroideries, candlesticks, Torah mantles and shields, as well as books and manuscripts. He presented his collection to the community just before his death. It was displayed on

The rural Baroque Hornburg Torah shrine is preserved within the walls of the former church of the Pauline monastery, which serves as Braunschweig's Jewish museum today.

69

the ground floor of the synagogue and then handed over to the Patriotic Museum in 1925. Today, a small part of Alexander David's collection is on display in Braunschweig's Jewish Museum. Much more is in storage or on loan to other museums.

The Jewish Museum is part of the Braunschweig Landesmuseum. The most remarkable exhibit is the small painted wooden synagogue, built in 1766, which was acquired in 1923 from Hornburg whose Jewish community had ceased to exist. This synagogue, which is a fine example of 18th century country Baroque, includes the carved Torah ark with decorative fruits, flowers, crowns, and arabesques; a small painted cupola; four ceiling paintings representing the ark, tabernacle, menorah, and shewbread table; as well as the bimah standing in the center of the room, under the cupola, as would be expected from a conservative community. The synagogue was installed in one of the halls of the church of the Pauline convent which had been converted to a museum some years before. The synagogue was on display during the Nazi years but was dismantled and hidden away after 1945. In 1987, it was re-installed as part of the new Jewish Museum within the Braunschweig Landesmuseum. The old, dark wood of the synagogue panels contrasts with the classicist white walls and arches of the convent church; photographs of the synagogue, as it was in 1923, line one wall and give a feeling for the serenity of this old place of worship.

In addition to the synagogue and the permanent Judaica collection, the museum displays documents and objects in connection with the persecution of Jews during the Nazi reign, the concentration camps, and Jewish life in Germany after 1945. There are also special exhibitions on Jewish themes. The Jewish Museum is located on Hinter Ägidien and is open daily from 10-5 and on Thursday from 10-8. Guided tours in English can be arranged by contacting Dr. Knauer, the director of the Jewish Museum.

St. Blasius cathedral in the center of town contains a 15 foot high seven-armed bronze candlestick, which is a copy of the one seen in Jerusalem by Henry the Lion, Duke of Bavaria and Saxony. It was donated by the duke, who also founded the cathedral in 1173, after his return from the Holy Land. The cathedral is open daily from 10-1 and 3-5. (Closed to sightseers during mass on Saturday at 12 and on Sunday at 10.)

The synagogue, built in 1875, was damaged in 1938, and torn down and replaced by a bunker in 1940. Today there is a commemorative tablet on the bunker which is located at the corner of Steinstrasse and Alte Knochenhauerstrasse. The Jewish Community Center, which includes a prayer room for 70 people, is next to it at Steinstrasse 4.

There are two Jewish cemeteries in Braunschweig. The older cemetery dates from the early 19th century and is located at Hamburgerstrasse 71 north of the city center. A visit is possible after contacting Dr. Piero Zamperoni, at Fasanenstrasse 30, telephone (0531) 33 86 96, in the evening.

The second cemetery dates from the late 19th century. It includes a memorial to the victims of the Nazi years and is located on Helmstedterstrasse 40. The cemetery is open, a visit to the taharah house can be arranged by contacting Dr. Zamperoni (see above).

BAD BUCHAU

is located about 110 km southeast of Stuttgart, on the Federsee lake, south of highway 312, between the A 30 and highway 311 (map 10, 11).

* Prayer room from the 17th century
* Cemetery from the 17th century

Jews are first documented in Buchau, then a Free and Imperial City, in 1382. In 1665 Baruch Moses Einstein from Wangen was permitted to settle in Buchau against the payment of the usual protection money; with some probability this is the ancestor of the Einstein family which still lives in Buchau, and also the ancestor of Albert Einstein (whose parents moved to nearby Ulm shortly before he was born in 1879).

According to tradition, the oldest known prayer room in Buchau (from the 15th century) was located on the second floor of Schustergasse 6; the ark was situated in the East wall, where a new window is now. A newer prayer room, from the 17th century, is partly preserved in Judengasse 6, on the second floor of what is now the Konrad shoestore. The most remarkable feature here is the painted

Painted furniture from a German farm? No - the ceiling of a room that could be opened for Sukkot!

wooden ceiling, parts of which can be opened, maybe to allow the sukkah to be erected in the prayer room, but still under an open sky. The former prayer room can only be visited after applying to the Konrad family.

In 1731 the small community built its first synagogue at the end of Judengasse. A century later Jews made up a third of the population of Buchau, and the synagogue became too small. A large, impressive, Classicist-styled synagogue was consecrated in Schussenrieder Strasse in 1839. It had an unusual little spire originally containing chimes, and then in 1854 the chimes were replaced with a bronze bell. This synagogue was destroyed by the Nazis, not on "Reichskristallnacht" November 9-10, 1938, when the arson did not succeed, but the following night. 122 Jews were deported from Bad Buchau, the last two in February 1945, and only four returned. The last camp survivor died in 1968 and is buried in the Jewish cemetery in Buchau.

The place where the synagogue used to stand, at Schussenrieder Strasse and Hofgartenstrasse, is marked by a commemorative tablet.

The Jewish cemetery is situated in Häselstrasse/Friedhofstrasse and was founded in 1659. The oldest gravestone is from 1675.

BUCHENWALD

lies about 30 km east of Erfurt, between highways 7 and 85, 8 kilometers from Weimar (map 5, 6, 7).

* Concentration Camp Memorial

Buchenwald is a former German concentration camp. About 60,000 out of about 250,000 inmates here were murdered or died from hunger, epidemics or exhaustion. About 11,000 Jews were among them. The camp was opened in July 1937 and liberated by US armed forces working together with the main camp resistance movement in April 1945. Today the site serves as a memorial for all the victims of Nazi terror. The Jewish victims are commemorated by a memorial erected in November 1993. Buchenwald can be visited from May to September from 9:45 to 5:15 and from October to April from 8:45 to 4:15. There is a brochure in English.

To each his own - cynical words on the entrance gate of the infamous Buchenwald camp.

CELLE

is located about 40 km northeast of Hannover, on highways 3, 214, and 191 (map 1, 3).

* Synagogue from 1740
* Cemetery from 1692

Jews settled in the village of Blumlage, now part of Celle, in the late 17th century. Initially the community used a school to hold services, but in 1740 they received permission from George, Elector of Hannover, who was also King of England, to build a synagogue. The synagogue is a Baroque half-timbered structure typical for the period and the area and is located in the backyard of the former school.

During the "Reichskristallnacht" pogrom in 1938, the synagogue was saved from arson by the local fire department who claimed that a fire would destroy the nearby houses and factory. However, they helped the SA break the windows and destroy the furniture and the books. The Torah was saved and hidden in a local museum. The cemetery and Jewish shops were also devastated.

In 1945, the synagogue was repaired by Chassidic survivors of the nearby Bergen-Belsen concentration camp. The rough and simple bimah and the steps to the ark, which these survivors constructed from boards salvaged from the ruins of bombed houses, remain. In stark contrast, the Baroque ark shows three gilded crowns in its elaborately carved scrollwork. Next to the entrance there is a small stone column, a collection box from 1740,

The bimah, in the bare, impoverished style of the late Forties, forms a stark contrast with the Baroque Torah shrine of the small Celle synagogue.

dedicated to the memory of Rabbi Josuah Feifelsohn Cohen by his son Aron. When visiting, be sure to ask to see the half-timbered exterior of the synagogue as well as it is also very interesting.

Today, the synagogue is one of the oldest in Germany and one of the very few DP (displaced person) synagogues to survive. Schoolchildren of Lower Saxony often visit this synagogue after going to the concentration camp memorial in Bergen-Belsen as part of their history curriculum. There is also a small museum in the former school building. The synagogue is located in the backyard of Im Kreise 24 and is open Tuesday to Thursday from 3-5, Friday from 9-11, Sunday from 11-1, or call 12452.

The 18th century Torah shrine of the Celle synagogue.

The cemetery dates from 1692 and includes richly decorated stones from the 18th century. The cemetery lies on a hill overlooking town on the other side of the Aller river at Am Berge 15. This cemetery is unusual for an old Jewish cemetery in many ways: for instance, the dead have not been buried in strictly chronological order as in most other old cemeteries, but many married couples are buried next to each other and there are even two old family burials. Along Am Berge there is a group of Cohen graves, close to the wall in order to let family members see the graves without entering the cemetery. The oldest graves are located at the highest part of the hill, while the graves from the 19th and 20th century lie at the foot of the hill. Some older graves have stones at the foot end of the grave. The cemetery is locked, but the wall is low so you can see into the cemetery easily. To visit, call 12343 for a guided tour or apply to the Landesverband der Jüdischen Gemeinden, Haeckelstrasse 10, 30173 Hannover 1, and obtain their permission in writing. With this document, go to the Stadtarchiv, Westerceller Strasse 4, 29227 Celle, between 8 and 12 from Monday to Thursday, and you can get the key from them.

COESFELD

is located about 140 km north of Köln, not far from the Dutch border, on highways 67 and 474 (map 4).

* Former synagogue from 1750
* Formerly two cemeteries

74

Although a letter of protection was granted by the Bishop of Münster to a Coesfeld Jew in 1323, it is thought that a community was not formed in Coesfeld until 1624. The influence of the Court Jew Abraham Isaac enabled the community to buy a plot for a cemetery in 1678. Only one 19th century stone and a memorial commemorate this cemetery. Today, there is a street where the cemetery used to lie, between the Süring gate and the Twent tower and opposite No. 7 on Gerichtsring.

A second cemetery was opened in 1896 on Osterwicker Strasse 75. It has a memorial stone to the victims of the Nazis. The cemetery is locked. The key is available at Osterwicker Strasse 77.

A synagogue was built around 1750. It was damaged but not destroyed in the 1938 "Reichskristallnacht", further damaged by WWII bombing and is being used as a Protestant church today; the Torah shrine has been renovated. There is a memorial plaque on the wall in front. The former synagogue is located on Weberstrasse 9 (behind Weberstrasse 7). According to an old tradition, the first synagogue was located in Schwerings Hof, opposite Weberstrasse 7.

CREGLINGEN

is located about 100 km west of Nürnberg and 15 km northwest of Rothenburg ob der Tauber (map 8, 9, 10).

* Former synagogue from 1799
* Cemetery from 1620
* Former synagogue in Archshofen

Jews did not settle in this area until around 1600. King Frederick William III of Prussia gave the community permission to build a synagogue in 1799. It was built in a combination of stone and half-timbering typical of the area and is attached to a 14th century fortification tower and part of the city walls. In 1938 it was converted into a youth hostel and since 1963 it has been a bistro. It is located on Neue Strasse 28.

Although the synagogue was small, the cemetery is quite large. It was established soon after 1620 and is located some distance away from Creglingen. Follow Streichentalerstrasse past the city limits and past two barns on the right and left of the

The former synagogue, leaning on the fortification wall, became a youth hostel in 1938 and is a bistro today.

street. After 150 meters take the asphalt path that turns right and then follow a gravel path about 20 meters beyond. The cemetery is at the edge of the forest, and protected by a high stone wall. It is locked (key at city hall where a memorial tablet to the Creglingen Jews is displayed), however, you can see into the cemetery from the gate. Older stones have simple ornamental scroll work. Jews from Archshofen are also buried here.

Archshofen is just a few kilometers down the road towards Rothenburg.

* Former synagogue

Jews began settling here around 1690. The synagogue used to be a stately building with unusual neo-Gothic windows. It was devastated in the 1938 "Reichskristallnacht" and is presently being used by the fire department which has cut two drive-in doors on the side and changed most of the windows. The stained-glass window in the east wall and the women's gallery are still there. The former synagogue is quite small. To get there, take the first left just before the bridge when entering town from Creglingen. Follow the road until it ends. The former synagogue is across from house number 38.

CRIVITZ

is located about 140 km east of Hamburg, on highway 321 east of Schwerin (map 1, 2).

* Former mid-19th century synagogue

It seems that the first Jews settled in Crivitz in the 18th century. The synagogue was a stately, neo-Romanesque building at Fritz-Reuter-Strasse 13. In 1919 the Crivitz community had become too small to maintain the building and sold it for use as a residence. Apart from a balcony over the entrance, chimneys, and television antennas, the exterior seems unchanged. Due to the addition of a floor and several walls to create rooms, the interior has been changed completely.

A small Jewish cemetery from the 18th century was destroyed completely during the Nazi years.

The former synagogue of Crivitz has been converted to a private residence.

DACHAU

lies about 15 km northwest of München on highway 304 (map 11).

* Concentration Camp Memorial

Dachau housed the first large-scale Nazi concentration camp. More than 200,000 human beings suffered at the hands of the Nazis here. Over 30,000 are known to have died from exhaustion, hunger, epidemics, torture, medical experiments, and murder. Thousands more, who were not registered, were brought here only to be executed. Today, the camp is a memorial to all those who suffered and died during the Nazi years. There is a museum, documentation center, memorials, two churches, a synagogue and the mass graves.

Many thousands of visitors from all over the world file quietly through the memorial every year. The memorial site is open Tuesday through Sunday from 9-5. An English brochure is available, some of the texts in the museum have also been translated. However, many of the exhibits documenting the terror and the day to day atrocities committed here have not been translated and can be read in German only.

The memorial on the former main square of the Dachau concentration camp serves to remind us of the tens of thousands who suffered and died here.

DAHN

is a small town about 100 km northwest of Stuttgart, about 150 km southwest of Frankfurt, on highway 427 (map 8).

* Former synagogue from 1872
* Former 19th century ritual bath in Busenberg
* Cemetery from 1833 in Busenberg

Jews settled in Dahn in the 18th century. They built their first synagogue in 1815, and the small neo-Baroque synagogue still surviving is from 1872. Because the community was shrinking, as in many other small towns in Germany, due to emigration and the move to bigger cities, the synagogue building was sold by the Jewish community before 1933. The building serves as a cabinetmaker's workshop today. Only the columns for the women's gallery and two round windows in the gable walls indicate the building's former use. There is a commemorative tablet to the Jewish community destroyed by the Nazis.

A few miles east of Dahn you will find Busenberg. Jews are first documented here in 1755 through records of the protection money they had to pay count Dürkheim; the ten men recorded by name paid about 80 florins a year, which amounted to about 5 % of the cash income the counts derived from Busenberg. On a short connecting road between Hauptstrasse and Talstrasse, the former mikveh has survived. It is located in a small, neglected building next to the road. The mikveh was closed around 1860 due to sanita-

DARMSTADT

lies about 30 km south of Frankfurt on the A 5 and A 67 (map 8).

* Synagogue and community center
* Memorials
* Early 15th century Pessach Haggadah
* Cemetery from 1680

Jews began settling in Darmstadt in the 16th century. They were forced to attend Christian missionary sermons as well as conform to the very strict ordinances governing Hesse Jews in the 16th and 17th centuries. Only after emancipation in the late 19th century did the Darmstadt community start to grow rapidly. By 1933, it numbered about 3,000 members. Today there is a small Jewish community in Darmstadt again.

Memorials to the synagogues destroyed in the 1938 "Reichskristallnacht" can be seen on Bleichstrasse/corner of Grafenstrasse, in the hospital grounds on Friedrichstrasse, and in Eberstadt, next to the Modau bridge. The Justus Liebig school in Julius-Reiber-Strasse 3 was used as a transit camp for Jews from Hesse in 1942 and 1943; there is a commemorative tablet.

A highly valued Pessach-Haggadah is one of the treasures of the manuscript department of the Hesse State Library in the Darmstadt castle (Schloss). It was written sometime in the early 15th century and contains 15 full page miniatures and 11 illuminated pages. The Hesse State Museum contains the gravestone of Abraham, son of Rabbi Gerson, who died in 1260. It is

The former synagogue of Dahn is a cabinet-maker's workshop today.

tion concerns. The building served as a poorhouse until the 1950's.

The cemetery of Busenberg is located just east of the little town, on highway 427, on a hillside in a very prominent position. The well-kept Moorish-style gravestones with their rich symbolism stand out here - not really surprising, since the first ever German synagogue in the Moorish style was built in Billigheim-Ingenheim, not far from Busenberg, in 1832. It was from this part of Germany that the Moorish style conquered Europe during the 19th century. The oldest stones in this cemetery stand at the higher eastern end, and all stones are oriented towards the east (as they would be in a small rural community) and face uphill.

located in an inner courtyard amongst many other gravestones. The museum is open Tuesday-Sunday 10-5, Wednesday 7-9 p.m.

The new synagogue, built in 1987/88 as a gift from the city and with additional donations from its citizens, stands in Wilhelm-Glässing-Strasse 26. There is a new community center that has a small museum with ritual objects from the home and the synagogue, as well as objects from the history of the Darmstadt Jews. Guided visits to the synagogue and the exhibition can be arranged by calling the community center (28897).

The cemetery on Steinbergweg was founded around 1680. Its oldest remaining stone dates from 1714. There is a memorial to the Jewish soldiers who died for their German fatherland in WWI and two commemorative tablets to the victims of the Nazis (near the gate). The cemetery is locked. The key is available at the community center in Wilhelm-Glässing-Strasse 26.

DEIDESHEIM

is located about 100 km southwest of Frankfurt and about 130 km northwest of Stuttgart, on highway 271 between Bad Dürkheim and Neustadt/Weinstrasse (map 8, 10).

* Former synagogue from 1854
* Cemetery from 1712

Deidesheim already had a large Jewish community in 1309, when its annual tax to the emperor was fixed at a considerable nine pounds of silver. The synagogue stood on what is Marktplatz today. During the Black Plague persecutions in 1349, the Jewish community in Deidesheim was destroyed like in many other German towns, and the synagogue became church property. However, Jews soon settled in Deidesheim again and a street and a city gate were named after them. The community stayed small and poor for the next few centuries. In 1852, the synagogue that was probably built in 1689 was condemned as unsafe (but not torn

The former Deidesheim synagogue was used as a garage for many years.

79

down until 1941). The small community consisting of fourteen families built a new synagogue that was finished in 1853. It was built in the simple neo-Romanesque style thought appropriate for synagogues at the time. Soon the community lost more members who moved to larger cities and could not raise the money necessary for maintenance any more. In 1935, the last four remaining Jewish families sold the synagogue for use as a garage. The building was not damaged in the 1938 "Reichskristallnacht", but the apartments of the Deidesheim Jews were devastated and two Torah scrolls from the synagogue that had been preserved by one of the families were destroyed. Only one Jewish inhabitant of Deidesheim survived the Nazi years. The Jewish woman had been interned in Gurs and came back to live in Deidesheim after 1945.

The former synagogue was bought by the city in 1992. It was standing empty and seemed to be in poor shape in 1994. Plans for renovation are being developed; however, the future use was not clear then. There is a commemorative tablet on the building, and both the former synagogue and the Jewish cemetery are mentioned in the city walk brochure. A visit to the former synagogue is possible by applying to Mr. Brandt at the Bauamt.

The small Jewish cemetery is from 1712 and is located on Platanenweg opposite number 18, next to the old Christian cemetery.

Thousands of gravestones from the old Jewish cemetery of Dessau are stacked up against its walls. They were saved from destruction by the private initiative of a young Christian from Dessau.

DESSAU

lies close to the A 9, on the Elbe river and on highways 184 and 185, about 80 km southwest of Berlin (map 2, 7).

* Cemetery from 1674
* Synagogue and community center
* Memorials

Little is known about the medieval history of the Dessau Jews. Apparently their community came to an end in 1348-1350 during the Black Plague persecutions, when so many other Jewish communities in Germany were destroyed. It was not until 1672 that Jews, after paying high protection fees, were allowed to settle in Dessau again. In 1759, 214 Jewish families lived in Dessau. The good conditions and the liberal views of the governing princes of Anhalt made Dessau a stronghold of liberal Judaism: in 1799, the Israelitische Freischule (the Jewish liberal school) under the management of David Fränkel was founded, and a publishing house and printshop supplied large parts of Germany with German translations of Hebrew literature and with Hebrew textbooks. David Fränkel also published *Sulamith* in Dessau, the first Jewish magazine written in German and printed in German-Gothic letters, which was widely read all over Europe.

In 1729, Dessau became the birthplace of Moses Mendelssohn, the great Jewish philosopher and reformer. His mother was buried in the large Dessau cemetery opened in 1674, and a memorial once stood opposite the train station. The memorial was destroyed by the Nazis and the cemetery was partially razed. Today, only a few stones, overgrown with ivy, are still standing in the cemetery. Hundreds of stones lie along the wall in neat stacks. The cemetery is being looked after by a young Christian living in the former guardhouse. He saved many stones from being destroyed by planned construction, learned Hebrew to make a catalogue of remaining stones, and works as a stonemason. The address of the cemetery is Am Leipziger Tor 4. It may be entered through the door of the house to the right.

The post-war synagogue and community center of the Dessau Jewish community are located at Königendorfer Strasse 76.
A memorial stele stands on the corner of Askanische Strasse/Kantorstrasse, where the neo-Romanesque synagogue from 1908 stood until it was destroyed in the November 1938 "Reichskristallnacht". There is a tablet to Moses Mendelssohn at Askanische Strasse 16; he was born in one of the houses then forming the neighborhood in 1729. A small post-war memorial to Moses Mendelssohn stands in the Stadtpark.

DRANSFELD

is located about 120 km south of Hannover or about 40 km northeast of Kassel, on highway 3 west of Göttingen (map 3, 5, 6).

* Former synagogue from 1810
* Cemetery from before 1850

The small 1810 synagogue of the Dransfeld Jews became a Catholic church after the Nazi years, later it was made part of a cabinetmaker's workshop. A commemorative tablet next to the entrance serves as a memorial to the Jewish community of Dransfeld.

The synagogue in Dransfeld was built in 1810 and is located at Gerlandstrasse 7. It was converted to a Catholic chapel after 1945. Today the building is a workshop for a cabinetmaker. Like in many other German rural synagogues, the niche for the ark emerges from the east wall of the building. There is a commemorative tablet in front.

The cemetery probably dates from before 1850. To get there, leave town taking highway 3 in the direction of Münden. Turn left onto a narrow asphalt road going up the hill about 500 meters after the last houses of Dransfeld. Turn left at a frame house and follow the metalled road leading through the forest. The cemetery is about 200 meters up this road, at the edge of the forest, overlooking Dransfeld.

There are four rows of massive grave plates with Hebrew inscriptions, unusual for Ashkenazi cemeteries. There are also about 50 standing stones from the early 20th century. Some of the stones were damaged but have been repaired.

DRESDEN (map 7)

* Synagogue (former taharah house)
* Two cemeteries
* Memorials

Little is known about the medieval history of the Dresden Jews. In 1349 Jews from Dresden were burnt at the stake during the Black Death perse-

82

The small synagogue serving Dresden's Jewish community today was once a very modern burial chapel.

cutions. The small community that remained was expelled in 1430. Apart from a few court Jews and their retinue, Jews could not legally live in Dresden from 1430 until well into the 18th century. A new Jewish community was founded in 1803, and the first post-medieval synagogue was built by Gottfried Semper in 1840 in a very successful neo-Romanesque style; however, a prayer room existed a hundred years before that.

In 1933 about 4,400 Jews lived in Dresden. About half left Germany before 1940, and the remaining Jews were deported to the German camps in 1942 and 1943. After the Nazi years, a small community was founded again. In 1950, it managed to rebuild the former taharah house as their synagogue. In the following years the community shrank, until the immigration of Russian Jews in 1990 brought new life to the community.

The taharah house of the cemetery at Fiedlerstrasse 3 was built in 1866 and enlarged in 1903. During WW II it was badly damaged and rebuilt as a synagogue in 1950. The gold-plated star of David crowning its cupola had been saved from the rubble of the Semper synagogue (which was destroyed during the 1938 "Reichskristallnacht") by a fire brigade worker. There are two commemorative tablets to the victims of the Nazis inside the synagogue. To the right of the entrance there is an impressive memorial to sixty Jewish soldiers from Dresden who died in WW I.

The cemetery surrounding the synagogue was opened in 1867. It looks like any city cemetery, thereby showing the assimilation of the Dresden Jews in the late 19th and early 20th centuries. The cemetery can be visited Monday to Thursday 8-5, Friday 8-2 and Sunday 9-4 (except on Jewish holidays).

The cemetery at Pulsnitzerstrasse 12 is the oldest Jewish cemetery in Saxony and was founded in 1751. Here, all the stones are still facing East. The cemetery is overgrown in a peaceful way. Many stones are weather-beaten and their inscriptions are no longer legible. The key is available from the Jewish community (see below) or from Hatikva at Pulsnitzerstrasse 10 (Monday-Thursday 9-12 and 1-4, Friday 9-12). Guided tours can be arranged by calling Hatikva (567 04 89) well ahead of time. Hatikva is an association building a library with a special focus on the history of Jews in Saxony and is pursuing several projects in this area.

The Jewish community center is located at Bautzner Strasse 20. The building also houses the offices of several Jewish organizations.

There is a memorial stone with a remarkable six-branched menorah where the Semper synagogue used to stand until its destruction on "Reichskristallnacht" at Brühlscher Garten.

Next to the entrance of the 13th century Kreuzkirche on Altmarkt a commemorative tablet to the Jews of Dresden persecuted and killed by the Nazis was unveiled in 1988.

Part of the oldest Jewish cemetery in Saxony can be seen on Dresden's Pulsnitzerstrasse.

DÜSSELDORF

is located at the edge of the most industrialized part of Germany, the Ruhr area, on the Rhine and about 40 km north of Köln. The A 46, A 52 and A 59 lead there (map 4).

* 1955 synagogue
* Memorials
* Paintings by Jewish artists in City
  Museum
* Cemetery from late 19th century

Historically, Düsseldorf has been a city of prominence, first serving as the capital of the dukes of Berg and later as the residence of the powerful Electors of the Palatinate. Jews began settling here in 1418 but expulsions and residence restrictions kept the community small until the new civil liberties, introduced early in the 19th century, enabled some of Düsseldorf's Jews to realize their potential and become important merchants and bankers.

The Jewish community of Düsseldorf suffered more than most other German communities during the 1938 pogrom known as the "Reichskristallnacht", because vom Rath, the diplomat assassinated by Herschel Grynszpan in Paris, happened to be a citizen of Düsseldorf. The main synagogue from 1905 and two smaller Orthodox synagogues were destroyed as well as the Ulmenstrasse taharah house. Eventually more than half of the 1939 Jewish population of almost 2,000 were deported in 1941 and 1942. Only 58 Düsseldorf Jews survived and returned after 1945. A new synagogue was built at Zietenstrasse 50 in 1958.

There are many memorials in Düsseldorf to remind both citizens and visitors of its Jewish past. The great German poet, Heinrich Heine, was born in Düsseldorf in 1797. As controversial in posterity as he was during his lifetime, the city has erected many monuments and memorials to his name in spite of continued dissent and opposition. A monument to Heine by Maillol is in the northern part of the Hofgarten park and another more modern monument is in Schwanenmarkt. The house that replaced his birth house bears a commemorative tablet at Bolkerstrasse 53. There is also a Heinrich Heine Platz and the main thoroughfare through the shopping area is called Heinrich Heine Allee. Maybe the best measure of his popularity, however, is the large number of restaurants and pubs named after him.

There is a memorial to the synagogue destroyed in 1938 on Kasernenstrasse at the corner of Siegfried-Klein-Strasse which was named after a Düsseldorf rabbi who was killed in Auschwitz. Across the street from the synagogue memorial is a small commemorative tablet at Kasernenstrasse 40 for Luise Dumont and Gustav Lindemann who founded the Düsseldorf Schauspielhaus (theater) and were its mentors from 1905 to 1932. Their archives are now in the theater museum on Jägerhofstrasse.

The city museum at Bäckerstrasse 7-9 exhibits works of Jewish artists from Düsseldorf and documents the fate of those persecuted by the Nazis. The museum also exhibits drawings by Jewish children from Düsseldorf. The museum is open Tuesday, Thursday, Friday, and Sunday from 11-5; Wednesday from 11-8; and Saturday from 1-5. The Kunstmuseum at Ehrenhof 5 also displays the work of German-Jewish artists from the 19th and 20th centuries. The museum is open Tuesday-Sunday from 11-6.

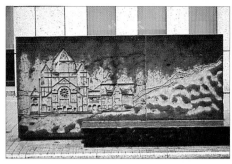

The Neo-Romanesque main synagogue of the Düsseldorf Jews stood here until it was destroyed by the Nazis; today a memorial marks the site.

The cemetery at Ulmenstrasse 236-187 was established in the late 19th century and is surrounded by the Christian cemetery. The cemetery has memorials to the Jewish soldiers who died for their fatherland in WWI, to the victims of the Nazi persecutions, and to Rabbi Klein and other members of the synagogue council who were killed in German camps. The cemetery is open Monday-Thursday from 9-6; Friday from 9-4:30; and Sunday 9-5:30 from April 1 to September 30. It closes 90 minutes earlier from October 1 to March 31.

EISLEBEN

is located about 90 km northeast of Erfurt, on highways 80 and 180 (map 3, 5, 6, 7).

* Former 19th century synagogue
* Former medieval ghetto
* Memorial at Market Church
* Cemetery from 1877
* Remains of an earlier cemetery

The former ghetto and the former synagogue of the Eisleben Jews lie close to the houses where Martin Luther was born and died. The former ghetto is a small square off the large market square of Eisleben; although the houses are all younger, the closed shape of the square with its one exit to the market and the name, Jüdenhof, reflect its former use. The house where Luther died lies a few steps from here, at the upper end of the market. Opposite this Luther

Only the arched windows high up in the facade of this run-down building reveal that it once housed the synagogue of the Eisleben Jews.

memorial house, there is a memorial to the Jewish community of Eisleben at the gate of the Gothic market church of St. Andrew. This memorial shows a menorah and the Sh'ma Jisrael prayer in German and Hebrew.

The former synagogue lies on the first floor of Judenstrasse 25, a few steps from the house where Luther was born. The teacher and cantor lived on the ground floor. The synagogue also served as a school. You can still see the high arched windows, and two round windows remain in the gable walls, although they have been crudely bricked up. The former synagogue is a residence today, and the interior has been changed.

The cemetery on Magdeburger Strasse 6 was opened in 1877 as part of the city cemetery. During WW II, Polish slave workers were buried here. At the entrance there is a memorial stone for the Jewish victims of the Nazis.

On Rammbergstrasse there was an older cemetery that was destroyed during the Third Reich. Some gravestones can still be seen in one of the gardens that have replaced the cemetery.

ELLINGEN

is located about 50 km south of Nürnberg and about 130 km northwest of Munich, on highways 2 and 13 (map 9, 10, 11).

* Former prayer room with 18th century Baroque ceiling paintings
* Former synagogue from 1759

The Jewish community of Ellingen must have been quite well-to-do during the 18th century; the community built a rather large synagogue complex in 1759, and the Landauer family built a remarkable Baroque house which displayed the lions of Judah over the entrance and also housed their private prayer room. Although Bavaria was very anti-Jewish at the time, Ellingen belonged not to the dukes of Bavaria, but to the Teutonic Order which admitted Jews (against proper fees or "Schutzgelder") in all its possessions.

The Landauer house at Weissenburger Strasse 17 became an inn in 1776, but the lions and the prayer room remained. In 1815 it became the property of the prince of Wrede. The family still owns it today. The prayer room lies in the middle of the first floor (the American second floor), in the center of the building. A marvel-ous oak staircase leads up to it. The place where the mezuzah used to be can still be seen at the entrance to the prayer room. The prayer room is ornamented not only with Baroque stucco, but also with seven ceiling paintings with biblical themes, unique in Germany as far as the authors know; the depiction of human beings is strictly prohibited by the Jewish faith, at least in a religious context. The inn has been standing empty since 1993, but a restoration was being planned in 1995. Until further notice the former prayer room can only be visited after contacting the Fürstlich Wrede'sches Rentamt in Ellingen.

The stately synagogue of Ellingen was built in 1759 in Neue Gasse 14, very close to the Landauer house. It had to be sold by the Jewish community under pressure in September 1938. The new owner prevented the burning

A Baroque ceiling painting (Abraham about to sacrifice Isaac) in a synagogue? Impossible, unheard of, but nevertheless, you can see it in the former Landauer synagogue in Ellingen!

The Lions of Judah adorn the entrance to the former Landauer house in Ellingen.

of the building during "Reichskristallnacht", but the furniture and the ritual objects were destroyed. The former synagogue is a residence today; hardly anything besides the traces of the mezuzah on the right-hand side of the entrance door reminds the visitor of its former use.

ELMSHORN

is located about 40 km northwest of Hamburg off the A 23 (map 1).

* Exhibition on the history of Jews in Elmshorn
* Cemetery from late 17th century

Jews began settling in Elmshorn in 1685. In 1838 almost ten percent of Elmshorn was Jewish; after emancipation many Jews left Elmshorn to go to larger towns. In 1933, only about 50 Jews lived here. Many succeeded in

leaving Germany, but at least 21 Elmshorn Jews were killed in German camps. There is a memorial to the synagogue built in 1845 and destroyed in the 1938 "Reichskristallnacht" at Flamweg 45.

The cemetery, dating from the late 17th century, is located on Feldstrasse near the central railway station and next to a Catholic church. It is well-kept and has a little taharah house built in 1906 with German and Hebrew inscriptions over the door. In the former taharah house there is a special exhibition on the history of Jews in Elmshorn on display. The key is available at the police station at Moltkestrasse 2.

The small taharah house of the Elmshorn Jewish cemetery today houses an exhibition on Jewish life in Elmshorn. A short time before the authors took this picture, swastikas were sprayed on the door.

This old wall half hidden behind some bushes was once part of the medieval synagogue of Erfurt. A small room is preserved behind this wall, part of a restaurant today.

ERFURT (map 5, 6)

* Wall of a 14th century synagogue
* Former synagogue from 1834
* Medieval depictions of the Synagogue Defeated and the "Judensau" in the cathedral
* Synagogue from 1952 (sole postwar synagogue in the former German Democratic Republic)
* Cemetery from 1873

Hidden behind parked cars and bushes on a small square at the end of Kramerbrücke, the last remains of a Gothic synagogue from the 14th century still stand. Traces of pillars and the outlines of two doors and windows can be seen on the remaining wall of this synagogue which was the third one built in Erfurt in the Middle Ages.

It was built in 1357, after survivors of the Black Plague massacres (that killed more than 100 Erfurt Jews and

about 3,000 Jews from the Thuringia province) were allowed to return to Erfurt. It stood very close to the Krämerbrücke (merchant's bridge), an ancient and important Gera river crossing.

The Jewish community of Erfurt is first documented in the 12th century, but it may be even older; some think the first Jewish community already existed when the bishopric was founded in 742. After the Black Plague persecutions, the new community prospered until the end of the 14th century when it was impoverished by the special taxes and moratoria ordered by king Wenceslav. In 1458 the com-

At the Lady's Gate of the Erfurt cathedral this Gothic statue of the Synagogue Defeated can still be seen. Unlike many others of its kind, there is little dignity in the defeat here.

One of the Gothic benches in Erfurt's cathedral shows this Jew riding a sow.

munity was expelled. Jews were not allowed to settle in Erfurt again until the early 19th century.

Today, the wall of the Gothic synagogue forms the outer wall of the Feuerkugel restaurant on Michaelisstrasse. One of the smaller rooms of the restaurant may also have been a part of the synagogue complex. The small, square room with its Gothic vaulting has been heavily plastered over and shows no trace of its former function. The former synagogue wall is located at the corner of Fischmarkt 22 and Michaelisstrasse.

During the early years of the 19th century Jews returned to Erfurt and built a new synagogue in 1834 on a street subsequently called An der Judenschule, directly on the Gera river and only a few steps away from the remains of the former Gothic synagogue. This building was used as a synagogue until 1884 when a new synagogue was built. The old synagogue was then sold and used as a vinegar factory, among other uses. Later the building was converted into apartments. The building, whose former Torah niche still hangs over the river, can best be seen from the road bridge parallel to Krämerbrücke. Its address is An der Stadtmünze.

The synagogue from 1884 was burned down in November 1938 "Reichskristallnacht". The Erfurt Jews had to pay for the gasoline used in the arson, as well as for the cost of removing the rubble and clearing the site. On this plot a new synagogue, the only newly-built synagogue in the German Democratic Republic, was built in 1952. This synagogue and the Jewish community center are located at Juri-Gagarin-Ring 16. The community center is open Monday to Friday, 9-4.

The Erfurt cathedral was built in the 12th century on a steep rock overlook-

The small synagogue from 1834 was sold by the Erfurt community after a large new synagogue was built. It is a residential building today.

ing the city. Two witnesses of the conflict between medieval Christianity and Judaism can be seen here. The Virgins' Gate shows the Church Triumphant and the Synagogue Defeated in connection with the Wise and Foolish Virgins. The Church Triumphant stands to the left, smilingly lifting the chalice, while the Synagogue Defeated, standing to the right of the gate, is contorted and tries to hide a lamb, the symbol for the burned offering of the Old Testament, behind her.

The second depiction, a Judensau, reflects almost 2,000 years of conflict between the two religions. Although very rare today, they were once common in Germany and other European countries during the Middle Ages. Inside the cathedral, on the side of a choir stall, a Jew riding a sow is shown being defeated by a Christian knight riding a horse and wielding a lance. The Jew wears the pointed medieval Jewish hat and the knight displays a fish, probably a symbol of Jesus, on his shield (the Greek initials of the name and attributes of Jesus spell out "fish" in Greek). The scene is carved on a choir stall from the 14th century. It is at the bottom left hand side panel of the stalls as you stand at the entrance looking towards the altar. The cathedral is open Monday to Saturday from 10 to 11:30 and from 12:30 to 5 in summer and to 4 in winter and 2 to 4 on Sunday and holidays.

Nothing remains of the first Jewish cemetery which was located close to the synagogue wall. The gravestones from that cemetery were used to build city fortifications, one of them, for rabbi Elaser, from 1289, can be seen in the Angermuseum. A second cemetery from the early 19th century, on Cyriakstrasse 3-4, was destroyed by the Nazis in 1938 and is a parking lot today. Some late Baroque gravestones from this cemetery were later taken to the new cemetery established in 1873 on Werner-Seelenbinder-Strasse 3. The stones stand to the right of the large taharah house today, close to a memorial for Jewish soldiers who died during WWI. There is also a memorial to the victims of the Nazi terror to the left of the taharah house. To the right there are many post-war graves of Erfurt Jews. The cemetery is open Sunday to Friday, 9 to 3.

After the end of the Third Reich, the Jewish community of Erfurt had about 600 members, mainly Eastern European survivors of the death camps. During the 1950s many Jews emigrated from the German Democratic Republic, and the community dwindled. In 1989 the community had 26 mostly elderly members. In 1990, there was an influx of Jewish families from the Soviet Union which gave the community new hope.

ERLANGEN

is located 20 km northwest of Nürnberg, on A73 (map 9, 10).

* Former synagogue from 1707 in Bruck
* 16th century mikveh in Bruck
* Mikveh in Büchenbach
* Cemetery from 1891

There was a Jewish community in

Bruck, now a suburb of Erlangen, from the 17th to the 19th century. This community built its synagogue in the backyard of Schorlachstrasse 23a in 1707. In 1872 the small community had to abandon its synagogue. However, the building still remains and there are still traces of its former use in the interior.

A mikveh, probably built in the 16th century, lies in the basement of a house in Fürther Strasse 36. In Hintere Gasse 5 in the Büchenbach suburb there is another mikveh, however, it may not be visited.

The cemetery of the Jews who settled in Erlangen after having been emancipated in 1861 lies behind Rudelsweiherstrasse 85. It was founded in 1891. There is a taharah house and a memorial to the victims of persecution by the Nazis.

All of these sites (except the mikveh in Büchenbach) can only be visited in the course of guided tours arranged by the city of Erlangen. These tours are held on an irregular basis, partly depending on demand. Please apply well ahead of time to the Bürgermeister- und Presseamt, Ms. Sponsel, in Erlangen city hall.

ERMREUTH

is located about 30 km northwest of Nürnberg, north of highway 2 close to Gräfenberg (map 9).

* Former synagogue from 1822
* Cemetery from 1711
* Former synagogue from 1766 in nearby Dormitz

The first Jews may have settled in Ermreuth soon after 1548. In 1548 the right to let Jews settle on their estates against the payment of fees was first granted to the knights of the empire, and many knights, members of the lesser nobility, eagerly accepted this new source of income. However, a Jewish community did not take shape in Ermreuth until the early 18th century. The small rural community had 230 members in 1825, which was equivalent to about 40 % of the population of Ermreuth. Like most rural communities, it dwindled in the second half of the 19th century due to emigration and migration to larger towns; in 1933, only 21 Jews lived in Ermreuth. Fifteen Ermreuth Jews died in Nazi camps.

The new synagogue was built in 1822 in Wagnergasse 8, where a half-timbered synagogue from 1738 had stood. Unlike other rural commu-

The massive sandstone walls of the former Ermreuth synagogue have weathered decades of neglect.

nities, the Ermreuth Jews were comparatively well-to-do, and that showed in the synagogue: it was built from massive sandstone blocks that withstood the ravages of time in spite of the lack of maintenance it received during the Nazi years and into the 1980's. The tall and stately synagogue was built in the spare Baroque style used in many Protestant churches of the times. During "Reichskristallnacht" it was not burned down because it was closely surrounded by houses; however, the interior was devastated, and the ritual objects were destroyed. In the following years, the building was used as a storehouse, and the remaining furnishings were destroyed. In 1988 Neunkirchen am Brand, the market town that Ermreuth is a part of now, started renovating the building, and in 1994 it was opened as a cultural center. The interior was reconstructed from descriptions and excavations, with a circular bimah in the center of the room and a women's gallery on three sides of the room. Many religious and secular books and manuscripts as well as tefillim and mesusoth were found in a genisah in the attic. These were still being examined and prepared for exhibition in 1994.

The cemetery of Ermreuth is located about 1.5 km north of the village, at the edge of the forest. The oldest remaining stone, at the upper end of the cemetery, is from 1719, and the last burial took place in 1937. Judging from the high number of Levite pitchers on the gravestones, the tribe of Levi must have been exceptionally numerous here.

The former synagogue and the cemetery can be visited after contacting city hall in Neunkirchen, or on the first Sunday in the month between 2 and 5.

In nearby Dormitz, in the courtyard of Hauptstrasse 18, there is a small and dilapidated former synagogue from 1766. The synagogue was sold in 1919 and has been decaying for several years; apparently the owner wants to tear it down eventually. Remains of Rococo stucco are supposed to still exist in the interior. The owner does not allow visits to the former synagogue.

ESCHWEGE

is located about 50 km east of Kassel on highway 452, on the Werra river (map 5, 6).

* Former synagogue from 1838
* Cemetery from mid-19th century

The first Jewish community in Eschwege was probably founded before

The former Eschwege synagogue from 1838 is a Protestant church today.

94

1200. Persecutions are documented for 1295 and 1349, but in 1367 a new community was established again. Apparently this community existed without interruption to the 1940's. In 1880 it had 531 members and then shrank to 390 in 1932. Due to the forced resettlement of many rural Jews, there were 535 Jews in Eschwege in 1939. About 300 were deported to extermination camps and about 200 were able to emigrate.

In 1687 the first documented synagogue of Eschwege was built. A later synagogue, built in 1838, is now a Protestant church. It was built in the classicist style and is located on the corner of Schulstrasse and Vor dem Berge. Because of its proximity to other buildings, the synagogue was not burned down but devastated during "Reichskristallnacht". There is a tablet near the entrance to commemorate the outrage. The former synagogue was changed and adapted to its new use as a church in 1954, but the women's gallery and the ark niche still remind us of its former use.

The Jewish cemetery of Eschwege, from 1859, is located on Elsa-Brandström-Strasse behind the hospital parking lot which used to be an unused part of the cemetery. The key is available Monday-Friday 8-12, 2-4 from the City Garden Department on Höhenweg 1 or at the city hall telephone exchange on Obermarkt 22, at other times at the reception desk of the hospital. Until 1859 the Eschwege Jewish community buried its dead in the cemetery of Jestädt.

ESENS

is located about 250 km west of Hamburg, between federal highways 210 and 461, about 3 km from the banks of the "Wattenmeer" (map 1).

* Former community center with ritual bath from 1899, now a museum and memorial
* Cemetery from 1702

Ostfriesland, or Eastern Frisia, lies far from the centers of Jewish life in Germany. The first Jews settled here around 1550. In Esens, the former Jewish community center built in 1899 has survived. It used to house the school, the teacher's apartment and the mikveh. From 1938 to 1940, the building was used as a "Judenhaus", a house where Jews expelled from their houses or apartments were forced to live until their deportation. Today, the building is named after the teacher and community president August Gottschalk and houses a small museum dealing with the history of the Jews of Eastern Frisia. The museum is open from March to October on Tuesday, Thursday and Sunday from 2-5. At other times, a visit can be arranged by calling (04971)2102.

Next to the former community center you can still see the walls of the synagogue of Esens built in 1828 and burned down during the "Reichskristallnacht" pogrom in 1938. The ruin is being used as a garage today. The community center was to be torn down to create parking lots, but was saved by a very active citizens´ association. There is a memorial stone for the Esens Jews killed by the Nazis in front of the synagogue ruin.

The Jewish cemetery of Esens lies at Mühlenweg. It was almost completely destroyed during the Third Reich. There are only a few gravestones left; there is also a memorial for the Jewish community of Esens.

ESSEN

is located in the heart of the industrial area of Germany, the Ruhrgebiet, about 70 km north of Köln, on the A 40 and A 52 (map 4).

* Former synagogue from 1913 with memorial and exhibition
* Synagogue from 1959
* Thousand year old menorah in Essen Minster
* Cemeteries

Jews settled in Essen in the 13th century but the community did not achieve prominence until the mid-19th century when new liberties coincided with the growth of the steel industry and enabled Jews to participate in its development. The community grew rapidly throughout the 19th century and by 1930 numbered 5,000.

A synagogue, one of the largest and most beautiful in Germany, was consecrated in 1913 and gutted by fire in the 1938 "Reichskristallnacht" pogrom. Two commemorative tablets were attached to the ruined walls of the synagogue in 1949, glossing over the genocide committed during the Nazi years. One tablet read "This house, the former synagogue of the Jewish community, is a mute witness of terrible events. We have the duty to make up

for them." The second text read "More than 2,500 Essen Jews had to lose their lives 1933-1945." After much criticism, the text was changed in 1981 to read as follows: "To the memory of more than 2,500 Essen Jews who were murdered by the Nazi regime in the years 1939 - 1945." From 1959 to 1979 the building was used as an exhibition hall for industrial design by the city of Essen; the interior was changed beyond recognition. After that, the building was partly restored. Today, the former synagogue on Steeler Strasse 29 is a memorial and documentation center and displays an exhibition on the "Stations of Jewish life in Essen" as well as other exhibitions and lectures on Jewish themes. It is open Tuesday-Sunday from 10-6. A brochure in English is available.

In 1959, a new synagogue was consecrated at Sedanstrasse 46 and may be

The Essen synagogue, built in 1913, was considered one of the most beautiful of the modern German synagogues.

visited by contacting the Jewish Community Center at the same address.

The Essen Minster, a much venerated church founded in the 9th century, has a six foot bronze menorah which is almost one thousand years old.

There are several Jewish cemeteries in and around Essen. The newest one, still used by the present-day Jewish community, is the 1935 Parkfriedhof cemetery on Plantenbergstrasse off Steeler Strasse. The early 19th century cemetery on Lazarettstrasse was razed to make room for a bunker in 1940/41 and 34 of its stones were transferred to the Parkfriedhof cemetery where there is a memorial to the Lazarettstrasse cemetery.

Nearby, on Hiltrops Kamp opposite No. 4, there is a small cemetery from the early 19th century. The cemetery lies several meters below street level under a thick canopy of old trees and can easily be seen by looking over a wall from a driveway leading down to a garage. The key is available from Mr. Mücke at the Grünflächenamt, weekdays 7-3:30.

The small and isolated cemetery in Werden, today a suburb of Essen, lies in the middle of a forest on Pastoratsberg (pastor's mountain). It was founded around 1700 but the oldest remaining stones seem to be from around 1850. The center path has a magnificent row of old beeches and the ground is covered in thick ivy. The cemetery can be reached by walking a hiking path marked with a square standing on its corner which starts on An der Stadtmauer in Werden, or you can drive up Klemensborn and then follow the signs leading to the La Buvette restaurant for a few hundred meters. The cemetery is in the forest to the right of the path. It is surrounded by a chain-link fence and can easily be seen from the outside. You can get the key from Mr. Mücke at the Grünflächenamt, weekdays 7-3:30.

ESSINGEN

is located about 110 km northwest of Stuttgart and about 130 km south of Frankfurt, next to highway 272 and not far from the A 65 (map 8, 10).

* Former synagogue from the early
   19th century
* Cemetery from 1618

Not much can be seen of the former synagogue of Essingen built around 1820 and sold in 1937. The building stands at Gerämmestrasse 48, but all you can see there is a bricked-up arched window over a new barn door. From the small garden to the left you can still see the west wall and another arched window; the roof also looks fairly typical. The former synagogue is a barn today, and the former ark supposedly a tool cabinet.

The large, old cemetery of Essingen, which served several other communities in the area, is still very impressive today. Follow first Gartenstrasse and then the rough farm track that succeeds it. About 200 meters after the last houses of the village you will find the cemetery. The new part (from 1889) lies to the left of the track. The old part that was started in 1618 lies to the right. The gateposts of the old part have Hebrew inscriptions, and many old stones stand under tall horse-chestnut trees. This part of the cemetery is long and narrow and lies much lower than the track. The cemeteries are locked. The key is available from the town hall in Essingen.

EUTIN

is located about 100 km northeast of Hamburg, on highway 76 not far from the A 1 (map 1).

* Cemetery from 1850

The small Jewish graveyard in Eutin lies under tall trees looking out over the little Eutin lake (Kleiner Eutiner See). Ten gravestones of Eutin Jews remain. The oldest is from 1886 and the most recent from 1940.

The Nathan family whose members are buried here lived in Eutin from 1801 on. Five stones are for Hungarian Jewish women whose transport passing Eutin on the way from Bre-men was strafed by Allied planes; 38 prisoners died on the spot and were buried in Lübeck-Moisling, five survivors died from their wounds a few days later and were buried here. One grave from 1954 lies by itself.

The cemetery is accessible from Plöner Strasse, between 71 and 73. Walk down towards the lake and keep left upon reaching it. The cemetery lies on the hillside a few hundred meters down the path.

The tiny Jewish cemetery of Eutin lies far from town, on the bank of the Kleiner Eutiner See. Next to the members of Eutins' only Jewish family, Hungarian Jewish women are buried. They were killed in an Allied air-raid on their transport.

FLOSS

is located about 120 km northeast of Nürnberg, between highway 15 and the Czech border, about 15 km northeast of Weiden (map 9).

* Early 19th century synagogue
* Late 17th century cemetery
* Flossenbürg Concentration Camp Memorial and Documentation Center

Jewish cloth merchants were the first Jews to settle near Floss in 1684. They built their homes on a hill opposite the small market town and later enclosed their hill with a stone wall. The Jewish community governed itself until 1869 when the village of Judenberg was incorporated into Floss.

The first synagogue was built in 1722 but soon became too small and was enlarged in 1780. In 1813, a fire destroyed most of Floss and Judenberg. Although the seven Torah scrolls of the synagogue were saved, everything else perished. A new synagogue was built in a late Baroque style over an octagonal floor plan between 1815 and 1817.

This remarkable synagogue stands in a commanding position above a creek and looks out across the red roofs of the little town to the Catholic and Protestant churches, each standing on hills at the same level as the synagogue. There are nine colorful windows with inscriptions in Hebrew on the ground floor and the bimah is located in the middle of the room in the old style rather than near the

The synagogue of the formerly independent village of Judenberg proudly stands on its hill at the same altitude as the churches of Floss.

Torah ark in front. Both a corner stone outside and a stone donation box at the entrance inside have the date 1815 carved on them. The women's gallery stretching along three sides of the synagogue is supported by twelve columns set in granite and is reached over an arched stone bridge from a second story level street north of the synagogue.

Although the synagogue was heavily damaged in the 1938 "Reichskristallnacht" pogrom, it was not destroyed, partly due to its four foot thick walls. In 1942, the last two Jewish families of Floss were deported. After years of decay, the synagogue was bought by the Association of Jews in Bavaria in 1964 and restored with financial aid from the Floss council in 1980.

The consecrated synagogue is located on the corner of Bergstrasse and Judengasse. The key is available in the Floss city hall Monday-Friday 8-12 and also on Thursday 1:30-5.

The plot for the cemetery was bought in 1692; the cemetery has been enlarged several times. It lies on a steep slope and is enclosed by a massive stone wall. The cemetery includes many old stones near the gate as well as a grave for 33 prisoners from the nearby Flossenbürg concentration camp. This grave is marked by a memorial to the Jewish victims of the Nazi regime.

The cemetery is located on Flossenbürger Strasse just outside of town after house no. 44. The key is avail-

The octagonal interior of the Floss synagogue was restored after the devastations of the Nazi years and serves as a place of prayer again.

This stone with a sleeping lion can be seen in the old Jewish cemetery of Floss.

able from city hall. The cemetery can easily be seen over the wall.

The Flossenbürg Concentration Camp Memorial is located about 5 km east of Floss. Out of the estimated 100,000 prisoners who had to work in the granite quarries or in armament factories nearby, more than 30,000 were killed or died of exhaustion, disease, or hunger. The site includes memorials to the Jewish victims of the camp, to the victims from 18 European countries, and to prominent members of the German Resistance Movement who were executed here in April 1945. There is a documentation center as well as cemeteries for many thousands, mostly nameless, who are buried here or whose ashes were dumped close to the crematorium. In 1994 a memorial to the Jewish victims of Flossenbürg was dedicated.

Two guard towers, a stretch of electrical fence, and part of the crematorium are still standing. The church was built from the stones of demolished guard towers by camp survivors between 1946-48. The memorial may be visited daily 8-6 in summer, and 9-5 in winter. There is a leaflet in English.

FRANKFURT (map 4, 8)

* Jewish museum and archives
* Philanthropin school
* Two mikvoth (one from 1462) and foundations of old ghetto
* Synagogue from 1910, community center and school
* Library collections
* Memorials
* Cemeteries

Frankfurt, a free and imperial city, commanded an ancient ford over the important Main river. It was also here that, from the 16th century on, the German kings and Roman emperors were not only elected by the electors of the empire, but also crowned in the cathedral (the elections had usually been held in Frankfurt, while until then the coronations had taken place in Aachen). Moneylending, one of the few occupations allowed Jews, grew in importance as candidates for the imperial crown, always short of cash, sought to influence the votes of the electors. Frankfurt is still the financial center of Germany today.

The development of the Frankfurt Jewish community parallels the development of Frankfurt itself. Earliest documents mentioning Jewish merchants in the city date back to 1074; a Jewish community, however, was probably founded only after 1150.

Destroyed on many occasions, the old Jewish settlement lay directly at the foot of the imperial palace which was later replaced by the cathedral. The Jews were serfs of the imperial chamber, and, through the payment of taxes, under the emperors' special, though often worthless, protection.

In 1460, the Council built a Juden-gasse away from the cathedral and forced the Jews to move there; the community unsuccessfully resisted and dubbed the Judengasse "New Egypt". Originally set up to house 180 Jews, the area of this Judengasse, later one of the most famous in Europe, was never enlarged and eventually housed 3,500. Houses were not al-lowed to exceed four floors, resulting in extremely cramped conditions with virtually every square inch being used to house people. For example, the narrowest house in the Judengasse was 1.67 meters (5 1/2 feet) wide and 24 meters (80 feet) long with one window at each end of each floor, leaving the rooms in the middle totally dark. While conditions like these were not totally unknown in fortified cities of the time, the Frankfurt Judengasse was particularly cramped.

One of its more notable houses, built in 1712, was shared by the Rothschild and Schiff families from 1720 on. (This house should not be confused with the early 19th century Rothschild palace which still stands.) The Roth-schild house, destroyed by bombs with most of the center of Frankfurt during WW II, once housed 60 to 70 people within its four floors and was about 30 feet wide. It had a green shield (grünes Schild) over one of its doors, so the Rothschild family name pre-dates the house and was derived from another house in the ghetto. It was here that Mayer Amschel Rothschild (along with his wife Gutle and their 10 surviving children as well as the Schiff family mentioned above) lived and started his banking business. (Incidentally, if you ask a German about the Rothschilds be prepared for a blank stare unless you pronounce the name "Rot-shield" instead of "Roths-child".)

Frankfurt achieved prominence as a Jewish religious center in the 16th century. The movement for reform and assimilation in Judaism became quite strong in the 18th century and by the beginning of the 19th century, after the Napoleonic reforms had broken the walls of the Judengasse and given the Jews citizen's rights, the Reformists founded the Philanthropin school. It was there that much of the work for reform was carried out. Later in the century the struggle between the conservative Jews and the Re-formers resulted in Rabbi Samson Raphael Hirsch joining the Israeliti-sche Religionsgesellschaft, which under his leadership became the spearhead of the neo-Orthodox movement all over Europe.

Little remains today of historical Jewish Frankfurt. What progress during the 19th century or the Nazis didn't destroy, the bombs did during WW II. All that survives of Jewish medieval history lies in a recently uncovered mikveh and in the tomb-stones of the 13th century cemetery on Battonstrasse.

During excavations for the construction of new buildings in Börneplatz, some foundations and basements of the former Judengasse were uncovered, including a mikveh built in 1462. There was considerable debate concerning this excavation, resulting in an agreement that the foundations of five medieval Jewish houses, the mikveh, and a well would be restored and made accessible for public viewing. Since then, a second, later mikveh has been uncovered.

These finds are displayed as outposts of the new Jewish Museum which opened in 1988. Its collections include ritual and secular objects, some of which were salvaged from the old Jewish museum founded in 1922, and the synagogues destroyed by the Nazis during "Reichskristallnacht", as well as contributions received from German-speaking Jews and their descendants around the world. The bulk of the collection is housed in the Rothschild Palace, which is located on

The massive structure of the Westend synagogue, from 1910, serves the Frankfurt Jewish community as their place of worship again.

Untermainkai 14-15, overlooking the Main river. There is also a large documentation exhibit on the history of Frankfurt and German Jews. The museum is open Tuesday-Sunday 10-5, also on Wednesday 5-8.

The Jewish Archives, which have been incorporated into the Museum, have collected thousands of old photographs of synagogues in Germany, Austria, Czechoslovakia, and Poland as well as documents relating to the German Jewish past. As a service to families with Frankfurt ancestors, a catalogue has been developed containing information about names, birth and death dates, and occupations as well as photographs. The large museum library is also at the disposal of the museum's visitors.

The Westend synagogue on Freiherr-von-Stein-Strasse was built in 1910, burned in the 1938 "Reichskristallnacht", restored in 1948, and consecrated again in 1950. A new elementary school was opened in 1986 in the Jewish Community Center between Westendstrasse and Savignystrasse.

An exhibition on the history of the important Reform Jewish Philantropin school can be seen at Hebelstrasse 15-19, Monday-Friday 8 a.m.-9 p.m. and Sunday 9-1.

Frankfurt's 13th century cemetery served the community until 1829. This cemetery is described in a 1933 book as having 7,000 red sandstone tombstones still standing and maybe 20,000 more sunk into the earth. Some of these were saved by the custodian of the Art History Museum who successfully pleaded their historical value. Most of the others were broken up on the spot or carted away during the Nazi years.

Today, about 2,000 of the old tombstones can still be seen standing beneath the canopy of tall trees at one end of the cemetery while others, brought back from where they were dumped, lie piled in the center. The gravestones from the museum are lined up along the wall. Two 13th century gravestones used in building the cathedral were moved to this medieval cemetery when the cathedral was renovated. Among the graves is that of Phinehas Horowitz, who denounced Moses Mendelssohn for translating the Torah into German in 1782. You may see the cemetery through a barred gate on Battonstrasse. For the best view, walk to your right and around the cemetery to the

area on Rechneigrabenstrasse 2-8. The wall isn't so high there. If you want to go inside, you may get the key from the Jewish Community Center at Westendstrasse 43.

Two Jewish cemeteries are located next to the city cemetery located on Rat-Beil-Strasse. The older section dates back to 1828. It is locked. However, there is a man who takes care of the cemetery so ring the bell. He also has an alphabetical register of graves. (If there is no answer, you can get the key from the flower shop across the street.) In addition to having both Orthodox and Reform gravestones from the last century, there are memorial stones to the victims of the Holocaust and many stones giving only the name, the notation "Beerdigt" (meaning buried) and a date. These stones mark the graves of some of the almost 700 Frankfurt Jewish suicides during the Nazi years.

Only a few stones remain standing in the medieval cemetery of the Frankfurt Jews, most were carted away by the Nazis.

The newer section, on Eckenheimer Landstrasse, still serves the community today. Stones here are of this century and include many memorial stones both for the victims of the Holocaust and for former Frankfurt Jews who died and are buried in Israel or elsewhere.

Information on other Frankfurt Jewish cemeteries may be obtained from the Jewish Community Center on Westendstrasse 43.

The Stadt- und Universitätsbibliothek (City and University Library) on Bockenheimer Landstrasse contains a large collection of Judaica and Hebraica, as well as German Jewish literature from the exile and pictures of Jewish writers. The Deutsche Bibliothek at Zeppelinallee 4 has a large collection of "Literature in Exile".

A number of memorials to Frankfurt's Jewish victims of the Holocaust and to the destruction of their synagogues have been established throughout the city. In addition to the memorials mentioned above, there are memorials on Börneplatz, Friedberger Anlage 5-6, behind St. Paul's Church on Berliner Strasse, in Rödelheim, and Höchst. A memorial tablet may be seen on the front of Anne Frank's birthhouse on Ganghoferstrasse 24.

FREIBURG

is located about 200 km southwest of Stuttgart off the A 5 and on highways 3 and 31, close to the southern Black Forest (map 10).

* Memorials
* Three Gothic statues depicting Jewish themes on the cathedral
* Synagogue and community center
* Cemetery

These low stones showing not the date of death, but of burial ("Beerdigt"), mark the graves of Jews who took their own lives during the Nazi years.

105

First mention of Jews in Freiburg concerns their imprisonment by a local prince and their release by King Henry VII in 1230. Documents later on usually deal with the right to the revenues created by the Jews of Freiburg and what interest rates Jews could charge. Only pregnant Jewish women and children escaped massacre during the Black Death persecutions in 1349 and the community was fully expelled in 1424. Jews were allowed to return in the early 17th century, but the community grew slowly. Several Jews became prominent at Freiburg University in the 20th century until the Nazis forced them to give up their academic posts.

There is a memorial for Freiburg's synagogue, consecrated in 1885 and destroyed during "Reichskristallnacht", on Werthmannplatz.

The Jewish cemetery, located on Elsässerstrasse 35, contains a memorial to the Jewish soldiers killed in WWI and a memorial to the memory of the Freiburg Jewish community of 1933-45.

Three late 13th century Gothic statues depicting the Synagogue Defeated (to be found on the right side of the main portal, facing the Church Triumphant), the Sacrifice of Isaac, and King David and his harp (in the southwest corner, behind a birch) can be seen on the outside walls of the cathedral on Münsterplatz.

The Freiburger Rundbrief, a journal dedicated to Christian-Jewish understanding, is published in Freiburg.

A post-war synagogue and Jewish community center are located at Engelstrasse/Nussmannstrasse 14.

The Synagogue Defeated of the Freiburg Minster stands stiffly, her eyes blindfolded and her scepter broken.

FREUDENTAL

is a small village located about 30 km north of Stuttgart, west of highway 27 and south of Brackenheim (map 10).

* Former synagogue from 1770
* Cemetery from 1811

The first Jews settled in Freudental in 1723 and already outnumbered Christians in the early 1800's. However, the community declined like so many other rural communities in Germany, until it numbered about 50 in 1933. The last 14 Jews to remain in Freudental were deported to the German death camps in 1941.

The former synagogue, built in 1770 in an austere Baroque style, was dese-

The colorful chuppah stone on the facade of the former Freudental synagogue shows the Hebrew abbreviation for "the voice of bliss and the voice of joy, the voice of the bridegroom and the voice of the bride".

cultural center since 1985. Set into the wall next to the entrance is a colorful red and yellow chuppah stone with a Hebrew abbreviation for "the voice of bliss and the voice of joy, the voice of the bridegroom and the voice of the bride". Outside stairs, now enclosed in glass, lead up to the former women's gallery. There is a small plaza in front. The former synagogue is located at Strombergstrasse 23.

crated in the 1938 "Reichskristallnacht" pogrom and later used as a storehouse. In 1979, the building was in such bad shape that the council decided to have it torn down. At the last moment, the former synagogue was saved by a civic action group. It has been carefully restored and has been a pedagogical

The Jewish cemetery was originally established in 1723, but in 1811 King Friedrich of Württemberg had it razed and built a pheasant farm instead. A new cemetery was set up the same year. The cemetery is small and well-kept with all stones standing. There is a memorial to five Jewish soldiers who died in WWI. One gravestone from 1970 has an inscription to two former Freudental Jews who died in New York. The German inscription reads "Oh my little village".

The former synagogue of Freudental was built in 1770 and houses a pedagogical-cultural center today.

The cemetery lies on the side of a hill on the edge of a forest looking down on the village. Drive out on Strombergstrasse past Gartnerstrasse and turn left at the end onto Stutenweg. There is a signpost "Zum Friedhof" with a Star of David.

(The memorial close by is for Helene, favorite horse of King Friedrich of Württemberg, buried here in 1812, from which Stutenweg, or Mare's Lane, derives its name.)

FRIEDBERG

is located about 30 km north of Frankfurt, on highways 3 and 455, close to the A 5 (map 4, 5, 8).

* 13th century mikveh
* Memorials
* Remains of two cemeteries, a cemetery from 1934

Probably the most beautiful of the surviving mikvoth in Germany, and certainly the deepest, is the 13th century Gothic mikveh (or Judenbad) in Friedberg.

The founder's tablet from 1260, immersed in the living water where it is deepest, gives evidence of Friedberg's medieval Jewish community.

From its dark entrance gate, adorned with a pointed arch in the Gothic style, five flights of ancient stone steps, 72 in all, lead the visitor down past columns with Gothic capitals. This magnificent subterranean bath was wrought from

25 meters (82 feet) of basaltic rock more than 700 years ago. It must have been incredibly difficult to build, given the primitive tools and lack of machinery and artificial ventilation at the time. Looking down into the darkness from the top, one sees what appears to be the moon shining brightly in the waters below. This moonlike image is created by the octagonal opening in the vaulted ceiling above - the sole source of daylight - and its reflection in the water below.

In the entry hall of the mikveh is a memorial listing the Friedberg Jews who gave their lives for their German homeland in WWI, along with old photographs. One photograph shows Karl Neuhof receiving a medal from Kaiser Wilhelm II in 1915. Underneath

Eighty feet below ground the light from the cupola is reflected in the living water of the Friedberg mikveh.

this photograph, a small note indicates that Mr. Neuhof was murdered in 1943 by the Nazis. A small stone commemorates another Friedberg son, Ernst (later Sir Ernest) Oppenheimer, who found fame and fortune in the gold and diamond mines of South Africa. There is also a memorial to the synagogue destroyed in the 1938 "Reichskristallnacht" and to the victims of the Nazi regime. The mikveh is located at Judengasse 20 and is open Tuesday-Friday 9-12 and 2-5; Saturday 9-12; and Sunday 10-12.

A few feet from the mikveh, a wall of the synagogue destroyed in the 1938 "Reichskristallnacht" pogrom still stands. In 1992 a commemorative tablet to the Friedberg Jews killed in German camps was attached to this wall. There is another memorial tablet at the Augustine school gym used as a transit camp by the Nazis.

The Wetterau museum displays a 14th century Jewish gravestone and a cast of the mikveh's founder's tablet. It is located on Haagstrasse 16 and is open Tuesday-Friday 9-12 and 2-5, Saturday 9-12, Sunday 10-5.

The old Jewish cemetery used to lie to the left and the right of Ockstädter Strasse, below the hospital, until it was totally destroyed during the Third Reich. There are only a few old gravestones left to the right of the street. A newer Jewish cemetery was opened in 1934 close to highway 3 going in the direction of Ober-Wöllstadt; it is in good condition.

The Gothic arches and columns of this grandiose structure were built by the same stonemasons who also built the town church.

FRIEDRICHSTADT

is located on the Eider river, about 130 km northwest of Hamburg, on highway 202 close to highway 5 (map 1).

* Former synagogue from 1845
* Cemeteries

This romantic little town, unique in Germany, is surrounded by water and crisscrossed with canals. It was built by the Dutch who were invited here in 1621 by the Duke of Holstein to cultivate the marshy land. Jews were living here at least since 1677.

Though it was not destroyed, the synagogue, built in 1845, was badly damaged in the 1938 "Reichskristallnacht" pogrom. Today it is being used as an office building. It is located on the corner of Westermarktstrasse and Am Binnenhafen. Opposite the building is a small memorial stone commemorating the synagogue. Next door is the former Jewish school.

The old cemetery on Treeneufer, in the northwest corner of the old part of town, was destroyed almost completely by the Nazis. Only a few chipped and broken stones remain and have been arranged in a circle with a memorial stone in the center. A memorial for the victims of the Nazis stands at the Westersielzug end of the cemetery. The cemetery is locked.

The new cemetery on Schleswiger Strasse is part of the city cemetery founded in 1888. About 70 old stones remain. Some of the stones are decorated with stone garlands of flowers and stylized roses. The former taharah house shelters a transformer today.

The former Friedrichstadt synagogue serves as an office building today.

FÜRTH

is located about 10 km west of Nürnberg on highway 8 (map 9, 10).

* Synagogue from 1884
* Community center
* Memorials
* Future Jewish regional museum
* Two cemeteries

First documents about Jews in Fürth stem from the mid-15th century and give their profession as moneylenders. They were eventually expelled; then a Jewish family was given permission to settle in Fürth in 1528. A new community was established and flourished in the 17th century due to the rivalry existing between the Margrave of Ansbach, the Nürnberg council and the Prince Bishop of Bamberg, jointly lords of Fürth. These rulers granted competing privileges to get tax-paying Jews to settle in their respective areas of Fürth, which attracted Jewish settlers from all over Germany, as well as large numbers of Austrian Jews after they were expelled from the

Habsburg possessions in 1670. By the end of the 18th century, the Jewish community numbered around 3,000 out of a total of 13,000 inhabitants of Fürth. For the times, conditions in Fürth were more favorable than anywhere else in Germany. For example, the community had a vote in the city council, self-regulated the settlement of Jewish immigrants, and could build as many synagogues as it could afford to maintain. Consequently, Fürth became known as another Little Jerusalem.

These favorable conditions resulted in a rich religious life. A yeshiva flourished here for more than 130 years, until 1830. Many rabbis schooled here went to other German and Eastern European communities. The Fürth community had seven synagogues. Many Hebrew and Yiddish books were printed in Fürth.

In 1763, a Jewish orphanage, with its own synagogue, was founded. It was the oldest such institution in Germany. This synagogue (which had been rebuilt in 1884) was the only one of Fürth's seven synagogues to survive destruction in the 1938 "Reichskristallnacht". Today, the orphanage has been turned into an apartment building. The synagogue is located at Hallemannstrasse 2. In the hall there is a memorial to Dr. Isaak Hallemann, the last headmaster of the orphanage, and to the 33 orphans he accompanied when they were taken to Izbica and their death in 1942. The synagogue can be visited after applying to the Jewish Community Center (see below).

The Jewish Community Center at Blumenstrasse 31, site of the former Jewish high school, has a memorial to the victims of the Nazis.

In Schulhof, where four synagogues stood before the 1938 "Reichskristallnacht", there is a memorial to the Jewish community and to the destroyed synagogues sculpted by Kunihiko Kato, a Japanese sculptor living in Fürth. The memorial is made of pink granite in the shape of a flame with Hebrew and German inscriptions around the bottom.

The Fromm family of court Jews built a small palace in Königstrasse 89; this is where the Jewish museum for Central Franconia will open in 1997. Central Franconia was unusually rich in rural Jewish communities, and much of this past remains. A branch of this museum will be opened in Schnaittach (see below).

There are two Jewish cemeteries in Fürth. The cemetery on Schlehenstrasse dates from 1607 and contains massive gravestones near the entrance made from the local gray sandstone like the houses in the neighborhood. The stones are quite simple, undecorated, with Hebrew inscriptions. Many of the stones are half sunken and only a few are visible from the locked gate. Further inside the cemetery there are many gravestones from the 19th century. The key is available from the Jewish Community Center. The cemetery at Erlangerstrasse 99 was established in 1906 and includes a memorial to Fürth's Jewish victims of the Nazi years. The caretaker can help you locate graves.

FUSSGÖNHEIM

is located about 100 km south of Frankfurt and about 130 km northwest of Stuttgart, between the A 61, A 65 and A 650 (map 8, 10).

* Former synagogue from 1842
* Cemetery from 1820

The former synagogue of the Fussgönheim Jews was sold before 1938 and was not damaged during "Reichskristallnacht". After being altered to some degree, it was used for grain storage. The building stood empty in 1994. It may be used to house part of the German potato museum. All windows and doors are bricked up, but their outlines can still be seen; the Hebrew inscription over the former entrance is still there, and there is still another inscription and remains of wall paintings inside. The former synagogue is located behind the Raiffeisen- und Volksbank building on Hauptstrasse opposite number 63.

There is a small cemetery between Ellerstadter Strasse and Bahnhofsstrasse. Many older stones are still standing, and they have all been catalogued and numbered. The key is available from the Fussgönheim town hall.

The former Fussgönheim synagogue stands empty today, in the backyard of a bank.

112

GELNHAUSEN

is located about 50 km east of Frankfurt, on the A 66 and highway 43 (map 4, 6, 8, 9).

* Former synagogue from 1734 and exhibition
* Cemetery from 1616

The first record of Jews in Gelnhausen concerns their tax payment to the emperor and to the Wetterau city coalition in 1241. The entire community was burned on the stake during the Black Death persecutions in 1349. A new community was established in 1361, was expelled in 1576, and resettled yet again in 1599. The community grew rapidly in the 18th century, augmented by Frankfurt Jews whose Judengasse had been destroyed by fire. In 1833 the Gelnhausen Jews received full citizen's rights. By the mid-19th century, it was in decline through emigration or settlement in larger German cities, as in most other small towns and villages in Germany.

In the 1930's, the speed of emigration increased and by 1938 the community had ceased to exist. More than 50 former Gelnhausen Jews, who by then had already moved elsewhere, were deported and killed in German camps.

Gelnhausen's old synagogue was rebuilt in 1601. (The chuppah stone formerly in the outside wall was from this period.) The synagogue was destroyed during the Thirty Years War, rebuilt in 1656 (three stone money boxes survive from this period), rebuilt again in 1734, and renovated in 1834. It was sold in early 1938 and used as a storeroom. It is now a

Only a few years after Gelnhausen was founded by emperor Friedrich Barbarossa, the first synagogue of Gelnhausen stood on this site.

113

cultural center. There is a copy of the old chuppah stone in the outside wall (the inscription is an abbreviation for "the voice of bliss and the voice of joy, the voice of the bridegroom and the voice of the bride") and the original Torah ark, one of the few Baroque arks surviving in Germany today. The entry hall contains a small exhibition on Gelnhausen's former Jewish community.

There is an unusual memorial of three interlocking rings in an open bronze door in the small plaza in front of the synagogue. It also shows a quotation in Hebrew, German, and Arabic from "Nathan der Weise", a play by the 18th century German playwright G. E. Lessing: "So may each man believe his ring is true—and act according to his uncorrupted love!" The play brings together a Christian knight, Sultan Saladin, and the Jew Nathan in Jerusalem. Saladin asks Nathan which of the three monotheistic religions is the true religion; Nathan tells him an old tale about a ring that had the power to make its owner "pleasant to god and men" and was passed on from generation to generation in a royal family. One of the kings, however, had three sons, so he had two exact copies made and left three rings to the three princes. The sons try to find out which of the rings is genuine and take the case to court, where a wise judge decides that all three rings, symbols for the monotheistic religions of Judaism, Christianity, and Islam, have the same power—if the owners act in accordance with their religious tenets. The play is an unusually early appeal for human and religious toler-ance and is often performed today.

The synagogue is located on Brentanostrasse 10 which was once called Judengasse. The key is available from the Stadtarchiv, in the Rathaus on Obermarkt. You can also join a guided tour of Gelnhausen starting at the Rathaus every Sunday at 2:30 from May to September, which includes the synagogue and the cemetery.

The oldest gravestone in the cemetery on Am Escher, which is behind the Schifftor, dates from 1616. The cemetery contains 836 gravestones, mostly made from red sandstone. There are a few 19th century stones in the back, but most stones appear to be from the 17th and 18th centuries. The cemetery is locked but you can easily look over the surrounding stone wall. The key is available from the city archives (Stadtarchiv) in the Rathaus on Obermarkt.

GEORGENSGMÜND

is located about 30 km south of Nürnberg off highway 2 (map 9, 10).

* Former synagogue from 1734
* Cemetery from mid-16th century

The synagogue in Georgensgmünd was built around 1734. Its survival is due to the talents of persuasion of the local school teacher, who convinced the villagers they shouldn't destroy it or the old cemetery, although he was a Nazi functionary. While the synagogue was in very poor condition serving as a storeroom for the old farmer who lived in the attached former Jewish school in 1989, it has been beautifully restored since and serves as a cultural center today. During renovation, several layers of wallpaintings were found and partially preserved; 19th century ornaments stand next to Baroque inscriptions and scrollwork today.

The former synagogue is a massive stone building and has three small windows over the Torah ark. The wooden women's gallery looks down from two sides. The former bimah's location is indicated on the tiled floor. There are separate entrances for women and men with an inscription in Hebrew ("Open the door, for I will come into the house") over the men's entrance. The old mikveh, which is

Wall paintings from the 18th and 19th centuries were found in the former synagogue.

The former Georgensgmünd synagogue was used as a shed for many years. Then it was restored. and serves as a cultural center for the small Bavarian town today.

115

fed by ground water, is in the second basement, though the newer mikveh on the ground floor is covered in concrete. Books, papers, a Torah mappah, and various calendars from the 18th and 19th centuries were found in the attic of the former synagogue in 1987. The former synagogue is located at Am Anger 9. It can be visited by applying to the mayor's office.

Behind the synagogue, a small street called Judenbastei (Jews' bastion) leads up to the very grand mid-16th century cemetery overlooking the village from behind the high stone walls that gave it its name. The cemetery once served the nearby communities in Roth, Schwabach, Thalmässing, and Windsbach also. Several unique styles can be seen amongst the 1,800 ancient stones.

The oldest stones, from 1605 on, are downhill behind the taharah house. The taharah house is from 1723 and has a prominent founders' tablet on a covered porch. It is now the residence of the caretaker.

How did small rural Georgensgmünd get to be an important Jewish settlement? The answer is both geographical and political: Georgensgmünd was almost totally surrounded by Eichstätt territories, where Jews were not allowed to live. They could, however, buy and sell in those territories. The distance from Georgensgmünd to the main settlements was short, about two hours walk, and the roads were safe. All this made Georgensgmünd an ideal place to live in for Jewish merchants. Much later, rural Georgensgmünd also became the home town for an unusually high number of Bavarian Nazi "Gold Pheasants" (top brass).

The old Jewish cemetery of Georgensgmünd lies on a hill overlooking the town.

GLÜCKSTADT

is located on the Elbe river about 60 km northwest of Hamburg, on highway 431 (map 1).

* Portuguese Jewish gravestones from 17th-19th centuries

Portuguese Sephardic Jews, then living in Hamburg, were granted special privileges by the Danish King Christian IV in 1618 to induce them to settle in Glückstadt. The community prospered, operating a sugar refinery, soap factory, and salt works, as well as

There are both Hebrew and Portuguese inscriptions on the gravestone of Ester Abessur, from 5418 (1658).

being active in foreign trade. The leader of the community was granted the operation of a mint. By the end of the 17th century, German Ashkenazi Jews were also admitted.

In 1732, the special privileges enjoyed by the Portugese community were withdrawn after the community had declined. Their synagogue was sold in 1785. The Ashkenazi community built their own synagogue in 1768; however, this community also declined throughout the 19th century and their synagogue was sold and torn down in 1895.

The two communities shared a cemetery, each following their own particular burial styles. A pre-war reference indicates that at that time there were more than 500 stones. However, today there are only eleven vertical Ashkenazi gravestones with Hebrew and German inscriptions and nine rows of 89 very remarkable horizontal Sephardic grave plates with Portuguese and Hebrew inscriptions surviving. Many of the Portuguese stones are elaborately carved, depicting biblical scenes, skulls, coats of arms, or symbols for the name of the deceased. Of particular interest is Eve, daughter of Isaak Palache, whose stone shows the biblical Eve receiving the fruit of the tree of knowledge of good and evil from the snake entwined in it. These 17th, 18th and 19th century gravestones are located on Pentzstrasse behind the railroad station.

Moses smites water from the stone surrounded by heraldic ornaments that might have done honor to a Spanish or Portuguese nobleman.

The biblical Eve receives the fruit of the tree of knowledge on this gravestone of her Portuguese/Northern German daughter Hava.

The gravestone of Rachel Kahanet from 5413 (1653) shows the blessing hands symbolic of her priestly tribe of Kohen.

The coat of arms of a knight is combined with an inscription in Hebrew on this stone from 5466 (1706).

118

The columns of the Temple of Solomon as well as hour-glass and skull adorn the gravestone of Ester, the wife of Benjamin Dionis de Caseres in a perfect synthesis of Jewish and Catholic symbolism.

GOLDBERG

is located about 160 km east of Hamburg, or about 160 km northwest of Berlin, on highway 192 (map 2).

* Former synagogue from 1845, now a Catholic church

The small Jewish community of Goldberg built a synagogue in 1845; soon, however, the community started declining and around 1900 the synagogue could no longer be maintained. After being used as a workshop and a warehouse, the former synagogue was converted to a Catholic church in 1925. The impressive facade goes back to a renovation in the 1950's and has nothing to do with the former synagogue.

The small church is located at Jungfernstrasse 36. In the courtyard, under the bells, there is a commemorative tablet with a menorah and the year 1845, and a cross and the year 1925. The former east wall of the synagogue was destroyed when the church's choir was added.

The Jewish cemetery of Goldberg was razed in the 1950's.

GÖRLITZ

lies about 100 km east of Dresden on the border with Poland, on highways 6 and 115 (map 7).

* Former synagogue from 1853
* Partly restored 1911 synagogue
* Cemetery from 1849

The oldest preserved documents about Jews in Görlitz are from the 14th century, however, the community may be older than that. A Judengasse and a cemetery are mentioned around 1300, and a synagogue in 1344. This community was destroyed in the 1349 Black Plague persecutions. Jews again settled in Görlitz in 1364, but the new community was expelled again in 1389 and 1395. Not until 1847 were Jews allowed to settle in Görlitz again.

In 1853 the new community built a synagogue. Soon this synagogue became too small and had to be enlarged in 1869. It served the community until a new synagogue was built in 1911. The old synagogue building still stands in the backyard of Obermarkt 17, formerly the White Horse hotel. From here the neglected side facade of the building can be seen; the west front can be seen from

The old Görlitz synagogue houses the workshop where scenery for the Görlitz theater is painted.

Langenstrasse 23. The former synagogue is a massive, two-story brick building with a small garden in front. Today it is being used to paint the backdrops for the city theater.

In 1911 the Görlitz community was able to consecrate a new and very grand synagogue. The monumental Jugendstil building emerged from a contest in which ten architects participated. The synagogue seated 280 men on the ground floor and 220 women in the gallery as well as 40 choir singers. In the 1938 "Reichskristallnacht" pogrom the building was damaged by fire, but saved from total destruction by the fire brigade. After the war the ruin was used as a depot for the theater's sets. Today the partly restored ruin of this imposing synagogue stands near Otto-Müller-Strasse, close to a park. Next to the entrance there is a tablet to the victims of the persecutions by the Nazis. Both synagogues can be visited after applying to the Kulturamt of the city of Görlitz on Untermarkt 6-8.

A cemetery was started in former Biesnitzerstrasse, today's Promenadenstrasse, in 1849 and was enlarged several times. The grave register kept from 1852 to 1942 has survived and is kept at the city archives. The former taharah house was renovated a few years ago, but is still being used by the city's construction department.

A memorial to the victims of the nearby Biesnitzer Grund concentration camp was erected in the cemetery. The address is Promenadenstrasse/Büchtemannstrasse.

Near Görlitz, in Biesnitzer Grund, the Nazis had a small concentration camp from 1943 on. Prisoners from Auschwitz and Gross-Rosen were brought here and about one quarter of the inmates died.

The ruin of the grand new synagogue of Görlitz is to be restored, but due to the weak economy of the region the time frame is uncertain.

A slave labor camp for Jews and half-Jews from Görlitz was started in the Zoar infirmary in Rothenburg in 1941. The prisoners were deported to the death camps in 1942/43.

The city of Görlitz has published a brochure on the persecution of the Görlitz Jews by the Nazis and about Erich Mühsam, a poet from Görlitz. A history of the Görlitz Jews may also be published.

GÖTTINGEN

is located about 50 km northeast of Kassel and about 120 km south of Hannover, off the A 7 (map 3, 5, 6).

* City museum has Jewish exhibitions
* Library collection of Hebrew manuscripts
* Memorials
* Cemetery from 17th century

Although it is thought that Jews settled in Göttingen much earlier, first mention is made in 1289. The community was destroyed during the Black Death persecutions in 1349 but Jews returned in 1370 under new protection agreements, this time concluded with the municipal authorities instead of with the distant emperor or the duke of Braunschweig. They were even given the southeast corner of the city fortifications to maintain and defend.

However, the Jews were expelled again in 1459, resettled in Göttingen in 1553, were expelled again in 1796 after many changes in city and ducal policies, returned in 1808, briefly enjoyed the fruits of emancipation

granted them by the occupying French and the short-lived kingdom of Westphalia, but lost their citizen's rights and were expelled yet again when the Hannoveranian authorities returned after a few years.

In 1848, the few remaining Göttingen Jews received equal rights along with Jews over most of Germany.

Göttingen is an important university town. The poet Heinrich Heine studied here along with many other Jews. Jewish professors increased the fame of Göttingen university with two Nobel prize winners, Max Born and James Franck.

Göttingen's city museum at Ritterplan 7/8 has three permanent exhibition rooms with Jewish themes. Room 38 on the first floor shows the rise of the Nazis and the fate of Göttingen's Jewish community. On the second floor, there are two exhibitions. One contains Jewish ritual objects such as a Torah mantle, mappahs, shofar, circumcision instruments, seder plates, wedding rings, a menorah, besamim boxes, and sabbath and Chanukah lamps. The other exhibition depicts the history of Jews in Southern Lower Saxony. The museum is open Tuesday-Friday from 10-5 and Saturday and Sunday from 10-1. Guided tours are available and advance arrangements can be made for tours in English.

The Niedersächsische Staats- und Universitätsbibliothek at Prinzenstrasse 1 contains an important collection of Hebrew manuscripts and rabbinical literature. It is open

The impressive memorial for the Jewish community and the synagogue of Göttingen (both destroyed by the Nazis) is a pyramid formed from Stars of David.

Monday-Friday from 10-1 and 2-5; Saturday from 10-12.

The cemetery is located on Groner Landstrasse and contains stones from the middle of the 18th century on, and a memorial to the former Jewish community. If the cemetery should be locked, you can get the key at the Preissler flower shop at Groner Landstrasse 31.

There is a very impressive memorial to the synagogue destroyed in 1938 and to the victims of the Nazi years on the corner of Obere Maschstrasse and Untere Maschstrasse which consists of groupings of Stars of David in a pyramid form.

GRÖBZIG

is located about 120 km northeast of Erfurt, between highways 6 and 183, about 15 km southwest of Köthen (map 3, 5, 6, 7).

* Former 18th century synagogue
* Jewish museum
* 17th century cemetery

The Jewish community of Gröbzig, a small town close to the former residence of Köthen, was founded in 1660. Soon the community gained importance in the economic life of Anhalt. A synagogue - only the third in the state of Anhalt - was built in 1788-92 and remodeled in 1859. After the advent of the railroads and the emancipation of Jews in Anhalt, the Gröbzig community lost its economic base and started to decline. In 1934 the small Jewish community of Gröbzig, like many other rural communities, dissolved and the ritual objects from the synagogue were taken to Dessau, only to be destroyed there during "Reichskristallnacht".

The synagogue building was leased to the Gröbzig council and used as a local museum. When the museum opened in 1935, Jews were already prohibited from visiting. During "Reichskristallnacht" in 1938 the mayor, who was also chief of police and of the fire brigade, prevented the destruction of the building. However, the "provocative" entrance building with its Hebrew inscriptions of "House of Jacob, let us walk in the light of the eternal" and "There will be light in the evening" as well as the house for the hearse were torn down in 1939. After 1945, both buildings were restored.

In 1981 the Gröbzig council decided to renovate the former synagogue as well as the house of the cantor, the Jewish school, the library and the Jewish community center. In 1988 the complex was opened as a museum again. The former synagogue now houses an exhibition on the history of Jews, the school has an exhibition on the development of Jewish schools in the 19th century, and the cantor's house is the local museum (Heimatmuseum) today. The museum is open Tuesday-Thursday and Sunday 10-12 and 2-5, Friday 10-12.

Near the Akazienberg, on the Fuhne river, the large Jewish cemetery of Gröbzig is located. It was started shortly after the community was first founded and enlarged at the beginning of the 19th century. During the Third Reich the cemetery was repeatedly desecrated, but restored after 1945. The older gravestones are carved from sandstone, badly weathered and illegible. The key to the cemetery can be obtained at the museum.

GRONAU

is located 40 km south of Hannover, on the Leine river east of highway 3 (map 3, 5).

* Former synagogue complex from early 18th century
* Cemetery from 1758

The former synagogue complex, built after the big fire of 1703, survived the "Reichskristallnacht" pogrom. It is a small half-timbered building and included a prayer room, two women's

The former synagogue of Gröbzig was sold to the town in 1934 and converted to a local museum. Today it houses a Jewish museum.

124

galleries, a Jewish school and a teacher's apartment. After 1938, the synagogue was converted into a Protestant church. The former syna-gogue has been a private home since 1987. It is located at Südstrasse 14. The school and teacher's apartment are visible from the street. However, the synagogue is in the back and only partly visible from a side street.

The cemetery dates from around 1758 and has 57 stones. Most of the stones are half sunk into the ground and have Hebrew inscriptions. A few also have German inscriptions. The cemetery is located next to Hoher Escher 3 and is open.

The town originally planned commemorative tablets for both the synagogue and cemetery, but was prevented from attaching them by the current owners and their neighbors. However, both sites are included in the tourist map.

GROSSKROTZENBURG

is located about 30 km east of Frankfurt, close to the A 45 and on highway 8 (map 8).

* Former synagogue from 1826
* Cemetery from around 1700

The former synagogue, built in 1826 and enlarged twice, was devastated but not destroyed on "Reichskristallnacht". It was used as a Protestant church until 1974, and since then as the meeting and exhibition hall for the local aquarium club. Visits may be made on Sunday 10-1. Plans are underway to restore it as a memorial

and cultural center. The former synagogue is small and built from the local sandstone. It has tall arched windows on the north and south sides and the outlines of three small windows and doors on the west front can still be seen. The former synagogue was once part of a complex including the school, the mikveh building, and the taharah house. The school, at Steingasse 12, was built at the same time as the synagogue and is now an apartment building. The mikveh building which was next to the school has been torn down as well as the taharah house next door. The former synagogue is located at Steingasse 10. On the face of the building is No. 50 1/2, the old house number. There is a commemorative tablet to the former use of the building.

The cemetery, which was established around 1700, is located outside of town. Drive out Waitzweg in the direction of the forest. Just before you

The modest former synagogue of Grosskrotzenburg was once part of a larger complex of buildings, consisting of the synagogue, school, ritual bath and taharah house.

125

reach the forest there is a track leading off to the left. Follow this track, which is rather rough, to the edge of the forest. Another track leads off to the left. The cemetery is enclosed by a red sandstone wall and contains a number of red sandstone gravestones, most of which are standing. The cemetery is locked. The key is available at city hall.

GRÜNSTADT

is located about 90 km southwest of Frankfurt, on highway 271 off the A 6 (map 8, 10).

* Former synagogue from 1790
* Cemetery from around 1700

The former synagogue building dates from 1790. The interior was damaged and its ritual objects destroyed during "Reichskristallnacht" in November 1938, but the building itself has survived. It is located on the corner of Post Strasse and Östlicher Graben and is now a wallpaper, carpet, and curtain business. The former synagogue is now light green and has three small circular windows over five arched windows. There has been a memorial plaque for the Jewish community and its synagogue since 1988. The cemetery, established around 1700 in a former sandpit, is located east of town on Max Planck-Strasse off Obersülzer Strasse. Take the first left immediately after leaving Grünstadt and then the second right. The cemetery is in a grove of trees behind a factory. The oldest remaining stone is from 1743 and stands over a family grave which is very unusual for older Jewish cemeteries; in 1743, Rebekka and six years later her husband Simon were buried here. Most stones are from the 18th and 19th century and appear to be in fairly good condition. The last burial took place here in 1969, and since 1989 the cemetery has been a protected site.

The former Grünstadt synagogue houses a textile shop today.

HAGEN

is located about 70 km northeast of Köln, between the A 1 and A 45 (map 4).

* Former synagogue from 1859
* Synagogue from 1960
* Two cemeteries

Jews began settling in Hagen in the early 18th century. The community grew in the 19th century, occupied primarily in the manufacture of textiles. The former synagogue, built in 1859 in an unusual neo-Renaissance style in the suburb of Hohenlimburg, was heavily damaged by the SA in the 1938 "Reichskristallnacht". It was used as part of a factory and by 1980 was a near ruin. A group of Hagen citizens undertook the necessary red tape, raised funds through the state,

city, and private donations, and had the synagogue restored as a memorial and documentation center. The former synagogue is located on Jahnstrasse next to no. 46. The key is available from city hall.

A new synagogue was consecrated in 1960 and includes a community center. It is located at Potthofstrasse 16, where the synagogue destroyed on "Reichskristallnacht" used to stand.

There are two cemeteries in Hagen. The cemetery in the suburb of Eilpe is located on Hohle Strasse at the corner of Strassburgerstrasse and contains stones from the old cemetery on Böhmerstrasse at the lower end. This cemetery can be visited at the usual times. Another cemetery on a hill overlooking Elsey is at the corner of Wiedenhofstrasse and Heidestrasse.

The small former synagogue of Hagen/Hohenlimburg was built in an unusual Neo-Renaissance style and carefully restored in the 1980's.

127

There is a row of old stones along the right side. There are also numerous Russian POW graves at the lower end and a Russian memorial at the top. The key is available from the Städtischer Bauhof at Elseyer Strasse 71.

HAINSFARTH

is located about 70 km southwest of Nürnberg, close to highway 466, just outside of Oettingen (map 9, 10, 11).

* Former synagogue from 1857
* Cemetery from mid-19th century

The former synagogue was built in 1857 and is set back from the street between Jurastrasse (formerly Judengasse) 12 and 14. Two earlier synagogues used to stand in this place from the late sixteenth century on, serving the rather large Hainsfarth community. The building was in very bad condition

The former synagogue had been used as a storeroom for construction equipment.

Unusual for small towns, the former synagogue of Hainsfarth was built in the Moorish style...

128

in 1988, but the exterior has since been restored and there are plans to restore the interior. There are several plans for the former synagogue: it may serve as a center for research into the history of Jews in rural Swabia, a cultural center, a conference venue and a synagogue for the small Oettingen community living nearby.

The doors and windows show a Moorish style unusual for a rural synagogue and there is Moorish decoration around and on the two doors. The Hebrew letters over one door had been torn away but you could still see their outline in 1988; the renovation has removed all traces. Inside, remains of the decorative painting on the ceiling and walls could be seen in 1988 as well as the Ten Commandments in Hebrew on both sides of the Torah ark. The former Jewish school stands next to the synagogue and was

restored for use as a residence in 1988, but has been abandoned in the meantime. The key to the former synagogue can be obtained at the mayor's office or at the Wittig grocery to the right of the former synagogue on Jurastrasse.

The mid-19th century cemetery is located on the outskirts of the village. Follow Jurastrasse all the way out to no. 43 which is the former taharah house and present guardhouse. The cemetery is locked. Should the caretaker not be available, you can still easily see over the surrounding wall. The stones are very elaborate and stand quite tall, giving the appearance of a small stone forest. The cemetery is in good condition with all the stones standing. However, most stones are badly weatherbeaten and the inscriptions are difficult to read.

... and restored in the 1990's. The former Jewish school is on the left.

129

HALBERSTADT

is located about 120 km north of Erfurt and about 120 km southeast of Hannover, on highways 79 and 81 (map 3, 5, 6).

* Former Klaus synagogue from 1709
* Remains of the 1716 community synagogue
* Former ritual baths
* Former Jewish school from 1899
* Former Jewish old-age home
* Three cemeteries
* Memorials

Jews are documented for the first time in 1146, after they were expelled from nearby Halle. The first letter of protection for Halberstadt Jews is documented for 1261, but a synagogue could not be built until 1456. The community was expelled by the bishops, the rulers of Halberstadt, in 1493 and in 1594, but returned within a few years. The president of the community, Jeremia, built a new synagogue in 1645, only to have it destroyed during an uprising of artisans in 1669. According to a contemporary inscription, the city museum still preserves a hammer used in the destruction of the synagogue. Later, Jews from Austria, who had been expelled in 1670, moved to Halberstadt in large numbers. The influential court Jew, Behrend Lehmann, built a yeshiva with a small synagogue, the Klaus-synagogue, in 1709 and a new community synagogue in 1716. In 1795 the parnas Hirsch Isaak Borchard founded a school for poor and orphaned children, one of the first of its kind in Germany. During the 19th and 20th

centuries, Halberstadt became the focus of Orthodoxy in Germany; the Union of Orthodox Communities in Germany existed here until 1939.

The Jewish community had about 1,000 members in 1728, out of a total population of about 10,000. In 1933, about 700 Jews lived in Halberstadt, only about 240 in 1939. 186 Jews from Halberstadt were deported to German camps in 1942, none returned.

The synagogue from 1716 was devastated during "Reichskristallnacht", and the Jewish community had to pay to have it torn down. Only parts of the tiled floor and a small part of the outer wall still exist in the courtyard of Bakenstrasse 56. There are plans to make these remnants part of a memorial after the current restoration of the quarter is finished.

A little way back from the street the

The former Klaus synagogue in Halberstadt was built in 1709 and used as a residence for many years.

tall and slim former Klaus synagogue still stands at Rosenwinkel 18. The building houses apartments today.

The former mikveh of the Halberstadt community still lies at Judenstrasse 26. It also will be accessible to the public after restoration. Until a few years ago the mikveh served as a coal cellar. It was only found during the visit of a former Halberstadt Jew in 1990. Two older mikvoth have been found at Seidenbeutel 7 and on Bakenstrasse.

Close to the former synagogue, at Westendorf 15, the former Jewish school is still standing. This building from 1899 served as an apartment building and now stands empty.

The former Jewish old age home can be seen on Strasse der Opfer des Faschismus (often abbreviated OdF-Strasse) 14a-15. In 1942, its last inhabitants were deported to Theresienstadt. Today the building serves as a residence.

There are three Jewish cemeteries in Halberstadt. The oldest, from 1644, lies on the corner of Sternstrasse and Am Berge. During the Third Reich it was destroyed almost completely, only about a hundred mostly 18th century stones remain, the others were used in construction. The entry gate is ornamented with two stars of David.

Only a narrow path separates this cemetery from the second oldest Jewish cemetery in Halberstadt, from 1696. In spite of this proximity the newer cemetery remained almost unharmed during the Nazi years. Most stones here go back to the 18th or 19th

century. Some gravestones salvaged from the older cemetery were brought here and laid flat; among them you can see the magnificent stone of the court Jew Behrend Lehmann with the Levite pitcher held by the two lions of Judah. Entrance is through the Catholic cemetery next door. The keys for both cemeteries are available from Cecilienstift across the road, from the Franciscan church of St. Andrew, or from the very active Association for the Preservation of the Jewish Heritage in Juri Gagarin-Strasse 10.

The third Halberstadt cemetery, from 1895, is in Klein Quenstedter Chaussee, next to the city cemetery. The taharah house was destroyed in the 1938 "Reichskristallnacht", otherwise this cemetery was hardly damaged. Because the Halberstadt community was very conservative, even 20th century stones show almost exclusively Hebrew inscriptions. You can enter the cemetery from the city cemetery, through the cemetery gardener's courtyard. There is a memorial to the Jewish victims of Fascism in the city cemetery.

Two memorials to the Halberstadt Jews can be seen in front of the cathedral (Dom) of Halberstadt. The one on the wall to the right of the entrance shows a burned-out menorah and a commemorative tablet; it was unveiled in 1982. The other, more prominent memorial consists of a bundle of square concrete pillars emerging from the pavement in front of the entrance to the cathedral. These pillars show the names of the Halberstadt Jews deported from here in 1942.

About 7 km southwest of Halberstadt, at Langenstein, there is a memorial to the auxiliary camp of Buchenwald; about 8,000 inmates died here.

HALDENSLEBEN

is located about 160 km west of Berlin and about 140 km east of Hannover, on highways 71 and 245 and on the Ohre river (map 2, 3).

* Former synagogue from 1822
* Cemetery from the 18th century

The small Haldensleben community built a tiny synagogue close to the market in 1822. However, the community did not escape the fate of many rural or small town communities elsewhere in Germany: in the course of the 19th century the community shrank due to emigration and a move to larger towns that provided better means of livelihood. Around 1900, the community could no longer afford its synagogue and sold it to a citizen of Haldensleben, who rented it to the Neuapostolische Kirche, a Protestant sect. In the 1950's, the former synagogue was bought by the Christian community that had already used it as a church for about fifty years. The former synagogue stands at Steinstrasse 18 and looks abandoned. The street entrance lies close to the east wall and looks very much like a later addition; the former entrance was probably either through the neighboring building or the courtyard.

The former Jewish cemetery of Haldensleben, on Auf dem Trendelberg, was destroyed almost completely during the Nazi years. There is a memorial stone to the Haldensleben Jewish community, but hardly anything else remains.

The tiny former synagogue of Haldensleben has served as an Evangelical church since the 1950's.

HALLE an der SAALE

is located about 100 km northeast of Erfurt and 160 km northwest of Dresden, where highways 6, 81, 90 and 100 converge and at the end of A 14 (map 6, 7).

* Gate of a synagogue from the 19th century
* New synagogue, converted from former taharah house
* Two cemeteries

Jews are first mentioned in Halle in 1184. Since they already owned several houses, a synagogue and a mikveh then, the community must have been older. After many persecutions, the Jews were expelled from Halle in 1493. The "Judendorf" (Jewish village) was torn down and the Moritzburg built in its stead.

Not until 1688 could Jews settle in Halle again. The new community bought a plot for their cemetery in 1693 (this cemetery was to be used until 1870). Around 1700 the community built a synagogue in Grosser Berlin, a new square close to the old market, where many Jews lived at the time. This synagogue was restored and enlarged several times and rebuilt in the Moorish style in 1870. During "Reichskristallnacht" in November 1938 the building was not damaged, but it was burned down a day later. In 1940 the Jewish community had to pay to have the ruin torn down. However, a few walls and the former entrance at Grosser Berlin remained standing since the neighboring buildings were held upright by these parts of the destroyed synagogue.

Most of the 1,000 Jews of Halle became victims of the persecution by the Nazis.

The former entrance to the synagogue is still standing on Grosser Berlin, although it was moved from its original position during reconstruction of the square. It is now a memorial for the destroyed synagogue and the Jewish community of Halle.

When the Jewish community was forced to sell its almost 250 year old cemetery in Gottesackerstrasse 2 to the Nazi state in 1937, they at least got permission to transfer the bones and the stones from this cemetery to the new cemetery in Dessauer Strasse 24. However, they were not allowed the means to do this, so the gravestones had to be transported one by one on small handcarts. In view of these difficulties what was achieved is amazing: Not only were about 180 old stones taken to the new cemetery, but once there they were not piled up or left leaning against each other, but were set into the ground in a narrowing chessboard pattern, being dug in deeper and deeper towards the center. The remains brought from the old cemetery were buried in a collective grave. This new cemetery from 1925 also has a memorial stone for the victims of Nazi persecution as well as a former taharah house from 1929. From 1938 on, it served as a transit point for transports to Theresienstadt, as accomodation for "privileged" Jews married to Gentile partners, as a refugee shelter, as party offices and as an old age home. Along the cemetery wall are the graves of Jews who chose death by their own hands rather than deportation.

The Jewish cemetery from 1869 is at Humboldtstrasse 52. Its taharah house was converted to a synagogue for the small Halle community in 1953. This cemetery was not damaged during the Nazi years. Most stones are still there and some have been repaired in recent years.

The Halle community center is at Grosse Märkerstrasse 13.

HAMBURG (map 1)

* Memorials
* Synagogue and community center
* Former synagogue from 1931-32
* 19th century synagogue in former Jewish hospital
* Cemeteries
* Neuengamme Concentration Camp memorial and documentation center

Hamburg was a free and imperial city and an important member of the medieval Hanseatic League, governed by an elected senate and a mayor. Jews were not allowed to settle in Hamburg until the end of the 16th century. At that time, a group of wealthy Portuguese Marranos (converted Spanish or Portuguese Jews who were suspected of secretly observing Jewish rites) were admitted.

At first the strictly Protestant Hamburg citizens suspected the Portuguese of being Catholics; but when the citizens discovered that they were, in fact, still practicing Jews, their expulsion was demanded. The city senate allowed the Jews to stay, however, because of their important business and commerce connections. These Sephardic Jews retained their old Spanish and Portuguese dialects until about 1800. Many books in Spanish or Portuguese, but in Hebrew characters, were printed in Hamburg during this time. In the 1660s, the teachings of Shabbatai Zvi, a false messiah who had promised to lead the Jews into the promised land (and who later became a Muslim), reached Hamburg. The community was so certain of the impending move to the Holy Land that the synagogues and schools were offered up for sale.

In 1697, when the Hamburg senate suddenly tripled the tax levied on the Hamburg community, most of the Sephardic Jews moved to Altona, now a part of Hamburg but a Danish possession at the time.

German Jews settled in Wandsbek, now also a part of Hamburg, but then also a city under Danish rule, around 1600, and some moved to Hamburg around 1627. The German, or Ashkenazi, communities of Hamburg, Wandsbek, and Altona soon formed a union which lasted, with a few interruptions, until 1811. In 1649, most Ashkenazi Jews were expelled from Hamburg and also settled in Altona. The Altona Ashkenazi community and its rabbis were very important until well into the 19th century.

With the arrival of Napoleon's troops in 1811, the Ashkenazi and Sephardic communities in Hamburg, Altona, and Wandsbek were forced to form one large community, which soon became a model for the co-existence of very disparate movements and traditions in one Jewish organization.

The granting of citizenship in 1850 brought relief from the various restrictions that had governed Jewish life continuously since the 17th century.

This period also saw the conflict between Orthodox and Reform Jews erupt in Hamburg. Out of this conflict, several communities emerged, each building its own synagogue. The communities continued to grow and by 1933 formed one of the largest Jewish populations in Germany with about 20,000 members. Five thousand Jews from Hamburg managed to emigrate by the late 1930s. One thousand Jewish residents were expelled to Poland in 1938. Eight thousand Hamburg Jews were killed in German camps during the Nazi years and almost all of the synagogues were destroyed.

A synagogue built in 1931-32 survived and is now used by NDR, the North German Broadcasting Company, as a concert hall. An inscription in Hebrew can still be seen over the door. A memorial to this former synagogue stands in front, depicting a torn Torah shrine curtain and a desecrated Torah. The former synagogue is located on Oberstrasse 120.

On Poolstrasse, behind numbers 12 and 13, a few walls of the second Hamburg synagogue from 1844 remain standing. The community was forced to sell the temple in 1937 and the building was hit by bombs in 1944. The ruins are now privately owned.

A hospital on Simon-von-Utrecht-Strasse 2 used to be a Jewish hospital founded in 1841 by Salomon Heine, the uncle of Heinrich Heine and a major 19th century philanthropists in Hamburg.

A synagogue in the center on an upper floor of this hospital is the only surviving pre-20th century synagogue building in Hamburg.

The Altonaer Museum on Museumstrasse 23 exhibits a collection of Judaica on the second floor. The museum collection included parts of a Chanukah menorah from 1662, the oldest evidence documenting the presence of Jews in Hamburg. The names of the twelve community members who donated the menorah are engraved on it. One of the members is Chaim Hameln, the husband of Glückel of Hameln, whose memoirs offer a unique view of Jewish life in Germany in the 17th century. After the exhibition "400 years of Jews in Hamburg", the restored menorah was returned to the Jewish community.

Next to the Judaica collection is a room exhibiting portraits of the Heine family, including one of Salomon Heine mentioned above. The museum is open Tuesday-Sunday 10-6.

The Museum of Hamburg History (Museum für Hamburger Geschichte) at Holstenwall 24 has the memorial book for the Hamburg Jewish victims of the Nazis years.

The Hamburg Kunsthalle includes paintings by Lieberman and Oppenheim and is located next to the Hauptbahnhof.

The Talmud-Tora high school, a former Jewish school built in 1911, is located at Grindelhof 30. This school was one of the most modern Jewish schools in Germany. Next to the school, there is a memorial to the Bornplatz synagogue, built in 1906, destroyed in 1938, and torn down at community expense in 1939.

A new synagogue has been built to serve Hamburg's medium-sized Jewish community. The complex is located at Hohe Weide 34. The restored menorah from 1662 mentioned above can be seen there. The Jewish community center is located at Schäferkampsallee 29.

A new memorial to Heinrich Heine, who was connected to the city through his family and several visits, stands on Rathausplatz. The memorial consists of a statue of Heine and bronze reliefs depicting the book burnings by the Nazis and the destruction of the pre-war Heine statue.

There are several Jewish cemeteries in Hamburg and its suburbs. The very large 17th century cemetery at Königstrasse 8 in Altona, a few hundred feet from the far end of the Reeperbahn

This relief of members of the SA burning books reflects the prophetic words of Heinrich Heine: "Where one burns books, one finally also burns humans".

contains about 2,000 Portuguese Sephardic graves as well as 6,000 German Ashkenazi graves.

The Sephardic stones are rectangular flat grave plates and some coffin-like stones with Hebrew and many Portuguese or Spanish inscriptions and are richly ornamented. The Ashkenazi stones are vertical with Hebrew and some German inscriptions. The cemetery is locked, but its interior can be seen through a barred fence on Königstrasse. The key is available at the Jewish Community Center.

The Jewish cemetery on Ilandskoppel is from 1882 and is next to Ohlsdorf, which is probably the largest Christian cemetery in the world. This cemetery includes a memorial to the Nazi victims with an urn from Auschwitz. Opposite the crematorium in the Christian part, on Fuhlsbüttler Strasse, there is a large memorial to all Nazi victims with 105 urns, symbols for the 105 major Nazi death camps and prisons where human beings were murdered in an industrial fashion.

In Harburg, a part of Hamburg located on the other bank of the Elbe, a cemetery from the 17th century is located opposite Schwarzenbergstrasse 72-74. Most of the stones are from the early 20th century with some dating from the late 19th century.

The cemetery is located inside a park between a gardening school and the Gildehaus restaurant. When entering the park from Schwarzenbergstrasse, keep half-right. The cemetery is surrounded by a low fence and is locked. A memorial to 500 Jewish women who were forced to work in the Neuengamme concentration camp outpost in Neugraben stands on Falkenbergweg.

Harburg also has a commemorative tablet to the synagogue destroyed in the 1938 "Reichskristallnacht" on Eissendorfer Strasse/Knoopstrasse.

The cemetery in Wandsbek is on Königsreihe opposite no. 62 and was established in 1675, although most stones date from the 19th and 20th centuries. There is a memorial to Dr. Simon Bamberger, rabbi of Wandsbek from 1902 to 1938. The key is available through the Jewish Community Center.

The former Neuengamme concentration camp is located on Neuengammer Heerweg, a few kilometers from the center of Hamburg across the Elbe.

The site includes a memorial to the victims of the Nazis and a documentation center. About 55,000 of its 106,000 prisoners from all over Europe died from starvation or epidemics or were killed by guards or doctors who used them for medical experiments. Many more died when the camp was evacuated in 1945, either on aimless death marches crisscrossing Northern Germany or in the Cap Arcona disaster, where 7,000 prisoners from Neuengamme perished (see Neustadt). The Neuengamme memorial site can be visited daily from dawn to dusk. The documentation center is open Tuesday-Sunday 10-5.

The Janusz Korczak school on Bullenhuser Damm 92 has a memorial to 20 Jewish children and 28 Neuengamme prisoners who were hanged there on April 20, 1945, a few days before the war in Europe ended. They were killed to hide the fact that a camp doctor had been performing tuberculosis tests on them. The basement room where they died can be visited during the school year, Monday-Friday 8-1.

HANNOVER (map 3)

* Synagogue and community center
* Kestner museum has a small collection of Judaica
* Memorials
* Cemeteries

Jews are first mentioned in the old city in 1292 and because the city was both prospering and expanding, the presence and protection of Jewish moneylenders was encouraged until the Black Death persecutions in 1350 drove the Jews from the city.

However, by 1375 the city was encouraging Jews to return and resume paying taxes. After 1553 the community was disturbed periodically when orders for its expulsion were issued, canceled, ignored, reissued, canceled, ignored, etc. This turbulence continued on into the 17th century.

In the 17th century, life stabilized and wealthy Jews were allowed to live in the new part of the growing city as well. Synagogues were built, Hebrew printing presses established, and various cultural and welfare institutions were set up, making Hannover an important Jewish center of activity until the destruction and deportations of the Nazi years.

The Kestner Museum owns a small collection of Judaica amongst its ethnological collections including a prayer book, besamim boxes, and a double cup (the cup of the law and the cup of blessing). However, this collection is rarely on display.

The museum is located at Trammplatz 3 and is open Tuesday, Thursday, and Friday 10-4; Wednesday 10-8; Saturday and Sunday 10-6. It is recommended to ask whether any of the collection is on display before making a special trip to the museum.

There is a commemorative tablet to the synagogue destroyed in the 1938 "Reichskristallnacht" on the Protestant church administration building at Rote Reihe 6 and a memorial to the destroyed Jewish hospital at Ellernstrasse 39.

Hannover's Jewish cemetery on Am Judenkirchhof (near the university) is the oldest Jewish cemetery in or around Hannover. It was used from the 16th century until 1866. There are more than 700 gravestones, including the grave of Leffmann Behrens, who was Court Jew and who in 1704

The old Jewish cemetery of Hannover lies on a low hill, close to today's university.

opened a synagogue in his home, and graves of some of Heinrich Heine's ancestors.

There are also two "stones of protection" granted by Duke Johann Friedrich in 1671 at the entrance. The cemetery is locked and surrounded by a stone wall. You can see into the cemetery to the left of the entrance as the cemetery stands on the only small hill for some distance.

The key is available from the Jewish Community Center at Haeckelstrasse 10, which is also the site of the new synagogue.

The large newer cemetery, located at An der Strangriede 55 near Engelbosteler Damm, was started in 1864. There is a memorial listing the names of the Hannover Jewish soldiers who died in the Franco-Prussian War and in World War I. There is also a memorial to Moritz Simon, founder of an agricultural school in Ahlem, now a suburb of Hannover, which provided Jews a chance to get away from typical professions. Many of the school's students emigrated to Palestine as agricultural colonists. The school building, however, was later used as a transit camp by the Nazis. Next to Moritz Simon's grave is a long row of Cohen graves. The cemetery includes a taharah house and a guardhouse. It is open Monday-Thursday 8-4; Friday 8-3; and Sunday 9-12.

A third, even newer, cemetery was used from 1926 on and is located at Burgwedeler Strasse 90. This cemetery includes a memorial to the Hannover Jewish victims of the Nazi years.

HANNOVERSCH MÜNDEN

is located about 20 km northeast of Kassel or 150 km south of Hannover, off the A 7 and on highways 3, 80, and 496 (map 5, 6).

* Former mikveh built sometime between 1796 and 1834
* Former school used 1796-1938
* Two cemeteries

The Fulda and the Werra rivers join in this romantic little town to form the Weser river. Jews began settling here in the 16th century. The community grew during the Thirty Years War and was protected by the imperial army against the hostile Münden council as the Jews furnished provisions to the imperial forces. Again, in the 18th century, the Jewish community was caught between the opposing forces of the city and the French army; this time the Jewish community helped the city raise the money the French were demanding. Of the 84 Jews living in Münden in 1933, at least 25 were killed in the Nazi camps.

The synagogue was built in 1834 in the backyard of what is now Hinter der Stadtmauer 23. It survived the Nazi years due to its proximity to other houses. When the neglected building was torn down in 1973, a mikveh which had been built sometime between 1796 and 1834 was discovered in the basement of the school building. This school building, which was used from 1796 until 1938, stands before the courtyard where the synagogue once stood. It

The former Jewish school of Hannoversch-Münden once hid the synagogue from the street. In the 1970's the synagogue was torn down, and the old mikveh was found.

is a half-timbered structure four stories high and has been beautifully restored. There is a commemorative tablet on the facade. The mikveh can be seen by applying to the owner of the building, Mr. Schlingensiepen.

There are two cemeteries. One was established in 1928 and is located on Heidewinkel. There are very few stones left and it is locked. A second cemetery on Vogelsangweg, next to no. 13, was used from 1673 to 1928 and razed by the Nazis. No stones survive but there is a commemorative tablet. The keys for both cemeteries are available from city hall.

The tall, massive former synagogue of Harburg lies on the river and serves as an office building today.

HARBURG

is located about 100 km southwest of Nürnberg, or about 130 km northwest of München, on highway 25 and the Wörnitz river (map 9, 10, 11).

* Former synagogue from 1754
* Cemetery from 1671

Jews are mentioned as being persecuted in 1348 during the Black Death persecutions. However, it is thought that there was no community in Harburg then and that Jewish refugees from Pfalz-Neuburg formed the first community only in 1671. The community first grew rapidly until the 19th century, then dwindled due to emigration like most other rural communities and had declined to very few members by the 1930s.

The former synagogue, built in 1754, has a mikveh in the basement. It lies above the Wörnitz river at Egelseestrasse 8. It was heavily damaged in the 1938 "Reichskristallnacht", but appeals to the SA from the neighbors fearing for their own property prevented the synagogue from being burned down.

The synagogue housed a small private museum in the 1950's and 1960's and was then for a while converted into a residence and an office building. It was used as a cultural center from 1989 to 1991. Today, however, its future use is uncertain. It is a quite tall and imposing building with arched windows on the first floor. The protruding aron niche is still visible on the river side of the former synagogue.

The cemetery was established in 1671 and includes a taharah house. Later on, the cemetery was also used by communities in Degging and Ederheim. The stones surviving today are mostly from the 19th and 20th centuries. The cemetery is locked but you can see through the gate and over the wall in places. The key is available from city hall.

To get to the cemetery, take the road to Schaffhausen past the castle on up to the crest of the hill. Turn right at the radio communications tower. You can see the cemetery walls in front of the forest from the road.

140

HECHINGEN

is located about 60 km southwest of Stuttgart, just off highway 27 (map 10).

* Former synagogue from 1767
* Cemetery from mid-17th century

Jews began settling in Hechingen in the early 16th century. A synagogue is mentioned in 1546 but a boycott in 1592 forced the Jews to leave.

In 1701 six Jewish families received letters of protection. A new synagogue was built in 1767 and a yeshiva in 1796. Although the interior of the synagogue was heavily damaged during "Reichskristallnacht" in November 1938, the building itself survived intact and has recently been carefully and beautifully restored.

It is being used for concerts and other cultural events. It is located at Goldschmiedstrasse 20. The street opposite has been renamed Synagogenstrasse. The key is available from Mr. Eckenweiler, who was among those

The former Hechingen synagogue lies opposite Synagogenstrasse and serves as a cultural center today.

actively involved in the renovation, at Schwalbenweg 48.

The cemetery is from the mid-17th century and includes a memorial to the Jewish victims of the Nazi era. The cemetery is large and well-maintained. It is located at Am Fichtenwald 1 and is locked, with a surrounding wall. To get there take the road to Sickingen. Turn right just before the 1A shopping center on Kaulla Strasse. Take a left at the end of the asphalt street. You can see the cemetery walls from the street. The key to the cemetery is available at city hall.

Both the synagogue and the graves look towards the south instead of the customary east.

HEIDELBERG

lies on the Neckar river about 100 km south of Frankfurt and about 110 km northwest of Stuttgart, on the A 656 and off the A 5 (map 8, 10).

* Heidelberg University library has a large collection of Hebrew manuscripts
* Synagogue and mikveh from 1994
* College for Jewish Studies
* Cemeteries

Jews are first mentioned in Heidelberg in 1275. It seems unlikely that a Black Death massacre like those taking place in the rest of Germany also took place in Heidelberg, since records indicate that refugees from the Rhineland were taken in during that time; the Black Death plague, however, eventually took its toll among Jews and Christians alike.

141

A Jewish community was established again in 1357 but was expelled in 1391. All of their houses, synagogue, mikveh, cemetery, and manuscripts were given to the university.

The Oppenheimer family arrived in the mid-17th century, of whom Joseph Suess Oppenheimer, the powerful Court Jew, was born in 1698. The Jewish community suffered through the wars with the French in the 1690's, the Hep Hep riots of 1819, as well as the 1848 revolution. At the beginning of the Nazi years, there were 1,100 Jews living in Heidelberg. Almost 450 Heidelberg Jews were deported and killed in the German camps.

The University of Heidelberg library at Plöck 107-109 has a large collection of Hebrew manuscripts and books as well as the originals of the agreements between 12th century Jews and the local princes. The library also has the Manessische Liederhandschrift, or Manesse song manuscript, a 14th century collection of songs with 137 miniature pictures of poets and minstrels, among them the curious Jewish minstrel Süsskind of Trimberg. The library is open Monday-Friday from 8:30 to 3:30.

A new synagogue from 1994, with a mikveh, is located at Häusserstrasse 10-12.

The College for Jewish Studies is at Friedrichstrasse 9, the only college of its kind in Germany.

There is a memorial tablet to the synagogue destroyed in the November 1938 "Reichskristallnacht" on Grosse Mantelstrasse/Lauerstrasse, around

the corner from Alter Synagogenplatz, where it stood.

The old cemetery, established in the early 18th century, is located on Klingenteichstrasse opposite No. 20. It is locked and practically nothing is visible through the gate. Visitors are not admitted to the cemetery.

The Bergfriedhof cemetery on Rohrbacherstrasse was opened in the mid-19th century and is part of the city cemetery. It includes a memorial to Heidelberg's Jewish victims of the Nazi years. The cemetery is open during the same hours as the city cemetery.

HEILIGENSTADT

is located about 60 km east of Kassel or about 90 km northwest of Erfurt, on highway 80 (map 5, 6).

* Former synagogue from 1873
* Mid-19th century cemetery

There are no documents to prove that Jews lived in Heiligenstadt during the Middle Ages; however, there is a certain probability since there were Jewish communities in many towns belonging to the archbishopric of Mainz, which also owned Heiligenstadt. All these communities were destroyed around 1350 by the Black Death persecutions. It is not until the 19th century that there are any documents pertaining to Jews in Heiligenstadt. In 1870 the small community bought a house and converted it for use as a synagogue, but the community was already shrinking by then. During "Reichskristallnacht", the synagogue was devastated, but not burned down because it was surrounded by houses on three sides. After the destruction of the Jewish community by the Nazis, the former synagogue was used as a residence. The building still stands at Stubenstrasse 14 and shows hardly any sign of its former use. There is a commemorative tablet from 1988 for the synagogue and the Jewish community.

The small Jewish cemetery of Heiligenstadt lies in a short cul de sac off Schillerstrasse, opposite number 30. Some of the 19th century stones resemble lecterns with open books. The wrought iron railings are unusual today because most such railings fell victim either to the Reichsmetallspende, a scrap metal drive to feed the armaments industry of the Nazis, or scrap metal thieves in later years. The key is available from Heiligenstadt city hall.

HEINSHEIM

(part of Bad Rappenau) is located on the Neckar river about 60 km north of Stuttgart and about 15 km north of Heilbronn (map 8, 9, 10).

* Former synagogue from 1796
* Cemetery from 16th century

In 1597, a letter of protection to Jüdel of nearby Wimpfen was issued by the Teutonic Order, who owned a third of Heinsheim, for an incredible 1,000 florins. The reason given for this high figure was that other owners of the village had already issued such letters to other Jewish families and only in the most exceptional cases were such rights to be granted in the future. 1,000 florins would certainly qualify as exceptional.

This document indicates that several Jewish families lived in Heinsheim at the end of the 16th century. Not much else is known about this rural community, except that its numbers declined in the second half of the 19th century (a fate it shared with most rural Jewish communities of the time).

All but one of the Jews living in Heinsheim in 1940 were deported to Gurs.

The former synagogue, built in 1796, was sold to a Christian in 1937 and survived the Nazi years. It was used as a workshop and storeroom by a blacksmith until at least 1994; however, it has been bought by the town in the meantime and will be restored. It will be used for cultural purposes

The former Heinsheim synagogue was built in 1796 and then used as a blacksmith's workshop for many years. Apart from its architecture, the Star of David over the entrance reminds us of its former use.

143

after the renovation is complete. It has the typical synagogal roof and arched windows of the area, as well as a chuppah stone with a Hebrew inscription (abbreviation for "The voice of bliss and the voice of joy, the voice of the bridegroom and the voice of the bride"), and a star of David over the door. It is located on Schlossgasse, second building on the left after Gundelsheimer Strasse.

The very large, very grand and very interesting cemetery is from the 16th century and is located near the Mühlgrund. The cemetery served as a burial place for Jews from all the surrounding communities.

There are about 1,100 stones still standing, including many elaborately carved Baroque stones with the typical sculpted Cohen hands, Levite pitchers, lions, law tablets, or doves holding a heart.

Some of the "Lions of Heinsheim" really don't look like lions.

The lions are especially interesting. The tombstone sculptors had never seen a living lion, or a proper picture of one, so they copied the creatures from the stones sculpted by their

The Lions of Judah are often represented on the gravestones of the old and large Heinsheim Jewish cemetery.

Animals like this oxen are depicted on many Jewish gravestones of Heinsheim.

predecessors, and the lions turned into more and more mythical beasts. There is a wall in front but the cemetery is unlocked.

The cemetery is not easy to find. It is, however, worth the time and effort to do so as it is very beautiful and most unusual.

Leave Heinsheim on Gundelsheimer Strasse going north. Join the main road towards Rappenau. Pass the fortress, then leave the main road on a little asphalt road going to the right in the middle of a hairpin curve. The asphalt road crosses a wider road after 1.5 km, turns into a concrete road, and then a metalled road. When this ends after about 2.3 km, take the gravel path to the left towards the trees. There is a wooden sign "Judenfriedhof" and a little sign "Kurweg 6".

HEMSBACH

is located about 70 km south of Frankfurt, off the A 5 and on highway 3 (map 8, 10).

* Former synagogue from 1845 includes a mikveh and a small museum
* Cemetery from 1674

Although it is probable that a community existed as early as the 14th century, it is not until 1661 that Jews are documented as living in Hemsbach. The synagogue complex, built in 1845 in pink sandstone, included a synagogue, school, teacher's apartment and mikveh all of which have been carefully restored. There is an inscription in Hebrew over the door of the synagogue reading "What prayer and supplication soever be made by any man, which shall know the plague of his own heart, and spread forth his hands towards this house: Then hear thou in heaven thy dwelling place, and forgive, and do." Inside, the women's gallery is supported by two rows of columns. The colorful ceiling has been restored with the decorative patterns painted in the 19th century.

The former school serves for preparations for the cultural events held in the former synagogue.

Across from the school and synagogue building is the mikveh with a little museum. The museum exhibits a small collection of Judaica and a plaque of ceramic tiles with the name and year of deportation for the 29 Hemsbach Jews who were killed by the Nazis. The complex can be seen by going into the backyard of Mittel-

The interior of the former Hemsbach synagogue, beautifully restored today.

The small ritual bath of Hemsbach is now incorporated into a museum.

The former synagogue and Jewish school of Hemsbach serve as a cultural center today.

gasse 16 or entering from the other side opposite Bachgasse 26. The former synagogue and the mikveh can be visited from April to November on the second Sunday in the month, from 11 to 12 and from 2 to 5. The cemetery dates from 1674 and includes a few characteristic early

146

18th century stones. It is large, with about 1,200 graves, and set in a forest on the side of a hill. The cemetery is locked but you can see gravestones from the street. It is located after Oberer Mühlweg 50. You can get the key from city hall or from Mr. Ehret at Oberer Mühlweg 9.

HEPPENHEIM

is located about 70 km south of Frankfurt, on highways 3 and 460, off the A 5 (map 8, 10).

* Martin Buber House
* Former synagogue from around 1800
* Memorial stone for synagogue destroyed in 1938

The first documents mentioning Jews in Heppenheim are from 1318; however, they may well have settled in Heppenheim some years earlier. The community seems not to have suffered any losses during the Armleder persecutions in 1337, but was struck by the Black Plague persecutions in 1349; no details are known, however.

In 1387, if not earlier, Jews settled in Heppenheim again. Heppenheim was a possession of the archbishop of Mainz then. In 1429 all Heppenheim Jews were arrested by the archbishop, their goods were confiscated and their houses plundered; later that year, all Jews were released again and part of their property was handed back to them. In 1461 Heppenheim came under Palatinate rule, and most Jews were driven out; only two families

were allowed for the next 170 years. In 1620, Heppenheim was returned to Mainz, and some of the restrictions concerning Jews were lifted. Mainz was early among German principalities in emancipating the Jews in the late 18th century. In 1803 Heppenheim became part of Hesse, and in 1806 56 Jews lived in Heppenheim. The community reached its greatest numerical strength in 1890, with 148 members, then more and more Jews moved to larger cities and the number declined to 113 in 1933. In 1938 only 33 Jews were left in Heppenheim, and 22 of those were killed in Nazi camps.

Martin Buber, a prominent Jewish philosopher and author, lived in Heppenheim from 1916 to 1938, in a house on the corner of Werléstrasse and Graben. Buber left Germany for Palestine in March 1938 and decided not to return to Germany after "Reichskristallnacht", when part of his extensive library was destroyed together with so much else.

The Bergstrasse county bought the house from Buber after 1950 and used it as an office building until 1976, when it was declared a National Monument and renovated. In 1978 it was handed over to the International Council of Christians and Jews, who have been using it as a place of communication and encounter in the spirit of Martin Buber ever since. The library housed here can be used Monday-Friday from 9 to 4.

Around 1800, the Heppenheim Jews built a synagogue with a classroom and a teacher's apartment. This former synagogue is still standing at Kleinen Bach 3 and is a residence today. Nothing but the two round windows in the gable of the north wall reminds you of the former purpose of the building. Since the building was converted to a residence and a shop soon after 1900, when the Hirsch synagogue was consecrated, nothing from that period remains inside either.

A memorial marks the place where the Hirsch synagogue stood until it was destroyed on "Reichskristallnacht" in 1938. The memorial is on the corner of Starkenburgweg and Eisenpfad. The synagogue from 1900 was paid for by members of the Hirsch family, longtime Heppenheim residents, who had made their fortune in London.

The Heppenheim community buried its dead in the old and large Alsbach cemetery, which served more than 20 communities in the area (see under Auerbach).

HOFGEISMAR

is located about 30 km north of Kassel, on highway 83 (map 3, 5, 6).

* City museum has a large collection of Judaica
* Cemetery from 1695
* Mid-19th century cemetery in Hümme
* Commemorative tablets

The first Jew in Hofgeismar is documented in 1470, when David from Geismar pays a scribe in Kassel one gold florin "like every year". In 1616

The former residence of Martin Buber serves as a place of encounter (Begegnungsstätte) today.

two Jews are mentioned as paying taxes to the city of Hofgeismar.

In 1835 the Jewish community had 243 members, then the community shrank due to the attractions of larger cities, especially Kassel close by.

From 1920 on, religious service was already made impossible by the lack of adult Jewish men in Hofgeismar; in 1933, only 31 Jews lived here. During the 1938 "Reichskristallnacht" the interior of the synagogue built in 1764 was devastated, but the building was not burned down due to the danger for the surrounding houses. However, the synagogue was torn down in the following weeks. At least twenty of the Jews living here in 1933 were killed in German camps.

The City Museum at Petriplatz 2 has a collection of Judaica from the Hesse area that is well worth a detour. Besides an exhibition covering the history and the culture of the Jews from Northern Hesse and a memorial displaying the names of all known Jewish victims of the Nazis from the Kassel area, the museum also has a rich archive of texts and pictures and a library. The museum is open Monday, Tuesday, and Thursday 10-12; Wednesday 3-6; Friday 5-7; Sunday 11-1 and 3-6. Guided tours can be arranged by contacting the museum well ahead of time.

The Hofgeismar cemetery is located on the right side of Schanzenweg, about 100 meters up the hill from Otto-Hahn-Strasse. The cemetery was established in 1695 and includes stones from the 18th century. The last burial of a Hofgeismar Jew took place in 1935, but the cemetery was also used between 1946 and 1947 for Jewish displaced persons who died in a DP camp nearby.

In 1945, Jewish concentration camp survivors gathered here to bury a piece of soap and erect a gravestone. The text on the stone is in Hebrew and translates as: "For eternal memory! Here lies buried a piece of soap made from the fat of 6 millions of our brothers, the sons of Israel, who were martyred by the Nazis between 1940-1945 for the holiness of the almighty name. May their souls be part of the community of eternal life."

In Hümme, to the left of Hümmer Landstrasse as you come from Hofgeismar, there is a small Jewish cemetery that was founded around 1850.

At Petriplatz 4, opposite the museum complex, there are two commemorative tablets for the synagogue built in 1764 and torn down in 1939 and the former Jewish school, which still stands here.

ICHENHAUSEN

is located about 120 km west of München and 120 km southeast of Stuttgart, on highway 16 south of the A 8 (map 10, 11).

* Former synagogue from 1781 and small exhibition
* Cemetery from 1567

It's not known when Jews began settling in Ichenhausen. However, there are indications that Jews, expelled from Donauwörth in 1518, sought sanctuary here. It is known that the printer Chajim ben David Schwarz from Prague lived in Ichenhausen between 1543 and 1545 and published religious books in Hebrew and Yiddish here, in one of only a few Hebrew printing shops in Europe.

Expulsions of Jews from nearby Memmingen and Günzburg in 1559 provide the first documents concerning Ichenhausen Jews. Although they successfully avoided expulsion themselves, Ichenhausen Jews had to account for their debtors in those two communities before the magistrate. The Jewish community again avoided destruction and expulsion during the Thirty Years War (1618-1648) with a lot of luck and the help of a Letter of Protection granted them by the Habsburg Emperor Matthias. By this time, Ichenhausen was not only part of the Holy Roman Empire but a direct Habsburg possession as well.

In 1567, the Jewish community numbered 13 families. By 1657, the community had grown to 150 families. In addition to paying an annual fee to the ruling vom Stain family, the community had to provide 24 geese as well. The community continued to grow due to the complex local political situation. Ichenhausen was split between the Upper Castle and the Lower Castle of the barons vom Stain. The two barons competed against one another in an effort to get Jews to pay taxes and be governed under their own respective protection. The situation was further complicated by the claims of the Margrave of Burgau and church officials in a nearby monastery. Town administrators eventually entered the fray as well. All this led to many privileges and generally favorable conditions for the Ichenhausen Jews.

Most Ichenhausen Jews lived in apartments they bought from the barons vom Stain. The community lived in 35 such houses initially; by the beginning of the 19th century there were 104 houses with 216 apartments. While other houses in Ichenhausen were restricted to three floors, the Jewish houses generally had four.

But when the Wittelsbachers, the new Bavarian kings, took over Ichenhausen soon afterwards, they tried to introduce restrictions governing the actual number of Jewish families allowed in Ichenhausen. These new restrictions forced first sons to wait until the death of their fathers before establishing their own families. Second and further sons couldn't marry at all unless they could take the place of someone who died without sons and whose residence rights they could buy. Nevertheless, the community continued to increase,

The former Ichenhausen synagogue was built in 1781 and used by the fire brigade after the end of the Nazi reign. It was restored in the 1980's.

The light interior of the Ichenhausen synagogue, with its star-spangled firmament and the Classicist ornaments bears witness to a prosperous and stable Jewish community.

becoming the second largest Jewish community in Bavaria by 1843. With about 1,300 members the Jewish community made up close to half of the total population of Ichenhausen. Jews were then occupied primarily with textiles, used clothes, horses and cattle. A few Ichenhausen Jews were farmers.

The Jewish community began declining as more and more young Jews were able to seek opportunities in the larger cities or abroad as emigrants. Full civil rights weren't granted to Bavarian Jews until 1871 when Bavaria joined the newly formed German empire. Jews and Christians lived peaceably together throughout the early years of this century with Jews playing important roles in the social, political and economic life of Ichenhausen.

However, in the 1930s, with the rise of the Nazis throughout Germany, more and more Jews emigrated. On "Reichskristallnacht", November 10, 1938, the SA set fire to the synagogue but had to extinguish the flames because the Christian neighbors protested due to the danger the fire posed to the surrounding buildings. Jewish women were forced to tear up the Torah scrolls and books from the Jewish library were thrown into the river. The interior of the synagogue was devastated and the debris dumped in the cemetery where many gravestones were knocked over as well. Jewish men were beaten and arrested. Efforts to emigrate intensified after 1938 but the 116 remaining Jews were deported in 1942 and 1943. Forty more Jews from Ichenhausen

were deported from other German towns. Only two survived.

Although the synagogue was heavily damaged during the pogrom, it was not destroyed. It was used as a storeroom until 1953 when the city bought it and converted it to a fire brigade depot in an effort to save the building. Eventually an association of concerned citizens was formed and successfully raised 400,000 DM in private donations and 2.9 million DM in federal, state of Bavaria, county of Günzburg, and city of Ichenhausen funds to restore the synagogue as a memorial to the many centuries of peaceful Christian and Jewish coexistence in this small Bavarian town.

This beautiful synagogue was built in 1781 incorporating parts of an older synagogue from 1687. It is thought by some scholars that it is the work of Josef Dossenberger, an important Bavarian architect who also built Catholic monasteries and Protestant churches in the Rococo and Classicist styles prevailing at the time.

The synagogue walls and ceiling borders are a whirl of decorative paintings of fruits and flowers. Overhead, gold stars embellish the bright blue ceiling. The women's gallery is two-tiered and original. The aron niche, destroyed when the city converted the east wall of the building into garage doors for the fire department, has been restored from old photographs.

In the reception area there is a memorial to the 13 Ichenhausen Jewish soldiers who died for their fatherland in WWI along with an exhibition of photographs and documents of Ichenhausen's Jewish community. The former synagogue is used for exhibitions,- cultural programs, and concerts and in addition is open to visitors every fourth Sunday in the month from 1:00 to 5:00 with guided tours every full hour. Groups can arrange a visit to the synagogue by calling (08223) 2033. The synagogue is located at Vordere Ostergasse 24.

Across the street at Von-Stain-Strasse 8 is the rabbi's house which was built in 1894. Since 1992 the house has been undergoing renovation and will be used for Günzburg county archives.

The mikveh was originally at a creek, then it was in the basement of a Jewish house at Bahnhofstrasse 11 which is now a private home.

The old Jewish cemetery is one of the largest in Germany today. It originated in 1567 and contains hundreds of stones. A grove of oak trees in the center is thought to be of the same age as the cemetery. There is a cluster of rabbi's graves at the top of the center hill with elaborately carved stones depicting shofars, Levite ewers, Cohen hands, and circumcision implements.

There are many memorial stones for family members who died in concentration camps as well as several stones for Hungarian Jews who died as labor slaves in nearby Burgau and for Eastern European displaced persons who died in Leipheim. These stones display Stars of David entangled in barbed wire. Here you can also see a memorial for the Ichenhausen Jewish victims of the Nazi death

This old gravestone from the Ichenhausen Jewish cemetery shows the blessing hands of the priest, the circumcision implements of the Mohel, and the shofar of the cantor.

camps. The cemetery includes a taharah house from 1934 and is locked.

The key is available at the city hall of Ichenhausen. The cemetery is located on Am Birketle. Drive south on highway 16 and turn left just before the railroad crossing. Take the first gravel road on the right.

ISSUM

is located about 70 km northwest of Köln, on highway 58 close to the A 57 (map 4).

* Former synagogue from 1865
* Mikveh in former Jewish school
* Cemetery from 1838

Jews are first documented in Issum in 1764. The community stayed small and was never really accepted; after 1850, the community started shrinking like so many other rural communities.

Service in the synagogue had to be given up around 1930 because the community could not muster the necessary minyan, ten Jewish men, any more. In the Thirties, more Jews left Issum; thirteen Issum Jews lost their lives in German camps.

The first synagogue in Issum may have been built in 1791. The small building that still exists today was bought by the Jewish community in 1855, converted to a synagogue and consecrated in 1865. Probably services ceased here in about 1930, and the building was sold to a Christian in 1935. The former synagogue was not damaged during "Reichskristallnacht", either because it was already owned by a non-Jew or because its location in the middle of a closely built-up area would have endangered the neighboring buildings. In 1987, the former synagogue was bought by the Issum council and converted to a memorial for the Jewish community of Issum. The interior was remodelled to resemble a synagogue using modern furniture and architectural elements.

The former Jewish school next to the synagogue houses a documentation exhibit about the Jews of the area as well as a small collection of Judaica. In the basement, the mikveh has been rediscovered. The synagogue and school are located at Kapellener Strasse 30, close to the Catholic and Protestant churches. The complex can be visited every first Sunday in the month between 2 and 5, or after applying to Issum city hall (028 35/ 10 21).

The Jewish cemetery was founded in 1838 about 3 km northeast from the town on the side of a hill on Xantener Weg. The gravestones are badly weather-beaten. A visit is possible after contacting city hall.

KALLSTADT

is located about 100 km southwest of Frankfurt and about 140 km northwest of Stuttgart, on highway 271 (map 8, 10).

* "Egyptian" style former synagogue from 1837
* Cemetery of Kirchheim, from 1887, nearby on highway 271

The small synagogue of Kallstadt, at Neugasse 12, a few meters from the church, was built in an Egyptian style in 1837. Before the Moorish or neo-Oriental style became dominant for many European synagogues, some architects of the early 19th century experimented with other Oriental styles. The Egyptian style did not prove successful, probably because the time in Egypt was not considered one of the happier periods in the many centuries of Jewish history.

The Kallstadt Jews had to give up their synagogue in 1918, since the community had become too small to maintain it. The building has been a residence ever since. In spite of its long use as a residence, remains of the synagogue wallpainting can still be seen inside.

A few kilometers north of Kallstadt, on highway 271 north of Herxheim, is the small Jewish cemetery of Kirchheim. It was started in 1887 and has a memorial to the victims of the Nazis. The key is available from the Kirchheim town hall.

The former synagogue of Kallstadt was one of a few to be built in a Neo-Egyptian architectural style.

KASSEL (map 5, 6)

* City museum has a small collection of Judaica
* Wilhelmshöhe Castle has 17th century paintings with Old Testament Jewish themes
* Community center
* Cemetery from early 17th century

Jews probably began settling in Kassel in the 12th or 13th centuries. The oldest preserved document pertaining to the presence of Jews in Kassel deals with Jewish-owned property and dates from 1293. The community suffered from the Black Death persecutions in 1348/49, but by the end of the 14th century there was again an organized community with a synagogue and cemetery. Jews were expelled again in 1524 and during the Thirty Years War, but in each case readmitted a few years later. Thereafter, the life of the community was restricted, but fairly stable for almost two centuries.

After short-lived emancipation introduced by the French occupying troops in 1808 new repression followed, with final emancipation in 1866. Thereafter, the community grew rapidly attracting Jews from many other areas of Germany. By 1933, there were 2,300 Jews living in Kassel.

The Kassel City Museum (Stadtmuseum) on the corner of Ständeplatz and Wilhelmstrasse contains a small exhibition of Judaica in its lobby. Plans are being developed to enlarge the exhibition space. The museum is open Tuesday-Friday from 10-5; Saturday and Sunday from 10-1.

The state art collection in Wilhelmshöhe Castle contains a number of important 17th century paintings with Old Testament Jewish themes by Rembrandt, Victors, Horst, Jordaens, de Grebber, Wolffort, and Pepijn. The Museum is open Tuesday-Sunday, 10-5.

The Kassel Jewish community center is located in Bremer Strasse 9.

The Jewish cemetery dates from the early 17th century and includes gravestones of many different styles. At one end there is a memorial to the Jewish soldiers who died in WWI. In the middle there is a memorial to the Kassel Jews who were killed by the Nazis. The cemetery has a resident caretaker living in the guardhouse.

The cemetery is located at Fasanenweg 2-4 across the street from the Christian Bettenhausen cemetery. The entrance is a small gate in the low brick wall marked with the caretaker's name, Lehmann.

KIPPENHEIM

is located about 160 km southwest of Stuttgart, off the A 5 and on highway 3 about 5 km south of Lahr (map 10).

* Former synagogue from 1851 in Kippenheim
* Former synagogue from 1812 in Schmieheim
* Large cemetery from 1703 in Schmieheim
* Parokhet from 1881 in Ettenheim

Jews settled in Kippenheim in the 17th century. In the second half of the 19th century, the 300 Jews of Kippenheim made up about 15 % of the population.

Their number declined less than in most comparable rural settlements, and in 1933 about 150 Jews still lived here. Many Kippenheim Jews were able to leave Germany, but 31 were killed in Nazi camps.

The synagogue was built in 1851 in a neo-Romanesque style and devastated in the 1938 "Reichskristallnacht". After that, the building served as a POW camp, workshop, and storeroom and was changed considerably. The outside was renovated in the 1980's, and since then the law tablets crown the gable once again and two crenellated turrets stand to the sides of the impressive facade.

The building now serves as an artist's studio. The interior still shows the scars of the "Reichskristallnacht" devastations. The building stands at Poststrasse 17, behind a small park and next to a bus stop signposted "Synagoge". A visit can be arranged through the city hall of Kippenheim.

A former synagogue in nearby Schmieheim, at Schloss-Strasse 41, was incorporated into a small factory. Jews are first documented for Schmieheim in the 13th century, and in 1850 almost half of Schmieheim's population was Jewish. During the 19th century Schmieheim was the seat of the local rabbi, who served ten communities in the region. The synagogue was built in 1812 and partly destroyed in the 1938 "Reichskristallnacht". The remaining structure is hardly recognizable today as a synagogue.

The large cemetery in Schmieheim served several communities in the

The former Kippenheim synagogue was restored in the 1980's.

region and was founded in 1703. Approximately 2,300 gravestones, some of them from the 18th century, remain.

The cemetery is located on the highway between Kippenheim and Münchweier, past Schmieheim, and can be visited by contacting the Schmieheim town hall, Im Schloss, or the Protestant parsonage (Evangelisches Pfarramt), Schloss-Strasse 2.

In nearby Ettenheim, a Torah shrine curtain is still preserved in the meeting room of the city council in the former Palais Rohan. This parokhet, from 1881, can be viewed after contacting Mr. Oswald at the Rohan palace Monday through Friday, 8 to 12.

There is a very active German-Israeli Group in the area. Among many other activities, it has inspired a riding club in Kippenheim to offer covered wagon tours to Jewish memorials in the region (Kippenheim, Schmieheim, Altdorf with its school and mikveh and Nonnenweier with its cemetery and exhibition). Information is available from the Kippenheim city hall.

KIRRWEILER, Pfalz

is located about 110 km southwest of Frankfurt and about 120 km northwest of Stuttgart, on the A 65 (map 8, 10).

* Former synagogue from 1766
* 17th century mikveh
* Cemetery from 1849

In the 18th century the Kirrweiler Jewish community must have been exceptionally small since they built one of Germany's smallest synagogues in 1766. The building has only two arched windows. If you look into the narrow space between Schloss-Strasse 1 and 3, you can see these two windows. The former synagogue is located in the courtyard of Schloss-Strasse 1 and serves as part of a dwelling today.

The mikveh lies in the basement of Kirchenstrasse 4, close to Hauptstrasse and next to a small square with a fountain. There is a straight staircase about five meters long and leading down to a depth of three and a half meters. To the left of the staircase, about halfway down, there is a small alcove that may have served as a dressing room. The groundwater still flows through the bath today. The

owner, Mr. Fritz Roth, lives around the corner on Hauptstrasse 13. Visits to the mikveh are possible after contacting him at 06321/5042.

The small Kirrweiler cemetery lies on Neustadterweg.

KITZINGEN

is located about 90 km northwest of Nürnberg, or about 140 km southeast of Frankfurt, on the Main river and highway 8 (map 8, 9).

* Former synagogue from 1883

Jews are first mentioned in Kitzingen in 1147, although the community is older. It was first decimated by a local blood libel in 1243, then suffered from the Rindfleisch massacres in 1298, the Armleder persecution in 1336, and was wiped out by the Black Death persecutions in 1349. A small community was re-established and stayed in Kitzingen, although frequently threatened by riots or expulsions, until 1798 when it was finally expelled.

After emancipation in the middle of the 19th century, a new community came into existence and built a synagogue in 1883. (The synagogue building from the 16th century, left behind by the community expelled in 1798, had become a dwelling in Christian hands and still stood until it was destroyed by bombs in 1945).

In 1910, there were 480 Jews in Kitzingen. In 1939 only 165 remained. Almost 100 Kitzingen Jews were killed in German camps.

The large and imposing neo-Romanesque synagogue with two onion-domed

158

The small towers of the former synagogue of Kitzingen - reminiscent of a Baroque pilgrimage church - were reconstructed by the town.

turrets resembling a Baroque pilgrimage church was devastated in the November 1938 "Reichskristallnacht". Later the building was patched together and used as a slave labor camp, then as a factory, storeroom and rehearsal hall, before being renovated by the city for use as a cultural center named "Alte Synagoge". It stands at Landwehrstrasse 1 and has two commemorative tablets for the Jewish community of Kitzingen and its destroyed synagogue. On the ground floor, at the east wall of the building, the small new synagogue of the Kitzingen community is housed, while the large hall on the first floor is the auditorium of the cultural center today. The entrance hall was restored in its original 19th century style, with a star-studded sky on the ceiling.

The former Jewish school building also survived at Landwehrstrasse 23. There is a commemorative tablet at the entrance to the museum.

KLEIN-KROTZENBURG

is located about 30 km east of Frankfurt, on the Main river across from Grosskrotzenburg and off the A 3 (map 8).

* Former synagogue from 1913
* Mid-18th century cemetery

The first documents pertaining to Jews in Klein-Krotzenburg date to 1728. The community was small, but stable and numbered 33 in 1905. The synagogue in this little village was built (or rebuilt) in 1913 in a somber Jugendstil, or Art Nouveau style. It was devastated in the 1938 "Reichskristallnacht" and taken over by the council, which used it first as a

The small former synagogue of Klein-Krotzenburg stands empty

159

blacksmith workshop and then as a storeroom for the construction department.

The building is currently empty and decaying. The 1988 plans for renovation and for use as a memorial are apparently not being pursued any more. The ruin stands hidden in the back of Kettelerstrasse 6, to the right of a transformer station behind a parking lot. In 1994 remains of the decorative paintings around the ark niche were still visible through the empty windows.

The small Jewish cemetery of Klein-Krotzenburg probably stems from the middle of the 18th century.

KOBLENZ

is located about 90 km southeast of Köln, or 120 km west of Frankfurt, on the confluence of the Rhine and Mosel rivers and between the A 48 and A 61 (map 4, 8).

* Exhibition on the history of Koblenz Jews
* Cemetery from 1850
* Synagogue in former taharah house

Several documents regarding Jewish revenues in the 12th century provide evidence that Jews were already well established then in Koblenz. Around 1160, Benjamin of Tudela, an early Jewish traveler, described a large community there. In 1345, a Jewish tax farmer was appointed. Jewish tax farmers were precursors of the Court Jews in later centuries. During the Black Death persecutions of 1349, most of the community was mas-sacred by the Flagellants. However, a new community was established almost immediately as records indicate the periodic confiscation and sale of their property for the benefit of the Archbishop of Trier, who was lord of Koblenz from 1352 on.

The community was expelled twice during the 16th century. By the 18th century, life in the Jewish community had stabilized to some extent which allowed its population to grow, reaching 600 by 1900.

Today, little is left to remind Koblenz of its long Jewish history. There is a memorial to the synagogue destroyed in the 1938 "Reichskristallnacht" on the side of a building at Florinsmarkt 13. On the first floor there is an exhibition on the history of Jews in Koblenz. The exhibition is open Monday, Tuesday, Thursday, and Friday from 2-6. (See the librarian in the Stadtbibliothek in the same building.)

The Liebfrauenkirche, or Our Lady's Church, an old Catholic church nearby, displays a Jewish gravestone with Gothic ornamentation in the nave to the right of the altar. This stone of Hanna, daughter of Jehuda, dates from 1149 and was found when the choir of the church was renovated; it had been used as construction material there. Since the choir was built in the early 15th century, it may be assumed with some certainty that the stone came from the Jewish cemetery confiscated and used as a cheap quarry after the 1349 destruction of the Jewish community.

There is a memorial to the Koblenz Jewish victims of the Nazi years in the Jewish cemetery, which dates from 1850, at Schlachthofstrasse 5. Along the central path near the entrance are several very old stones and a row of broken stones. There is a second entrance on Moselweisser Strasse. The cemetery is open Sunday-Friday from 8:30 to 5. The new synagogue of the Koblenz community stands at the edge of the cemetery. It was once the taharah house.

KÖLN (map 4)

* Parts of walls and pillars of 11th century synagogue
* Remnants of old walls, foundation and staircase of 12th century mikveh
* Stadtmuseum shows permanent exhibition of Jewish religious and household objects
* Late 19th century synagogue and community center
* Memorials
* Cemeteries

The presence of Jews in Köln parallels the founding of Köln, or Colonia Agrippina, by the Romans. A surviving decree by the Roman emperor Constantine in 321 revoked an earlier decree which had exempted the Jews of Colonia from serving on the curia, or city council. Service on the curia entailed collecting taxes for the imperial treasury. Since any tax deficits had to be made up from the curia members' own pockets, exemption from this service was highly valued. Losing the exemption was probably very costly for the Jews of Colonia.

This decree is the first written document pertaining to the presence of Jews in what is now Germany.

When Köln was destroyed by looting Normans in 881, its ancient Jewish community also ceased to exist. There are indications that a community was formed again in the 10th century; however, actual documentation only begins in the 11th century with a reference to a Jewish cemetery, described as old even then. This cemetery, parts of which were uncovered in 1922, was used until the 15th century.

The bombings of WWII brought further evidence of medieval Jewish settlement in Köln by uncovering foundations and remains connected with the medieval Jewry just south of the old city hall on Judengasse.

During the Middle Ages, Köln was important both for its large Jewish community and for the numerous fairs which attracted Jews from all over the Rhineland. It is estimated that at the time of the First Crusade in 1096, there were about a thousand resident Jews in Köln, most of whom were killed by the camp followers of the crusaders in spite of the efforts of the archbishop to protect them.

During the Second Crusade in 1146-47, Archbishop Arnold managed to protect most of his Jews by hiding them in Wolkenburg fortress. After 1252, the Jewish community paid for an assortment of protections and privileges issued by the various archbishops. In 1266, one of the rulers of Köln, Archbishop Engelbert II, granted such a privilege, had it engraved in stone and inserted into a wall of the cathedral where it can still be seen. It is now in the northern nave next to the entrance to the Chapel of the Sacrament. Among other things, the privilege grants equality with Christians as far as customs and tolls payments were concerned, the expulsion of Christian moneylenders, as well as the right to a cemetery, unrestricted burials there, and freedom from executions in the cemetery.

The frequency with which these protections and privileges were issued belies the lack of security they provided. The Black Death rioters in 1349 overwhelmed the community, most were massacred or died by their own hands. A new community was formed in 1372 which struggled to pay for its protection and privileges every ten years until the expulsion of 1424, when medieval Jewry in Köln came to an end. Some of the exiles went to nearby Deutz and settled there. Jews were not allowed to return to Köln until the end of the 18th century.

With the introduction of equal rights in 1856, the Jewish community grew rapidly. By 1933, the Jewish population numbered 20,000. Anti-Semitic attacks began when the Nazis came to power in 1933 and steadily increased. By 1939, 40% of the 1933 Jewish population had left. The emigrants were quickly replaced by Jews from smaller cities throughout the Rhineland seeking refuge in Köln. More than 11,000 Jews were deported and killed from 1941 on. After 1945 a medium-sized community was reestablished.

This Romanesque window, part of the mikveh of the medieval Judengasse, lies below ground level.

Only a column and a few rests of a wall remain of the medieval synagogue of the Jews of Köln.

Remnants of old walls, foundations, and the staircase of a 12th century mikveh as well as parts of the walls and pillars of the 11th century synagogue were found after a WWII bombing in front of the old city hall on Judengasse. They have been restored in recent years and may be seen by obtaining the key from the porter at the Historic City Hall (Altes Rathaus) Monday-Thursday from 8-5; Friday 8-4; Saturday 10-4; and Sunday 11-1. The foundations of the Jewish quarter have been depicted in the pavement above.

The large, neo-Romanesque synagogue on Roonstrasse 50 was built in 1899, burned during "Reichskristallnacht" in 1938, and rebuilt in 1959. The impressive complex also houses the Jewish community center.

The Stadtmuseum (city museum) of Köln maintains a permanent exhibition of Jewish religious and household objects presented by German citizens who hid them for their Jewish friends in their homes, churches, and cemeteries from 1933 to 1945. Some pieces go back to the 15th century. The museum is located at Zeughausstrasse 1-3 and is open Tuesday-Sunday 10-5, and Thursday 10-8.

The large cemetery, opened in 1918 in Venloer Strasse/Militärring, resembles urban Jewish (and Christian) cemeteries elsewhere in Germany. It was laid out by garden architects and has mausoleums, family graves, and stone borders. Only the absence of crosses and the presence of occasional Hebrew letters or Stars of David distinguish it from Christian cemeteries of

The grand Neo-Romanesque Köln synagogue was damaged, but not destroyed in 1938.

163

the same period. When the medieval cemetery on Bonntor was rediscovered in 1922, some of the remaining stones were transferred to this cemetery where they may be seen in a wall in the center near the rear of the cemetery. Several of these 13th and 14th century stones had been used to build a winding staircase in a city fortification tower in later centuries.

This cemetery includes a memorial to the Jewish soldiers who died in WWI and a memorial to the memory of 11,000 Köln Jewish victims of the Nazis.

There is also a memorial to the Torah

Medieval gravestones that had been used in fortifications and as steps of a spiral staircase found a place of repose in the walls of this small hall in the new Jewish cemetery of Köln.

scrolls which were hidden in the cemetery in 1938, but could not be recovered and therefore decayed; they were rediscovered and buried in 1978.

The cemetery is open from May 1 to September 30 from 8-6 and October 1 to April 30 from 8-5 (except on Saturdays and Jewish holidays).

The cemetery in Deutz, now a part of Köln, from 1699, is well-preserved under tall old trees. It can be visited Monday-Friday from 8-3. It is located on Judenkirchhofsweg.

The Germania Judaica library, with its large collection of books on Jewish life and history in Germany, is located on the third floor of the Central Library on Joseph-Haubrich-Hof 1. It is open Tuesday and Thursday from 11:30-8; Wednesday and Friday from 9-6; and Saturday 10-3.

Part of the former Gestapo jail at Appellhofplatz 23-25 has been turned into a memorial and also houses an exhibition. The former cells in the basement, with hundreds of inscriptions left behind by Gestapo prisoners who were interrogated and tortured here, can be visited Tuesday-Sunday from 10-4. On the first Saturday of the month, there is a guided tour at 2:00. Ring the bell under the "Gedenkstätte" sign in the doorway if the door is closed.

The building also houses the Nazi Era Documentation Center of the city of Köln with a public library. The library is open Monday to Friday, 10 to 4, and Thursday until 6.

There is a large number of memorials to the Jews of Köln and their persecution throughout the city.

Memorials to the synagogues destroyed in 1938 can be seen on Glockengasse/ Offenbachplatz (named after the composer, Jacques Offenbach, whose father was cantor in Köln), St. Apern-Strasse/ Helenenstrasse, Reischplatz 6 in Deutz, Körnerstrasse in Ehrenfeld, and Mülheimer Freiheit 78 in Mülheim.

There is a memorial at the former transit camp in Müngersdorf on Walter-Binder-Weg. A memorial to seven prisoners killed and hastily buried by the Gestapo in 1945 is in Hansaring Park and includes a statue of a Mother and Dead Child by Mari Andriessen.

KRAICHTAL

is located about 70 km northwest of Stuttgart, between highways 3, 35 and 293 (map 8, 10).

* Former synagogue from 1776 in Gochsheim
* Former synagogue from 1870 in Menzingen
* Cemetery from 1629 in Oberöwisheim

Jews are first mentioned in Gochsheim in 1427. Gochsheim was a Württemberg fief then, but the local ruler, the count of Eberstein, was much less dogmatic than his prince who had forbidden Jews to settle in his lands.

In 1662, however, most Gochsheim Jews were expelled. The small remaining community was dissolved in 1882. It sold its synagogue which had been established in 1776. While the building still stands at Hauptstrasse 70, it was converted to a residence more than a century ago; very little survives today that would remind one of its past.

Menzingen, part of Kraichtal today, had Jewish inhabitants from at least 1546 on. The first synagogue was built in 1787. The Jewish population numbered about 60 at the time. As the community grew, plans for a new synagogue were made; however, lack of funds delayed construction until 1870 when the community was already in decline.

In 1921, the last Jewish family left Menzingen and the synagogue was sold to the city and used as a school until it was eventually sold again. Today it is also a private home like its Gochsheim counterpart. The building still stands at Mittelstrasse 6, the former Judengasse.

The Jews from the area began burying their dead in Oberöwisheim in 1629 even though there had never been a Jewish community there. However, the ground was poor and the hillside steep, so the price for the land was low and affordable. (This is a reason why many rural Jewish cemeteries lie far away from the little towns or villages they serve, on steep hillsides or in forests).

The old cemetery was not destroyed during the Nazi years. The cemetery is very overgrown with about 270 stones remaining. The oldest stones date from around 1850.

KRAKOW

is located about 160 km northwest of Berlin and about 160 km east of Hamburg, on highway 103 (map 2).

* Former synagogue from 1866
* Mid-19th century cemetery

Jews lived in Krakow during the Middle Ages. The Jörgenberg north of town reminds us of the fact that the Jewish community of Krakow died on the wheel here in 1325. The Jews were accused of a host desecration and were sentenced by the ruling prince, who happened to be heavily indebted to the Jews of Krakow.
In 1866 the new community built a grand neo-Romanesque synagogue in what today is Schulplatz, a few meters from the church. Like many other rural communities, the Krakow community dwindled around the turn of the century. After WWI, the community sold its synagogue which was used as a gym from then on.

This use was the reason why the building was not destroyed during "Reichskristallnacht". In 1994, the interior of the building was being renovated. It can be visited after contacting the town administration. The former synagogue will be used as a cultural center.

The small Jewish cemetery stems from the middle of the 19th century. It is located in the northeast corner of the Protestant cemetery on Plauer Chaussee.

The small synagogue of the Krakow Jews had already been used as a gymnastics hall for more than a decade by 1938.

BAD LAASPHE

is located about 140 km north of Frankfurt and about 120 km east of Köln, on highway 62 and close to highway 253 map 4, 5).

* Former synagogue from 1764
* Cemetery from 1750

Jews are first mentioned in Laasphe in 1640, although the Sayn-Wittgenstein counts, lords of Laasphe, issued bylaws concerning Jewish affairs as early as 1573. There may already have been a synagogue in 1682. A regulation concerning religious service was issued in 1717 and a rabbi is documented in 1750. The synagogue was first documented in 1764, when a house in Mauerstrasse was bought by the Jewish community and converted to a synagogue.

This former synagogue building is still standing. It is located in the northwest corner of the town against the city wall at Mauerstrasse 44. In the November 1938 "Reichskristallnacht" the interior was demolished, but the synagogue was not burned down. The building was then converted into a blacksmith's workshop. Nothing remains to remind one of the former use of the building, and there is no commemorative tablet. The attic is supposed to have housed the Jewish school; if that is correct, the arrangement would be fairly unique, since the school would be expected below and not above the synagogue.

In 1750, Count Friedrich zu Sayn-Wittgenstein leased land in Wittgenstein close to Laasphe to the Jewish community for their cemetery. The rent was to be paid to the poorhouse. The cemetery still exists.

LANDAU

lies about 100 km southwest of Frankfurt and about 130 km northwest of Stuttgart on the A 65 and on highway 10 (map 8, 10).

* Memorial at the Frank-Loeb house
* Former synagogue in Landau-Arzheim
* Remains of a synagogue from 1884 and memorial
* Cemetery from the 19th century
* Mid-16th century cemetery in Annweiler

There is a former inn from the 15th century at Kaufhausstrasse 9 in Landau where the grandparents of Anne Frank lived sometime after 1870. In 1987, the city of Landau opened a center for encounter and remembrance here which includes a small prayer room and an exhibition of the history of the Jews of Landau. This memorial is open Tuesday through Thursday from 10 to 12:30 and from 2 to 5, Friday through Sunday from 10 to 1. It is closed from the middle of July to the middle of August each year. For more information or a guided tour, please call the city hall (86 472/13171 or 13155).

The former synagogue, which was used until 1884, when the synagogue destroyed in 1938 was built, is still standing in the backyard of Hauptstrasse 36 in Arzheim, part of Landau today. The half-frame building has been used as a shed for a long time and is steadily deteriorating.

167

The synagogue built in 1884 was burned down on "Reichskristallnacht", only a few walls remain standing. At the site of the synagogue, a memorial stone was unveiled in 1988 on Xylanderstrasse, next to Savoyenpark.

The Jewish cemetery of Landau was opened in the middle of the 19th century and is part of the city cemetery at Zweibrückerstrasse 33.

Surrounded by car dealers and private homes, the mid-16th century Jewish cemetery of Annweiler lies at the foot of the Trifels and its fortress.

Coming from Landau take a left into Burgenring immediately after entering Annweiler. Turn right immediately into Industriestrasse and then turn left again on to an access road going uphill after a few meters. The entrance of the cemetery is just a few steps uphill, on the right. The cemetery is long and narrow. From the entrance you can only see a few late 19th/early 20th century stones in the background. The key is available from Annweiler city hall.

LAUFERSWEILER

is located about 130 km west of Frankfurt, 140 km south of Köln, in the Hunsrück mountains about 5 km east from where highway 50 joins highway 327 (map 8).

* Former synagogue from 1910

The former synagogue, built in 1910 in an imposing Protestant Baroque style, is located a few meters from the church of Laufersweiler on higher ground. It was devastated but not destroyed in "Reichskristallnacht" in November 1938. Today it is the only synagogue building to survive in the Rhein-Hunsrück area.

The former synagogue was renovated in 1987 and a memorial and exhibition on Jewish life in the region were planned. However, like in many other well-meaning projects, no new life has blossomed within the old walls and the former synagogue stands empty most of the time. In 1994, a Catholic prayer group used the former synagogue as a meeting place. The key is available from the mayor's office close by.

The Neo-Baroque Laufersweiler synagogue stands opposite the village church.

LAUINGEN

is located on the Danube about 130 km northwest of Munich and about 130 km east of Stuttgart on highway 16 (map 10,11).

* Former synagogue, probably from after 1367

Medieval Lauingen must have commanded either a ford or a bridge across the Danube, as it was an important commercial site and had a long Jewish street leading from the bank of the Danube up a low hill. Jews are first mentioned in 1293 but the community was probably much older. The community survived the

The medieval synagogue of Lauingen still stands at the upper end of the former Judengasse, called Hirschstrasse today.

Rindfleisch pogrom in 1298 but was overwhelmed by the Black Death persecutions in 1348/49. The Jewish houses were then turned over to the city and converted into a hospital complex. It is thought that the hospital chapel still in existence today may have been built where the synagogue once stood, and the spring running under the crypt of this chapel may have fed a mikveh.

Jews resettled in Lauingen in 1367 on their Judengasse (which is now called Hirschstrasse). The second Lauingen synagogue building, with an inscription in Hebrew over the door ("This is the door to God"), still exists today and is located at Hirschstrasse 19, at the highest point of the street. (The commemorative tablet on the building states that this is the pre-1348 synagogue, which the authors think highly unlikely.)

The Jews were expelled by the new duke of Bavaria, Ludwig IX, in 1450. A hundred years later, in 1550, Jews were again given the right to settle, then were expelled again in 1553, resettled again in 1630, and were expelled again in 1653 for the last time.

In the 19th century, when Jews were given full civil rights in Bavaria as in the rest of Germany, Lauingen had lost its former importance and no new community was formed.

The former synagogue building was used as a pilgrim's hostel and a poorhouse from 1450 on. Today it is a private dwelling. Nothing is left in the interior to remind one of the past use of the structure, only the Hebrew writing over the entrance remains.

169

LEIPZIG

is located about 120 km west of Dresden and about 130 km east of Erfurt, between A 14 and A 9 (map 6, 7).

* Synagogue from 1904
* Former synagogue from 1921
* Former elementary school and high school
* Memorials
* Machsor Lipsiae in University library
* Cemeteries

Leipzig is an old settlement that became a city almost 1,000 years ago and has had important market fairs for more than 500 years.

The first Leipzig Jews are documented for the year 1000. This community was decimated during the Black Plague persecutions in 1349, but it either survived the pogrom or Jews were allowed back to Leipzig soon after the plague subsided, since a Judengasse (Jewish quarter) outside the city walls is documented for 1359.

The medieval community came to an end around the middle of the 15th century due to excessive taxation and several persecutions. The Leipzig fairs were still visited by Jewish merchants, but they could not settle in Leipzig and were subject to special taxation.

It was not until the mid-18th century that Jews were allowed to live in Leipzig again in exchange for a heavy special tax. Only in 1814 could the emerging community acquire its own burial ground. Up until then, the dead had to be taken to Dessau or Naumburg and buried there. This old cemetery was destroyed by the Nazis during the Third Reich, and after 1945 gardens were laid out where the cemetery used to be. The gardens are still there, an area called Johannistal on Stephanstrasse. You can still see parts of gravestones that were used for the edge of a path or a wall.

In 1855, the Jewish community built an unusually large, moderately neo-Moorish synagogue. The synagogue was extra large to accomodate the many Jewish merchants visiting Leipzig during the fairs. It was burned down during "Reichskristallnacht". There is a memorial stone for the synagogue as well as for the 14,000 Jews from Leipzig who were victims to the Nazi persecutions on Gottschedstrasse/ Zentralstrasse.

The cemetery on Stephanstrasse soon became too small for the rapidly growing community. In 1864 a plot adjacent to the Nordfriedhof at Berlinerstrasse 123 was used for a second cemetery (which is called the Old Jewish Cemetery today).

In 1904, the Orthodox Jews from Brody living in Leipzig bought a house at Keilstrasse 4 and converted it to a synagogue. During the November 1938 "Reichskristallnacht", the synagogue was not burned down because of the other buildings on both sides. The building was devastated, however, and later used as a storehouse and a factory. In 1945, the Brody synagogue was reconsecrated and has served the Leipzig community ever since. The building also houses a Jewish library and reading room. From the outside, the stained glass on the ground floor and first floor indicates the special nature of the building, and so - alas - do the heavy steel bars in front of the windows and doors.

In 1913, a Jewish elementary and high school was opened at Gustav Adolf-Strasse 7. The building houses the German Central Library for the Blind today. There is a commemorative tablet in memory of the founder of the school, Dr. Ephraim Carlebach, and its former use as a transit camp by the Nazis.

Nearby, in the backyard of Färber-strasse 11a, lies the former Orthodox Beth Yehudah-synagogue built in 1921. After devastations on "Reichskristallnacht", the building was used as a shelter for the homeless, and then as a "Judenhaus", a house where the Jews evicted from their apartments and houses were crammed together. Today it is a small factory.

In 1928, an additional cemetery, now called the New Jewish Cemetery, was laid out at Delitzscher Strasse 224. This new cemetery had a very progressive taharah house which survived the "Reichskristallnacht" arson, but was torn down by the Nazi state in 1939. In its place there is a new taharah house built in 1955. A memorial to the Leipzig Jews killed by the Nazis can be found in the eastern part of the cemetery.

During the 1938 "Reichskristallnacht", Jews in Leipzig, as elsewhere, were arrested and taken to concentration camps. The Leipzig Jews were not taken to jail after their arrest, but to

The former synagogue of the Brody community is the main synagogue of Leipzig today.

the bed of the Parthe river which has steep banks. A memorial from 1988 reminds us of this barabarous event and the deportations that followed in which 14,000 Leipzig Jews were killed. The memorial is located on Parthenstrasse, close to Dr. Kurt Fischer-Strasse.

The Leipzig university library keeps the Machsor Lipsiae, a Jewish prayer book from the 14th century. The miniatures and illustrations of this book were probably painted in southern Germany before the Black Death pogroms. The library also has a large collection of Jewish manuscripts and prints. Leipzig was the most important publishing and printing center of Germany in the 19th and early 20th century.

The synagogue and the cemeteries can be visited by contacting the Jewish community center at Löhrstrasse 10. This house, by the way, is also a former "Judenhaus" where the Leipzig Jews evicted from their houses and apartments were given shelter until their deportation.

LICH

is located about 50 km north of Frankfurt, off the A 5 and on highways 488 and 457 (map 4, 5, 8).

* Former synagogue from 1886
* Former synagogue from 1866 in nearby Langsdorf
* 19th century cemetery

The small former synagogue of Lich may be used as a concert hall in the future.

172

Jews are first mentioned in Lich around 1622, soon after the Thirty Years War began. The first documented synagogue was built in 1810.

An inn built in 1886 was bought by the Jewish community in 1921 and converted into a synagogue. During the 1938 "Reichskristallnacht", the synagogue was devastated but not destroyed. Since then, it has been used to house a German army unit, prisoners of war, the city council, a rifle club, a music school, and a senior citizen's center.

The former synagogue is located at Amtsgerichtsstrasse 4. There is a commemorative tablet. After renovation, the building will be used as a concert hall. A visit is possible after contacting Lich city hall.

In nearby Langsdorf there is a former synagogue from 1866 at Erbsengasse 7. However, the building has been converted into a private residence and does not resemble a synagogue any more. Only a commemorative tablet reminds one of the building's history.

The small 19th century Jewish cemetery is now being looked after by the city of Lich.

LICHTENFELS

is located about 100 km north of Nürnberg, on the Main river and highways 173 and 289 (map 6, 9).

* Former synagogue from 1797
* Cemetery from the middle of the 19th century

The small synagogue in Lichtenfels is from 1797. It survived the Nazi years

The small Baroque synagogue of Lichtenfels was a pigsty during the Nazi years and is a warehouse today.

as a storeroom for scrap iron and a pigsty. It was returned to the Jewish Community in 1947, but the post-war community of Lichtenfels soon dissolved and the last remaining Jews sold the building before they left. It is now being used as a storeroom by a hardware shop. The former synagogue is located at Judengasse 12.

Only a few stones still stand in the mid-19th century cemetery, together with a memorial for the 25 Lichtenfels Jews killed in German camps.

To get there, drive up An der Friedenslinde and turn right after the Hallenbad (indoor swimming pool) parking area opposite the entrance to the Hauptschule (secondary school), which has a statue of a man with artificial wings. Then turn right again on to the farm road and drive past the fields and gardens until the road turns to the right.

The cemetery is at the corner. It is locked. The key is available at city hall. When the authors last visited, the cemetery looked well cared for, even though, as mentioned above, hardly any stones remain.

173

LIMBURG

This Gothic chapel housed the Limburg synagogue in the 19th century and is a Protestant church today.

is located about 70 km northwest of Frankfurt and 120 km southeast of Köln, on the A 3 (map 4, 5, 8).

* Houses and two mikvoth in the old Jewish quarter from the 13th century
* Former Gothic chapel used as a synagogue from 1867 - 1903
* Early 19th century cemetery
* Memorials

Several years ago, a simple Romanesque mikveh was discovered in this medieval town which lies on the slope of a large hill above the river Lahn. In the process of excavating and renovating the mikveh an even older mikveh was found. Consequently, the newer mikveh had to be filled in with sand to protect it and the very old basements around it from collapsing while work went on to research the older mikveh and the old houses above it.

These houses are among the oldest half-timbered buildings in Germany today; according to dendochronological tests they were built in 1289, after a devastating fire, and it is likely that they were owned by Limburg Jews then - the first document about a Limburg Jew is from 1278. The Jewish dance hall might have been located here. The site is presently closed to the public. The two mikvoth are located at Römer 2/4/6.

While renovation should be finished by 1996, there will be no public access to the mikveh in the basement. The mikveh in the courtyard had to be filled in, as mentioned above, and only four walls indicate its location. However, there might be a small memorial within these walls in the future.

Close by, on In der Erbach, stands a Gothic chapel that was bought from the Eberbach monastery in 1867 by the Jewish community of Limburg and converted into a synagogue. In 1903, when the new synagogue at Schiede 27 was finished, the chapel was sold to the Protestant community and has been used as a church ever since.

There is a memorial to the 1903 synagogue, which was destroyed in 1938, at Schiede 27.

The Limburg cemetery dates from the beginning of the 19th century. It is located at the foot of the Schafberg off Beethovenstrasse and includes a memorial to Limburg's Jewish community. The key is available from a gardener in Beethovenstrasse 12.

LÜBECK

is located on the Trave river about 70 km northeast of Hamburg on the A 1 (map 1).

* Synagogue from 1880
* Cemetery from the 17th century

Lübeck, an important port near the Baltic Sea, was a free and imperial city as well as one of the most important members of the Hanseatic League. Jews were not admitted to Lübeck until 1680 when two goldsmiths were allowed to settle, only to be expelled in 1699. However, from 1656 on, Jews were allowed to live in nearby Moisling, then under Danish rule and now a suburb of Lübeck. This situation did not change until the beginning of the 19th century when the occupation of Lübeck by the French in 1806 brought some relief and the possibility to settle in Lübeck. This possibility, however, was short-lived and the Jews were expelled again in 1822. Many Jews

The Lübeck synagogue, originally built in Moorish style and later devastated by the SA, was rebuilt in unobtrusive Northern German brick after the end of the Nazi years.

from Lübeck returned to Moisling, where they had left a few years before. Emancipation in 1848 brought their return to Lübeck but did not bring about community acceptance. The community numbered about 700 in 1913 but had decreased to 250 by 1937. About 85 Lübeck Jews were killed in the German camps.

The Lübeck synagogue at St. Annen-Strasse 13 was built in 1880 in a subdued Moorish style. It was badly damaged in the November 1938 "Reichskristallnacht", restored in a nondescript residential style and returned to the new DP community, mostly composed of eastern European Jews, survivors of death camps and death marches, in 1945. An old age home and mikveh are located next door at St. Annen-Strasse 11.

In the last few years the Lübeck synagogue has, alas, become well-known due to two arson attacks.

The large cemetery in Lübeck-Moisling dates from the mid-17th century, although most of the stones are from the 19th century. There is a memorial to the Jewish victims of the Nazi years and close to one hundred graves of Jews who died as a consequence of their ordeal after Bergen-Belsen was liberated. There is also a mass grave for victims of the Cap Arcona disaster (see Neustadt). The cemetery is located at Niendorferstrasse 45 in Moisling, now a suburb of Lübeck. There is a taharah house and a guardhouse. Admittance can be obtained through the resident guard.

LUCKENWALDE

is located about 70 km south of Berlin, on highway 101 (map 2).

* Former synagogue from 1897
* Memorial to the destroyed 1815 cemetery

The first Jews settled in Luckenwalde in 1735, probably in connection with an expulsion of unauthorized Jews from Berlin. In 1815 the small community bought a plot for a cemetery, which had to be enlarged several times in the course of the 19th century. In 1895 the community had 128 members and built a large synagogue and community center soon afterwards on Carlstrasse, now Puschkinstrasse 36. This former synagogue still stands and serves as the church of an Evangelical community today. There is a commemorative tablet for the synagogue and the Jewish community. Nothing remains of the interior decoration or furnishings.

The cemetery from 1815 was devastated during the Nazi years and destroyed either in 1943 or after the war, during the first years of the German Democratic Republic. There is a small memorial to the cemetery on Grüner Weg.

The former Luckenwalde synagogue is a Protestant church today.

MACKENSEN

(part of Dassel) is located about 80 km south of Hannover, about 80 km north of Kassel, and about 20 km west of Einbeck (map 3, 5, 6).

* Former synagogue from around 1800
* Cemetery from before 1835

Jews probably settled in Mackensen around 1670 after being expelled from Hildesheim. Many Jews left Mackensen after emancipation in 1850 as there were few opportunities in this poor agricultural area.

One of them, Georg Steinberg, a grandson of Zvi Hirsch ben Samson, who is buried in the local Jewish cemetery under a very ornate grave plate with a garland and the crown of the good name, wrote a book about his childhood in Mackensen in 1899. In his book he says that no big conflicts ever seemed to have existed between the Christians and the Jews since everybody was poor and life was hard enough without fighting.

A house at Mühlenanger 3, probably built around 1700 as an inn in a half-timbered rural style, was bought by the Jewish community around 1800 and converted into a synagogue. There was a bakery for mazzoth in the same building.

The house lies close to a creek and is a residence without any trace of its former use today. It was sold to a local Christian in 1913 when the last Mackensen Jew moved to Breslau. It is said that Jews used to bathe in the "Judenkolk", which is a natural pond formed by the creek going by the house.

It is not known exactly when the cemetery of Mackensen was established. The oldest stone dates from 1835. There are about 20 upright stones made of a blackish-red local stone in addition to the one grand graveplate for Zvi Hirsch ben Samson, from 1835, mentioned above. The cemetery is located on the second track to the left off Forststrasse on a hill overlooking Mackensen.

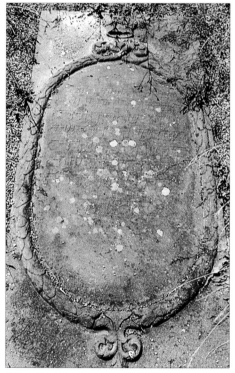

The splendid gravestone of Zvi Hirsch ben Samson, from 1835, lies in the small Jewish cemetery of Mackensen.

MAGDEBURG

is located about 160 km east of Hannover and about 160 km southwest of Berlin, on A 2 and A 81 and on highways 1, 71 and 189 (map 2, 3).

* Community center and prayer room
* Cemetery from 1816
* Memorials

Magdeburg was first mentioned almost 1,200 years ago, and Jews are first documented in 965. This makes Magdeburg the oldest Jewish settlement in non-Roman Germany. Until the beginning of the 13th century, the Jews lived around the Old Market and in Judendorf south of the city; after the "Jewish village" was destroyed the community settled in Sudenburg west of the city. During the 14th century several persecutions occurred, with the 1349 Black Plague pogrom being the worst. At the beginning of the modern era, in 1493, Jews were expelled from Magdeburg; it was not until 1705 that the first Jew was allowed back in exchange for a high tax. From then on to the beginning of the 19th century the number of Jewish families in Magdeburg was kept small by the authorities. After the Napoleonic reforms numerous Jews settled in Magdeburg and a community was founded in 1808. Among the immigrants was Israel Jacobsohn, who played a prominent role in the community and in the Reform movement and the modern Jewish school system.

In 1816 the first Magdeburg Jew was buried in the new cemetery of the community. Most gravestones in the large cemetery on Fermersleber Weg,

The glass in the doors of the Magdeburg taharah house shows the Star of David.

however, are from the years between 1850 and 1930; after emancipation, many rural Jews moved to the cities, Magdeburg among them.

The cemetery is well worth a visit. There is a taharah house with old stained glass windows. A room on the right-hand side of the building houses some unusual urns (the Jewish religion does not allow burning the dead). On the outside, a medieval gravestone, probably from the cemetery destroyed in 1493, is leaning against the wall. In front of the taharah house there is a memorial to the victims of the Nazis, and behind the taharah house, next to the children's graves and between two menorahs, there is a memorial to the million Jewish children killed in German camps.

Remarkably, a lot of metal grave ornaments are still in place; most cemeteries, Christian or Jewish, lost their metal to the "Reichsmetallspende", a drive for scrap metal to feed the Nazi armament machine.

In 1852 the community built a synagogue which was enlarged in 1897 in a Moorish (or neo-Oriental) style. This synagogue was devastated on "Reichskristallnacht" and torn down in 1939. Close to where it used to stand on Bremerstrasse, a memorial to the Jewish community and the synagogue was erected.

In 1928, the community reached its greatest numerical strength at 3,200. More than 1,500 Magdeburg Jews were killed in German camps.

Since 1968, the small post-war community has occupied a community center and a prayer room at Gröperstrasse 1a. The house is a large villa dating from the beginning of the 20th century, and nothing except the mesusah at the entrance door indicates its present use. On the gable there is an old inscription "Gott beschütze dieses Haus" (God, protect this building).

MAINSTOCKHEIM

is located on the Main river about 130 km southeast of Frankfurt or 90 km northwest of Nürnberg between the A 3 and highway 8 (map 8, 9).

* Former synagogue from 1836

A synagogue, school, and community center were built in 1836 in a simple neo-Romanesque style. The complex is located at Hauptstrasse 213 (in the cul de sac opposite Hauptstrasse 126) and is used by the Catholic church today. In the east wall the remains of a round window over the former Torah niche can still be seen; the niche itself

The former Mainstockheim synagogue serves as a Catholic church today.

was removed when the synagogue was converted to a church. A commemorative tablet to the synagogue and the Jews of Mainstockheim was set up in 1986.

MAINZ

is located about 45 km southwest of Frankfurt, between the Rhine and the A 60 (map 8).

* Landesmuseum has a collection of 18th and 19th century Judaica
* Memorials
* Community center
* Cemeteries

Only a few ancient red sandstone tombstones still bear witness to the rich vibrant religious life that flourished in Mainz in the early Middle Ages. Settled in the early years of the 10th century, Mainz was one of the foremost centers of Jewish religious learning. Rabbi Gershom ben Judah, Light of the Exile, taught here in the yeshivah founded by the Kalonymus family in the 10th century.

It is believed that the Jewish Kalonymus family moved from Lucca in Italy to Mainz sometime during the 10th century. Legend credits them with "bringing the Law from Italy, where it had been transported from the fading schools of Palestine". It is known that the family served the Mainz community as respected community leaders, rabbis, teachers, and in other capacities until well into the 13th century. They are particularly honored for the courage and leadership they displayed during the massacres of the First Crusade in 1096, and the social

upheavals that followed in the 12th and 13th centuries.

Although rich in historical importance to Jewish history in the Rhineland, the Mainz community has been destroyed repeatedly. After enjoying many years of freedom and protection in Mainz, the Jewish community was briefly expelled in 1012 and massacred in 1096 by the camp followers of the crusaders. By the early 12th century, a new Jewish community was established and together with the communities in Speyer and Worms formed the "Shum", a kind of supreme council which exercised strong influence over Jewish law and religious teaching in all German communities.

After blood libels led to several killings and the burning of the synagogue in 1281 and 1283, the community decided to move to the Promised Land under the leadership of Meir of Rothenburg in 1285. When that effort failed and rabbi Meir was taken prisoner by the emperor, the returning community found that the land and houses they had left behind had been taken over by the archbishop. The Jews of Mainz had to start building their lives and their community from scratch.

During the Black Death persecutions in 1349, many Jews were killed in a battle with the mob of Mainz, while 6,000 are said to have died by their own hands in the flames of their synagogue and houses.

The 11th century cemetery was dismantled in 1438 and its stones used as building material. (Some 200 of

180

these stones were discovered in 1922 and either taken to the Mombacherstrasse cemetery or placed in the museum.) In 1483, the Jews were expelled once more from Mainz, this time for a hundred years.

The new community remained small and endured extreme restrictions until the end of the 18th century, when some liberties were granted in the wake of the Enlightenment and the French revolution. Around 1900, after emancipation and an influx of rural Jews, the community had grown to over 3,000 members; in 1939, about 1,500 Jews remained, most of whom were deported in 1942 and 1943 and killed in German camps.

Among the gravestones on the wooded hillside of the Mombacherstrasse 85 cemetery, which was established around 1700, is the 11th century gravestone of Rabbi Gershom ben Judah. The cemetery lies behind the main train station.

For the best view of the old red sandstone tombstones, go to the top of the hill on Fritz-Kohlstrasse and the corner of Paul Denis Strasse. You can get the cemetery key at the Jewish Community Center at Forsterstrasse 2, Monday-Thursday from 8-2.

The mid-19th century cemetery located inside the Christian cemetery on Untere Zahlbacherstrasse/Xaveri-usweg includes a taharah house in the Moorish style and a guardhouse. This cemetery contains many very elaborate stones from the 19th century and a memorial to the Mainz Jewish victims of the Nazi years.

The Landesmuseum has a very good collection of 18th and 19th century ritual objects on display in a separate room on the third floor. Much of the collection was inherited from the Jewish Museum that was opened in 1926 by the Mainz Jewish community and partly destroyed by the Nazi mobs in 1938. The collection includes several beautifully engraved silver Torah shields and crowns as well as a rimon which displays a Napoleonic eagle on top.

On the first floor gallery overlooking the lapidarium there are a few medieval gravestones including that of Rabbi Meshullam ben Kalonymus who died in 1171.

What has long been thought to be a part of the Kalonymus house, a stone window frame with an imperial eagle

There is speculation that this Romanesque window may have been part of the house of the Kalonymus family that came from Italy.

181

and a scene interpreted as the dream of Adam, is displayed on the wall of the medieval wing. However, it is unlikely that a rabbinical family and leaders of their community would decorate their house with human figures as that would be a violation of their religious rules.

The museum is located on Grosse Bleiche 49-51 and is open Tuesday 10-8, and Wednesday through Sunday from 10-5.

There is a memorial to the synagogue destroyed in the 1938 "Reichskristall-nacht" at Hindenburgstrasse and Josefstrasse and a memorial to another synagogue, devastated in 1938 and destroyed by bombs in 1942, 20 meters from the corner of Margaretenstrasse and Flachsmarktstrasse.

MEISENHEIM

is located about 100 km southwest of Frankfurt, close to highway 420 (map 8).

* Former synagogue from 1866 and a small exhibition
* Cemetery in nearby Bauwald from 1880

The small Meisenheim community built a grand churchlike synagogue with two low towers in a mixture of neo-Classicist and neo-Romanesque styles in 1866. However, like many small-town communities, it declined to about 50 in 1925. In the 1938 "Reichskristallnacht" pogrom the synagogue was damaged and later used as a grain storehouse. The interior was changed completely and the two towers were also removed. The former synagogue was renovated by a group of concerned citizens in 1987 and now serves as a memorial and community center.

An exhibition on the history of Jews in the Meisenheim area is on display here. A visit to the former synagogue at Saarstrasse 3 can be arranged by contacting Meisenheim city hall.

There is also a cemetery from about 1880 in Bauwald.

The grand former synagogue of the Meisenheim Jews houses a meeting hall (Stätte der Begegnung) today.

MICHELBACH AN DER LÜCKE

is located about 120 km northeast of Stuttgart and about 90 km west of Nürnberg, five km north of the A 6, between the A 7 and highway 290. Road signs are also marked Michelbach/L. and Michelbach a. d. L. Take good note of these signs as there are several places called Michelbach in the area (map 8, 9, 10).

* Former synagogue from 1756/57 and an exhibition
* Cemetery from 1840

Jews settled in Michelbach in 1519 after they were expelled from nearby Rothenburg. Twenty-two families lived there before the Thirty Years War, but the number declined to seven families during the war. By 1869 there were 216 Jews living in Michelbach, making up about a third of the population, but due to emigration and the attractions of larger cities their number had declined to 35 by 1933.

Of those deported from Michelbach, 16 Jews were killed in Riga and Theresienstadt and only one Michelbach Jew survived to return after 1945. He eventually became a council member and died in 1968. His concentration camp uniform and Nazi era identity papers are exhibited in the small museum in the old synagogue.

The former synagogue, built in 1756/57, was not damaged in the 1938 "Reichskristallnacht" pogrom.

The small former Michelbach synagogue was carefully restored and made a museum. The typical niche in the eastern wall that shelters the Torah shrine is clearly recognizable.

It was used for storing ammunition during the war and soft drinks afterwards. Great care has been taken to restore this former synagogue to its original state. There is a Hebrew inscription over the door and a copy of the old chuppah stone inserted next to the door. The wall and border paintings in the interior have been refurbished.

Today, the synagogue is used as a memorial to the Jews of the Franken area and includes a small collection of Judaica as well as an exhibition of photographs and documents of Jews and their history in the region. The visitors' book indicates hundreds of visitors since its opening in July 1984. The synagogue is located behind Judengasse 4. You can get the key on workdays between 9 and 12 at city hall on Schloss-Strasse.

The cemetery, established in 1840, is large and well-maintained. A few stones have been broken and repaired but most of the stones are in good condition and all are standing. The cemetery is located on Rossbürger Strasse. Go towards Rossbürg to the crossroads after the end of the village. It is signposted "Jüdischer Friedhof". The cemetery in Schopfloch was used before 1840. The cemetery key is available from city hall on workdays between 9 and 12.

MICHELSTADT

is located about 70 km southeast of Frankfurt, on highways 45 and 47 (map 8, 9).

* Former synagogue from 1791 and a small exhibition of Judaica
* Cemetery from mid-17th century

It was not until the end of the Thirty Years War that Jews could settle in Michelstadt. The community grew

The former prayer room is used for various community events today. Therefore, the bimah was moved closer to the Torah shrine, an untypical place in a rural German synagogue.

184

The Baroque synagogue, where the Baal Shem of Michelstadt once officiated, stands close to the fortification walls. The former synagogue houses a museum today.

slowly and had about 100 members in 1790. The Michelstadt synagogue was built in 1791 in the Baroque style and stands very close to the city wall at what is now Mauerstrasse 19. Although the interior was devastated during the 1938 "Reichskristallnacht" by the Nazis, the building was saved from destruction due to its proximity to other buildings. After being used as a storeroom, it was restored as the Dr. I. E. Lichtigfeld-Museum and exhibits a small collection of Judaica and a display of photographs and documents related to Michelstadt's Jewish community. The inscription "How beautiful are the tents of Jakob and the dwellings of Israel" is preserved over the entrance. The museum synagogue is open between the second Saturday before Easter and November 1 on Thursday from 2:30-4 and every first and second Sunday in the month from 2-4.

The cemetery dates from the mid-17th century. It is located in the forest on Am Stadion, on the side of a steep hill across the street from a public swimming pool where you may pick up the key. The cemetery is quite large with stones of many different styles. Most of the stones have been knocked over and are in poor condition. The grave of Rabbi Seckel Löb Wormser, better known as Baal Schem, the miracle worker of Michelstadt, is to the right of the entrance and is frequently visited by Jews from all over the world. He is the author of a sentence often quoted and often misunderstood: "Remembrance is the secret of salvation." When the swimming pool is closed, you may pick up the cemetery key at the Verkehrsbüro, tourist office, in the center Monday-Friday 8-12 and 2-4.

The home of Baal Schem, where he lived from 1826 to 1847, can be seen at Erbacher Strasse 12 near the center. There is a commemorative tablet.

MILTENBERG

is located on the Main river about 90 km southeast of Frankfurt close to highway 469 (map 8, 9).

* Former synagogue from 13th or 14th century
* Remains of a synagogue from 1904
* Remains of a medieval Torah shrine in the city museum
* Cemetery from 15th or 16th century
* Cemetery from 1900

Jews settled in Miltenberg in the 13th century. They built a small Gothic synagogue around 1300. This synagogue has a feature that you can find only here and in the famous Altneuschul in Prague. Its two vaults have a fifth rib each, useless architectonically, but helping to avoid the depiction of the cross, the symbol of Christianity.

In 1429 the Jews were expelled from Miltenberg and their synagogue was handed over to one of the citizens. When a new community formed in the 18th century, it managed to buy back the old synagogue in 1754. In 1851, however, the building was declared unsafe and a new prayer room was established at Riesengasse 9.

The old synagogue was sold to a brewery in 1875 and is the oldest remaining former synagogue in Germany today. It is located in the backyard of Hauptstrasse 199-201 in Miltenberg. The Gothic building with its vaults and the traditional three windows in the east wall is being used as a storeroom by the Kalt-Loch-Brewery. A visit is impossible or requires great effort. If you go up Schlossgasse to

All you can see of the oldest remaining synagogue in Germany is this piece of the eastern wall.

No. 4, you can at least look down over the town and see the east wall of the former synagogue.

Nearby, in the basement of Löwengasse 1, there is a ritual bath from the 19th century. Visits are impossible here as well.

The house at Riesengasse 9, where the prayer room and the school used to be between 1851 and 1904, still stands, but has been radically changed. You can still see the place where the mesusah was fastened to the right of the entrance door.

The new synagogue from 1904, at Mainstrasse 57, was a stately and very impressive neo-Romanesque building with a cupola and a community center. On "Reichskristallnacht", the synagogue was partly destroyed and later remodeled several times. It is a private home today. The left part is not recognizable as a former synagogue, but the right part, the former community center, has not been changed on the outside.

The gable of the Torah shrine from the medieval synagogue has survived seven centuries. It was first moved from the old synagogue to the Riesenstrasse building and then to the new synagogue on Mainstrasse. In 1938, the stone was broken, but most parts were salvaged. A reconstruction of the oldest Torah shrine ornament in Germany can be seen at the Miltenberg city museum (Stadtmuseum). However, the museum will be closed for renovation until at least 1996.

The old Jewish cemetery from the

186

15th or 16th century, on Burgweg after house number 44, has many old stones, some of them almost completely sunk into the ground now. The newer cemetery, from 1900, is located on Monbrunnerstrasse.

MINDEN

is located about 60 km west of Hannover, on the Weser river and highways 61 and 65 (map 3).

* Minden museum has a small collection of Judaica
* Post-war synagogue and memorial
* Cemetery from 1895
* Cemetery from 1850 in nearby Porta Westfalica

In 1270, Jews lived in Minden under the protection of the bishop. In the early 14th century they had to pay taxes to both the town and to the bishop. The sole occupation authorized by the town officials was moneylending. This community was destroyed during the Black Death persecutions.

Jews were not allowed to return until 1550, but their presence in Minden was continuous from then on although they were subject to a variety of restrictions governing their residence and occupations until their emancipation in the 19th century.

In 1865 the community built a synagogue that was destroyed on "Reichskristallnacht". The remaining Minden Jews were deported from 1941 on, most were killed in German camps. After 1945 a small community was founded again.

The Mindener Museum has a small collection of Judaica as well as a gravestone from 1350. The museum is located at Ritterstrasse 23-33 and is open Tuesday-Friday 10-1 and 2:30-5; Thursday also from 5-6:30; Saturday 2:30-5; and Sunday 11-6.

The Minden cemetery was established in 1895 and is located on Jakobsweg/Erikaweg. Before the Minden cemetery was opened, an older cemetery in nearby Porta Westfalica was used. This cemetery is located on Kempstrasse on a hill above the Christian cemetery. The Porta Westfalica cemetery includes stones dating from the 1860s, some of which are very elaborate, and many memorial stones to victims of the Nazi years. Both cemeteries are open to the public.

There is a memorial to the victims of the Nazi years in the entrance hall of the new synagogue at Kampstrasse 6.

MÖNCHSDEGGINGEN

is located about 100 km southwest of Nürnberg, about 140 km east of Stuttgart and about 140 km northwest of Munich, off highway 25 about halfway between Donauwörth and Nördlingen (map 9, 10, 11).

* Mikveh from 1841
* Former synagogue used from 1684 to 1734
* Cemetery from 1833

Jews began settling in Mönchsdeggingen in 1684 after being expelled from nearby Höchstädt. They used a half-timbered house, built in 1542, as a synagogue from 1684 until 1734 when they built a new synagogue. The former synagogue building has long been a private home now and displays a memorial plaque. It is located at Albstrasse 20.

On the corner of Raiffeisenstrasse and Römerstrasse there is a memorial to the second and third synagogues from 1734-1828 and 1828-1879. The Jewish community moved to nearby Nördlingen in the 1870's and the synagogue building was sold and eventually torn down.

A rural-Moorish style mikveh was built in 1841. The small white building, with chimney, can be seen at Alemannenstrasse 17. The mikveh was converted into a police jail after the community had left. Today it houses a local museum. The former Jewish school is now the city hall and tourist office and is located at Albstrasse 30. The cemetery, opened in 1833 and closed in 1877, is located on the edge of town on Magerbeiner Steige. The stones are all in good condition, although some inscriptions are badly eroded. The cemetery contains stones of several different styles, a taharah house, probably of the same age, and is surrounded by a stone wall.

To get there, follow Albstrasse towards Niedermagerbein. The cemetery is on the left side, opposite the school complex. You may get the key at the city hall and tourist office building at Albstrasse 30.

MORINGEN

is located about 90 km south of Hannover or 70 km northeast of Kassel, on highway 241, close to the A 7 (map 3, 5, 6).

* Former synagogue from 1838
* Cemetery from mid-18th century

Moringen is a small town with a castle built by Henry the Lion in 1140.

Jews have lived here since 1748. The community grew until the middle of the 19th century and then declined due to emigration and the pull of the larger cities.

The former synagogue, now a private home, was built in 1838 and is a half-timbered two-story building with two entrances next to each other, probably the former men and women doors. The proximity to the creek indicates a mikveh. The building is located at Schneehof 1.

The cemetery, from around 1750, is located on the side of a hill in a dense

The Mönchsdeggingen mikveh was built in 1841, using elements of the Moorish style. Later, after the Jewish community dissolved, it was used as the town jail for a while.

188

forest outside of town. There is only one standing stone. All the rest of the stones that should be standing are broken and scattered. There are also 34 grave plates. A corner is reserved for four Russian POW graves. The cemetery has obviously been disturbed on many occasions and is untended. A low wooden fence surrounds the cemetery allowing entry at will. To get there, follow An der Mergelkuhle to the sewage treatment plant. Take the gravel road that turns off to the left. There is a big oak tree at the edge of the forest marked by a small red and white trail sign. Take the path leading straight up the hill and you will see a path leading to the cemetery off to the right.

MÜHLHAUSEN

is a small town about 60 km northwest of Erfurt, on the Unstrut river and highways 247 and 249(map 5, 6).

* Former synagogue from before 1870
* Late 19th century cemetery

Jews first settled in Mühlhausen in the 13th century. This first community was destroyed in the Black Plague persecutions of the 14th century, but a new community was founded a few years later. In 1543, following the Reformation, the Jewish community was expelled "for all eternity" from Mühlhausen, like from many other German towns.

The former Moringen synagogue, now a private residence, still shows traces of its earlier use: Two entrances (formerly one for men, one for women), a wide field of masonry on the east wall, where the Torah shrine used to be, and possibly the entrance to the former mikveh next to it.

It was not until the beginning of the 19th century that a new Jewish community could settle in Mühlhausen. The neo-Classicist former synagogue from before 1870 stands in a backyard of Jüdenstrasse (or Wahlstrasse) 24. The building forming the street front was the Jewish school. The synagogue can not be seen from the street. If you can't gain access at Wahlstrasse 24, you can see part of the east wall of the synagogue building with its prominent Torah niche and the round window above it from the courtyard of Wahlstrasse 22.

The former synagogue is a high half-timber building partly built with loam bricks. In the November 1938 "Reichskristallnacht" pogrom, the building, like many others in Germany, survived due to its proximity to other buildings. The round window over the Torah niche still has remains of the original blue glass. There are plans to renovate the building and use it as a museum and a cultural center.

The cemetery from the late 19th century is located on Eisenacher Strasse, next to the Protestant cemetery. The very urban cemetery still shows signs of desecration and serves as a memorial today.

The former Mühlhausen synagogue is a half-timbered building in the backyard of the former Jewish school, now a private residence.

MÜNCHEN (Munich)

is the capital city of Bavaria (map 11).

* Synagogue from 1931
* Memorials
* Cemeteries
* Bookshop specializing in Jewish themes
* Small private Jewish museum

Jews first settled in Munich in the 12th century. Although the community was soon stable enough to have a synagogue, mikveh, and hospital in their own quarter, this stability was repeatedly disturbed.

In 1285, 180 Jews were burned to death inside their synagogue as a result of a blood libel. The Black Death persecutions in 1348/49 forced the survivors to flee. Jews returned a few years later but were repeatedly faced with death or expulsion. Between 1442 and 1450, all the Jews living in the dukedom of Bavaria were expelled.

Jews were not officially allowed to return to Bavaria until the last quarter of the 18th century, although a few always managed to live in the country. Even around 1800, the restrictions were so severe that the number of Bavarian Jews remained small until emancipation in the 19th century. With emancipation, Jewish residence in Munich increased rapidly.

After WWI, anti-Semitism was particularly severe and wide-ranging, partly because the short-lived revolutionary Soviet government of Bavaria had several prominent Jewish members.

During the Nazi years, 4,500 Munich Jews were deported and very few survived to return.

Today, Munich again has one of the largest Jewish communities in Germany, but anti-Semitic acts and terrorism still plague the community with - among others - an arson attack on an old age home in 1970, in which seven Jews were killed, the massacre that killed eleven Israeli participants in the Olympic games in 1972, and repeated desecrations of the synagogue and cemeteries.

Hardly anything survives of Munich's Jewish past. There are memorials to the synagogues destroyed in 1938 on Herzog-Max-Strasse/Maxburgstrasse and on Herzog-Rudolf-Strasse 1. The main synagogue on Herzog-Max-Strasse was torn down in June 1938, long before "Reichskristallnacht", because the Nazi city authorities decided they needed a parking lot where the synagogue stood.

The Orthodox synagogue on Herzog-Rudolf-Strasse was destroyed during "Reichskristallnacht" in November 1938.

The synagogue of the Eastern European Jews at Reichenbachstrasse 27, built in 1931, was devastated, but not burned down during "Reichskristallnacht" as it was too close to adjoining buildings. It was restored after 1945, reconsecrated in 1947, and serves as Munich's main synagogue today.

There is a memorial to the Munich Jewish victims of the Nazi persecutions on Brienner Strasse/ Oskar-von-Miller-Ring.

The Bayerisches Nationalmuseum has a collection of ritual objects and other Judaica, but it is on perpetual loan to the Jewish Culture Museum in Augsburg.

The Jewish cemetery from 1816 at Thalkirchnerstrasse 240 has about 6,000 stones, including the graves of Jews who were victims of the Nazi camps. The early 20th century Jewish cemetery at Garchinger Strasse 37 has a memorial to the Jewish soldiers of WWI who died for their German fatherland as well as many stones for Munich Jews who were killed in the German death camps.

Munich had the first and for some time the only bookshop specializing in Jewish themes in post-war Germany. It is called Literaturhandlung (Literature Store) and is located at Fürstenstrasse 17 close to the Feldherrnhalle and Odeonsplatz. Dr. Rachel Salamander, the owner, is very active in bringing Jewish writers to Munich to read from their works.

Munich may have the smallest Jewish museum in the world, a private museum established in a two-room apartment by Richard Grimm, an enterprising non-Jew. The address is Maximilianstrasse 36, and the museum is open Tuesdays and Wednesdays from 2 to 6 and Thursdays from 2 to 8. Mr. Grimm describes his museum as a first step towards a larger Jewish museum, run by the city and/or the Jewish community.

The Bayerische Staatsbibliothek has an important collection of Hebrew manuscripts, among them a Babylonic Talmud. This collection, however, is not on display and only scholars can get access to them.

MÜNSTER (Westfalen)

is located about 200 km west of Hannover, 180 km northwest of Kassel, and 150 km northeast of Köln, on the A 1 and A 43 (map 3, 5).

* Westfälisches Landesmuseum has a small collection of Judaica
* Community center
* Memorials
* Cemetery from 1811

Jews began settling in Münster in sufficient numbers to maintain a synagogue, cemetery, and mikveh by the mid-13th century. However, the Black Death persecutions of the mid-14th century resulted in the death of some Münster Jews and the expulsion of the survivors of this pogrom.

After this expulsion, Jews were not allowed to resettle in Münster until the early 19th century. With emancipation, residence increased until the 1930's. Although some Münster Jews were able to emigrate, the majority were deported in the large transports of 1941 and 1942 and eventually killed in Nazi camps.

The Westfälisches Landesmuseum, at Domplatz 10, exhibits a small collection of Judaica. The museum is open Tuesday-Sunday 10-6.

There is a memorial to patients killed by the Nazis because they were either mentally or physically handicapped at the Westfälische Landeskrankenhaus (hospital church) at Friedrich-Wilhelm-Weber-Strasse 30. Tens of thousands of handicapped were killed by gas, injection or starvation in Hadamar, Brandenburg, Hartheim, or other institutions from 1940 on. Jewish patients were often killed first.

The cemetery was established in 1811 and is located at Einsteinstrasse and Forsterstrasse. There is a gravestone from 1324 from an earlier cemetery to the right of the taharah house. The cemetery is surrounded by a high wall but you can look into it through the gate. The key is available from the Jewish Community Center at Klosterstrasse 8-9, Monday and Tuesday from 8-12.

NAUEN

is located about 40 km west of Berlin, on highways 5 and 273 (map 2).

* Former synagogue from 1800
* Memorial to destroyed cemetery

Little is known about the history of the Nauen Jews. There was a medieval community, and an old field name "Jüdenkirchhof" (Jewish churchyard) indicates a cemetery destroyed long ago. In 1800 a new synagogue was built at Goethestrasse 11, in the shade of the parish church. In the 1938 "Reichskristallnacht", the synagogue was devastated and later used as a workshop. In 1994 the building was used as the office of an insurance salesman. There is a commemorative tablet to the Jewish community showing two Jews raising a Torah scroll.

The cemetery on "Am Weinberg" from 1819 was destroyed during the Nazi years. There is a memorial to the Jewish community.

BAD NAUHEIM

is located about 30 km north of Frankfurt, off the A 5 and on highway 275 (map 4, 5, 8).

* Synagogue from 1929
* Cemeteries

Jews were expelled during the Black Plague persecutions in 1348.

The tiny former synagogue of Nauen stands in the shade of the church.

The Nauheim synagogue from 1929 was reconsecrated in 1945.

194

Thereafter, documents concerning Jews living in Bad Nauheim primarily relate to their taxes.

Although they were expelled again in 1539, Jews continued to live in Bad Nauheim in small numbers until emancipation when the population increased.

The community built its first synagogue in 1867. Soon this synagogue became too small, especially since Nauheim became a fashionable spa and many Jewish guests from Germany and abroad visited it. In 1929 a new synagogue was built at Karlstrasse 34. This synagogue survived the Nazi years and was reconsecrated in 1945.

There are two large Stars of David on both sides of the entrance with a smaller one over the door. There is a memorial to the victims of the Nazi years, dating from 1945, inside. The synagogue can be visited Saturday mornings.

There are two Jewish cemeteries located on Homburgerstrasse. A small cemetery, opened in 1866, can be seen opposite no. 23. Further down, at Homburgerstrasse 82, the newer Jewish cemetery is located between the Catholic and the Protestant cemeteries. It contains a taharah house and several early 20th century stones of Russian Jews who evidently died while staying at the local spa.

If locked, keys to both cemeteries may be obtained at the Christian cemetery administration office.

NEU-ANSPACH

is located about 30 km northwest of Frankfurt, off highway 456 (map 4, 8).

* Hesse farm museum Hessenpark with former synagogue from 1874

Just outside Neu-Anspach lies the Hesse farm museum, Hessenpark, which displays a large number of representative old relocated farm houses, barns, a school, churches, and other village buildings from all over Hesse. Included in the museum is the former synagogue from Gross-Umstadt which was built in 1874. It is located to the left of the entrance, past the blacksmith and firefighting display.

The former synagogue is a massive stone building with a flat ceiling, a Torah ark not marked on the outside,

In the 19th century, the synagogue was as much part of the village in the German state of Hesse as the church, the school or the inn. Today more than 200 synagogue buildings remain in Hesse. The Hesse farm museum reflects this history and houses the old synagogue from Gross-Umstadt.

195

a round window over the entrance and arched side windows, and a tablet with an inscription in Hebrew reading "House of Israel's prayer".

Hesse had hundreds of Jewish rural communities in the 19th century. The synagogue then was as much a part of the village scene as the church or the school. The museum is open from March 19 until November 1, Tuesday-Sunday from 9-6.

NEUSTADT

is located about 100 km northeast of Hamburg, between the Baltic Sea and the A 1 (map 1).

* Cemetery and memorial

The cemetery on Grasweg, from 1945, contains the graves of some of the victims of death marches that preceded the Allied victory, as well as a memorial to the victims of one of the most tragic Allied military errors in the closing days of the war.

As the Allies advanced in northern Germany, thousands of concentration camp prisoners were loaded on to ships anchored in Neustadt Bay by their German guards, the largest ship being the Cap Arcona. The British, suspecting that these ships would be used to help Nazi top brass escape from Germany, decided to attack them on May 3. The prisoners, thinking the approaching planes brought liberty, hailed them with waving arms and shouted greetings. Then the planes opened fire and started bombing. Over 7,000 prisoners died that awful day only hours before British troops

took Neustadt without fighting. Several resorts around Neustadt Bay, including Grömitz, Haffkrug, Niendorf, Sierksdorf and Timmendorfer Strand, have graves of Cap Arcona victims.

NIEDERWERRN

is located about 120 km northwest of Nürnberg, or 140 km east of Frankfurt, on the A 303 just west of Schweinfurt (map 8, 9).

* Former synagogue from 1786
* Former Jewish school
* Cemetery in Euerbach

Jews probably first settled in Niederwerrn in 1555, after their expulsion from nearby Schweinfurt. First documents that refer to Jews in Niederwerrn date from 1657, however. Niederwerrn was then an estate of a minor noble family. Jews could obtain letters of protection against one-time payments and higher taxes.

After emancipation in the mid-19th century, the Jewish population of Niederwerrn, like that of most small rural communities, dwindled. The number of Jews in 1800 was about 300, but then rapidly declined to 52 in 1925 and 50 in 1933.

Thirty-nine Jews from Niederwerrn left the village during the first years of the Nazi reign, some emigrated, others moved to larger cities. The nine Jews still remaining in Niederwerrn in 1942 were all deported and killed in German camps.

The former synagogue built in 1786 was devastated in the 1938 "Reichskristallnacht", but not burned down

196

because it was too close to other buildings. It was built in the Baroque style by a Jew from Niederwerrn who had become rich in the Netherlands. After 1945 the building was handed over to the Jewish Restitution Fund, who later sold it to the Niederwerrn council. It was then used as a cinema and a storeroom after an annex on the south side was added and the windows were bricked up.

Plans for restoration and use as a cultural center are being developed. The former synagogue stands at Schweinfurter Strasse 23. There is a commemorative tablet that is now almost illegible. You can get a good impression of the building as it used to be by walking around to the left and viewing it from the north.

Across the street at Schweinfurter Strasse 54, the former Jewish school from 1878 is still standing. Today, it is the city hall. This building also displays a commemorative tablet.

A plot in nearby Euerbach was bought by the Jewish community in 1672 and used as a cemetery for the communities of Euerbach, Niederwerrn, Oppach and Westheim.

NOHFELDEN

is located about 150 km southwest of Frankfurt, on the A 62 (map 8).

* Former synagogue from 19th century in Sötern
* Cemetery from early 19th century in Sötern

Only the roof and a faded commemorative tablet remind us of the fact that this building used to be the Niederwerrn synagogue.

197

* Memorial on "Skulpturenstrasse" (sculpture road)
* Late 19th century cemetery in Gonnesweiler

In nearby Sötern, on highway 52, there is a 19th century former synagogue that has been converted to a home and bank office. It is located at Hauptstrasse 30.

An early 19th century cemetery is located on Weiherdammstrasse outside of town. To get there drive down Weiherdammstrasse under the motorway bridge past the Catholic cemetery. The cemetery is surrounded by a low stone wall and is unlocked. The stones are in good condition although the inscriptions are eroded; there are many different styles of stones. There are a few stones from 1939 and 1940. Broken stones have been repaired.

There is a memorial to the Jewish community of nearby Gonnesweiler on highway 269, in the form of a sculpture called "Requiem for the Jews" by Shelomo Selinger which was erected in 1980 on a former Roman road now called the "Sculpture Road". To get there, drive through Gonnesweiler towards Tholey. Turn right and drive down to "Römerhof" to the car park. The large stone sculpture stands next to the path leading around the lake, a few hundred meters from the car park. The inscription is in Hebrew "El male rachamin" (g'd of mercy).

Gonnesweiler also has a late 19th century cemetery which includes a memorial stone to the victims of the Nazi years.

This sculpture near an old Roman road in Gonnesweiler is called "Requiem for the Jews".

NORDHAUSEN

is located about 80 km north of Erfurt, on highways 4 and 80 (map 3, 5, 6).

* Former early 19th century prayer house
* Jewish gravestones from 14th and 15th century
* Cemetery from early 19th century

A Jewish community was first documented in Nordhausen in the beginning of the 13th century. Nordhausen had a Jewish street, a synagogue, a mikveh and a Jewish cemetery then. The Black Plague persecutions destroyed the community in 1349, but a new community had emerged by the end of the 14th century. This community stayed comparatively small until 1559 when Jews were expelled from Nordhausen.

Jews were not allowed back to Nordhausen until the beginning of the 19th century. A synagogue was built in 1845 and destroyed by the SA during "Reichskristallnacht". There is a memorial for this synagogue near St. Blasii church. A cemetery was established in 1827. The 13th century synagogue on Hüterstrasse/Frauenberger Stiege and the prayer house on Jüdenstrasse were destroyed by bombs in April 1945 as was the mikveh in Tuve'sche Haus on Arnoldstrasse.

A building with a former prayer room from before 1845 still stands at Dr. Külz-Strasse 3. The rooms are used for a music school today.

The mayor of Nordhausen plans to establish a Jewish museum there in cooperation with the Jewish community of Thuringia and the Protestant communities of Nordhausen.

Jewish gravestones from the 14th and 15th century could still be seen on the Judenturm am Rähmen, a ruined fortification tower, before the war. They were used as construction material after the 1559 expulsion. Today, these gravestones have disappeared under the rubble of destroyed buildings that was dumped here after the war.

The Jewish cemetery on Ammerberg was started around 1827 and badly damaged by bombs in WWII. However, it has been restored and is in good condition. The key is available

The numerous medieval Jewish buildings of Nordhausen were destroyed by bombs in WW II. Today, only this former 19th century prayer hall remains.

from the resident in the former guard house.

There was a Nazi labor camp in the suburb of Krimderode, north of town, where slave labor from many European countries, many Jews among them, were forced to work for the German arms industry in subterranean factories. Many of the slave laborers died from exhaustion or hunger. There is a memorial in Mittelbau Dora to the approximately 20,000 victims of this camp.

NÜRNBERG (map 9, 10)

* Memorial for synagogue destroyed in 1938
* Germanisches Nationalmuseum has a few medieval gravestones and a collection of Judaica (mostly in storage)
* 14th century fountain with Gothic statues depicting Moses and seven prophets
* New synagogue has part of the Gothic ark from the synagogue destroyed in 1499
* Cemeteries

Jews probably began settling in Nürnberg in the first half of the 12th century. The community was large and prosperous when an impoverished Franconian nobleman named Rindfleisch led his private crusade through large parts of Germany. His followers killed about 700 Jews in Nürnberg in 1298.

The 14th and 15th centuries were years of oppressive and often petty restrictions by the city authorities (such as prohibiting Jews from buying eggs or live animals before 9 a.m. in order to keep prices down).

There were also heavy taxes which involved an intense struggle between the emperor, burgrave and the municipal authorities over the rights to Jewish revenues, as well as years of being held hostage until ransom could be paid. There were also many temporary expulsions.

The Black Death persecutions took place although the plague itself bypassed Nürnberg; 560 Jews were burned, their synagogue and houses torn down, and their gravestones used for paving a street and building a church. The Marienkirche was erected where the medieval synagogue used to stand.

The frequent expulsions of the Nürnberg Jews were usually declared "for all eternity" but rarely lasted more than a few years since city officials, burgraves, and emperors quickly ran through what had been gained from the expulsion and sought to attract Jews back in order to collect the usual special taxes from them once again. The 1499 expulsion, however, following a 1498 decree giving the Nürnberg merchants moneylending rights, was to be in effect for 350 years.

Although after 1499 Jews were allowed to visit Nürnberg, subject to severe restrictions and the payment of tolls on any goods purchased, they were not allowed to resettle until the 1850's. After emancipation, however, the number of Jews living and working in Nürnberg increased rapidly until it was the second largest Jewish community in Bavaria, numbering 9,000 by 1933.

Throughout the 1920's and 1930's, Nürnberg was in the forefront of anti-Semitic violence in Germany. The fact that many Nazi party congresses were held here certainly contributed to this. Over 1,600 Nürnberg Jews were deported from their city, which had given its name to the infamous "Nürnberg laws", of the Nazis, and very few survived.

There is a very prominently positioned memorial to the synagogue which was built in 1874 and destroyed on August 10, 1938, three months before the November pogrom, on Hans-Sachs-Platz and Spitalbrücke. The new synagogue has the Judenstein, a Gothic arch with the Hebrew words "Keter Torah". It was once part of the Torah ark of the old synagogue destroyed in 1499. It was then displayed on the

There is a memorial to the main synagogue of Nürnberg which was destroyed in August 1938, three months before Reichskristallnacht.

house of a patrician family for 400 years, incorporated in the 1874 synagogue, put in a museum after 1945, and finally taken to the new synagogue in 1987. The Nürnberg synagogue is located at Johann-Priem-Strasse 20.

The Germanisches Nationalmuseum has four Jewish gravestones from the 13th century and one from the 15th century on display in the museum cloister. A small collection of ritual objects is in storage most of the time. The museum is located at Kornmarkt 1 and is open daily 9-5, Thursday also 5-9:30 p.m.

In 1986, a medieval mikveh was found at Königstrasse 18, in the basement of the Bally shoe shop; however, it can not be visited.

The 14th century fountain, the Schöner Brunnen, on the Marktplatz includes Gothic statues of Moses and seven prophets as well as David and his harp.

The old Jewish cemetery at Bärenschanzstrasse 40 (from 1864) is locked but you can see into the cemetery through the gate. The cemetery contains a taharah house, guardhouse and long rows of 19th century stones. The key is available from the Jewish community center at Johann-Priem-Strasse 20.

The new cemetery, established in the early years of this century, is located at Schnieglinger Strasse 155 behind the Christian cemetery. The taharah house contains four mid-14th century gravestones which were used to build the spiral staircase in the St. Lorenz church. The cemetery also has a memorial to the Jewish soldiers who died for Germany in WWI, with an addition for the Jewish victims of the Nazi years, and 31 graves of concentration camp prisoners.

ODENBACH

is located about 110 km southwest of Frankfurt, off highway 420 between highways 48 and 270 (map 8).

* Former synagogue from 1752
* Cemetery from 1850

The small former synagogue at Kirch-

hofstrasse 9, very close to the church and wedged in between houses, was not destroyed in the 1938 "Reichskristallnacht" but was in very poor condition until recently. The building was private property and stood empty and deteriorating until a local initiative started looking after the former synagogue and began renovations. So far, there is no concept for the future use of the building.

The ground floor was built of stone and the gable wall is half-timbered. There is an inscription in Hebrew over the men's door, "This is the gate of the Lord", which you can see through an iron gate around the

The small former synagogue of Odenbach was left to decay for many years...

202

corner. Inside there are remarkable fragments of late Baroque wall paintings and two columns in the center holding up the wide women's gallery. The orientation of the former synagogue is a surprise: the ark (still there) was not, as you would expect, placed in a gable wall, but in a long wall, and the prayer room is wider than it is long. The building can be visited daily, except Monday, at noon by contacting Mrs. Dittrich, the chairwoman of the initiative that restored it, at Untere Glanstrasse 2, a few weeks in advance.

Remains of Baroque wallpaintings in the former Odenbach synagogue.

The Jewish cemetery was opened in 1850. To get there, drive through town towards Adenbach. About 200 meters

before a local group of concerned citizens managed to get it restored.

after the last house and barn of Oden-bach, you can see hedges on the side of a gradual hill to the left.

The cemetery is small and all stones are standing and in good condition. If the cemetery is locked, you can get the key at city hall.

OFFENBACH

is located about 10 km southeast of Frankfurt, on the Main river (map 8).

* Former synagogue from 1916
* Synagogue from 1956
* Klingspor museum with collection of artistic Jewish prints
* Cemeteries

Offenbach Jews were massacred during the Black Death persecutions of 1348. A new community was not established until the 17th century, when the reigning family of Isenburg-Birstein searched to attract Jews to its possessions.

This community remained small until the arrival of Jacob Frank in 1788, who bought a castle from the indebted prince and called himself Baron of Offenbach. Frank was a follower of the teachings of the false messiah, Sabbatai Zwi, and became a false messiah himself. He later became a Christian. Nevertheless, he, and after his death his daughter Eva, attracted thousands of eastern European, pri-marily Polish, devotees to Offenbach to honor him. Unfortunately, the large sums of money loaned him by his fol-lowers to support his project to lead the Jews to the Promised Land disappeared upon his death.

The Offenbach community numbered about 1,000 Jews during the 19th century, about 1,400 in 1933 and 550 in 1939, most of whom died in the Nazi camps. A small community was re-established after 1945.

The former synagogue, built in 1916, was damaged in 1938 and then used as a movie theater. In 1959, it was converted into the municipal theater and has become a center for American-style musicals lately. It is a large building with a cupola, seating 850, and is located at Goethestrasse 1-5. There is a commemorative tablet. The new synagogue and community center are located across the street at Kaiserstrasse 109.

The former Offenbach synagogue is a musical theater today.

A synagogue in the suburb of Bürgel was also damaged in the 1938 "Reichs-kristallnacht", later sold, and is now a private home. It is located at Bürger-strasse 15. Nothing except one arched window remains in its appearance to indicate it was once a synagogue.

204

The Klingspor Museum specializes in 20th century book and lettering art. The museum and library collections include some of the work commissioned by Dr. Siegfried Guggenheim, a Jewish lawyer and patron of the arts in Offenbach.

The collection includes the famous Offenbach haggadah which was used by the Guggenheim family at their seder meals. The museum is located at Herrnstrasse 80 and is open Monday-Friday 10-5, Saturday and Sunday 10-1, 2-5.

The mid-19th century cemetery at Friedhofstrasse 2 contains some of the stones from the early 18th century cemetery on Bismarckstrasse. These stones have been joined together into two pyramid-shaped monuments. There is a memorial to the Jewish soldiers who died in WWI and many elaborately carved gravestones. The Jewish cemetery is part of the city cemetery and partitioned off from the

Gravestones from an older Jewish cemetery were assembled to form a memorial in the Offenbach city cemetery.

Christian cemetery by a hedge only, with several paths leading from the Jewish to the Christian part; it stands as an unusually early example of cooperation and tolerance, since at that time most cemeteries were still strictly segregated along religious lines.

There is an 18th century cemetery in Bürgel that was used by the Offenbach community until they managed to get their own cemetery.

OFFENBURG

is located about 140 km west of Stuttgart, off the A 5 motorway, on highways 3 and 33, and close to highway 28 (map 10).

* Mikveh from 14th century
* Former synagogue from 1875
* Cemetery from 1871

Jews probably began settling in Offenburg in the 13th century under Emperor Friedrich II. By the early 14th century, the community had built a remarkable mikveh.

All Offenburg Jews were probably killed during the Black Plague persecutions in 1349. After this, Jews were not allowed to settle in Offenburg until 1627, when a few letters of protection were issued to Jews from neighboring communities. The community grew until the invasion of the French in 1689, when it was once again destroyed, together with most of Offenburg. Thereafter, Jews did not settle in Offenburg again until the mid-19th century.

The Gothic mikveh was discovered around 1850. It had first served as a mikveh and then been used continuously as a well from 1349 to 1689.

The mikveh is 50 feet below ground and is reached by a long straight stone staircase under Glaserstrasse 8. The original building over the mikveh was burned down by the French in 1689 and a new house was only built in 1793. The entrance to the mikveh is on Bäckergasse, formerly Judengässchen until 1824 (although no Jews had lived here for almost five centuries), and may be visited on Sunday at 12 or Wednesday at 4:30.

The remarkable Offenburg mikveh served as a well from 1349, when the Jews were expelled, until 1689; then it was buried under the rubble of a destroyed building and only rediscovered about a hundred years ago.

In 1875, the growing new community bought the Salmen Inn in the courtyard of Lange Strasse 52 for use as its synagogue. The former main hall of the inn became the prayer room. The synagogue was renovated and changed to some degree in 1922 and devastated but not destroyed during "Reichskristallnacht". Today it is the storeroom of an appliance store.

There are still three tall windows on the second floor which are visible from the parking alley around the corner. There is also a small commemorative tablet to Offenburg's Jewish community on the refrigerator-lined staircase leading up to the former prayer room of the synagogue.

Offenburg's Jewish cemetery, opened in 1871, is located in the rear of the Christian cemetery on Friedenstrasse/Hansjakobstrasse, behind the school.

There are stones from an older cemetery (in use until 1813 and destroyed in 1836) along one wall. There is a memorial to 72 victims of the Nazis from eight nations and a memorial to Red Army soldiers. There are also many flat grave markers without a name or date.

PFUNGSTADT

is located about 50 km south of Frankfurt, between the A 5 and the A 67 and on highway 426 (map 8).

* Former synagogue from 1820
* Commemorative tablet for Jewish Institute for Learning and Education

206

The first known documentary evidence of Jews in Pfungstadt is from 1571 and, as so often, deals with the taxes that "the Jew at Pfungstadt" had to pay to the local ruler.

Around 1820 the Pfungstadt Jewish community had about 120 members and built a comparatively small synagogue. Due to the industrialization of Pfungstadt, the community grew to 236 members in 1871, which meant the synagogue had to be enlarged. However, many Pfungstadt Jews then moved to larger cities (as did many other small-town Jews all over Germany) and the community shrank to 91 in 1910. Probably more than eighteen of the Jews still living in Pfungstadt in 1938 were killed in German camps in the 1940's.

The synagogue was not destroyed, but devastated during "Reichskristallnacht" in November 1938. It was later used as a warehouse. After 1945, it was converted into apartments and later served as housing for foreign workers. Then the city bought the building, and in 1995 plans were being developed to restore it for use as a cultural center.

Visits are possible by applying to the city administration. The former synagogue stands at Hillgasse 8 (however, Hillgasse is really two parallel streets, and the synagogue is located on the eastern or, if you enter from Eberstädter Strasse, the left-hand branch of Hillgasse). There is a commemorative tablet, and the door leading to the women's gallery still remains.

The former Pfungstadt synagogue still retains the arched windows of the women's gallery.

The Jewish Institute for Learning and Education, a modern secular Jewish school, was founded in 1857 and contributed to the size of the Pfungstadt community. The address was Mainstrasse 6.

Chaim Weizmann, who went on to become the first president of Israel, was a teacher here while studying in Darmstadt; however, the assimilation-minded management of the school and the Zionist young teacher clashed and Dr. Weizmann did not have good memories of Pfungstadt. In 1907 the institute was closed again since by then there was little demand for a secular Jewish school. Today, a commemorative tablet reminds us about this important institution. The building itself has been torn down.

The Pfungstadt community buried its dead in the old and large cemetery of Alsbach an der Bergstrasse (see under Auerbach).

The "Reichskristallnacht" pogrom bypassed the former synagogue, but the building was badly damaged in 1939 and could not be used as a church until 1947. The church still leaves a synagogal impression in spite of the Christian symbols displayed today.

The location close to the lake indicates the former presence of a mikveh. The interior still displays a neo-Classicist Torah shrine with columns and a triangular gable, which serves as a frame for the altar today.

The former synagogue is located at Strandstrasse 10. Visits are possible after contacting the Catholic priest.

The Jewish cemetery on Klüschenberg was first used during the last years of the 18th century. It was mostly destroyed by the Nazi mobs, but restored as much as possible after 1945. It is maintained by the city of Plau and looks well kept.

PLAU

is located about 140 km northwest of Berlin, on highways 103 and 191 and on the Plau lake (map 2).

* Former 19th century synagogue, now a Catholic church
* Late 18th century cemetery

The former synagogue of Plau, a mighty neo-Baroque building from the 19th century, was sold in 1920 after the Jewish community dissolved and has served as a Catholic church since 1921.

POLCH

is located about 140 km west of Frankfurt or about 100 km south of Köln, off the A 48 (map 4, 8).

* Former synagogue from 1877

Although the synagogue, built in 1877, was damaged by arson during the 1938 "Reichskristallnacht", it was not destroyed. It has been restored and is now used for exhibitions.

The former synagogue, which is very small and simple, was built from the

Simple and rural, built in a conservative Neo-Romanesque style with a few hints of Gothic, the small former synagogue of Polch has survived the Third Reich.

local volcanic stone like the other buildings in the neighborhood. It was built in a simple neo-Gothic style which is rather unusual for the period because in the 19th century neo-Gothic (or Italian neo-Baroque, for that matter) was thought suitable only for Catholic churches, while synagogues were usually built either in a neo-Romanesque or in a Protestant Baroque or in a Moorish (neo-Oriental) style.

The former synagogue is located at Ostergasse 11 and may be visited during July and August, Tuesday-Sunday from 2:30-5; or, by getting the key from city hall at other times. In 1988,

a memorial to the Polch victims of the Nazi years was being planned for the former synagogue.

PRETZFELD

is located about 50 km north of Nürnberg, off highway 470 south of Ebermannstadt (map 9).

* 14th or 15th century mikveh
* Cemetery from 1632

Jews are first documented here in the early 14th century. From then to the mid-19th century there was a Jewish community at Pretzfeld, then emigration and the move to larger towns led to its dissolution.

The mikveh is from the 14th or 15th century. It is about four meters deep, and chiselled into the local limestone rock. A winding staircase leads down to the basin where the clear "living water" still flows. The mikveh is behind Am Schlossberg 5. In 1994 it was not possible to visit the mikveh because of the risk of it collapsing; however, the house next to the mikveh is to be renovated and the mikveh will be renovated, too. The synagogue from 1626 stood next to the mikveh, it was used until the dissolution of the community in 1876 when it was sold and torn down in about 1900. The 1826 school and apartment of the teacher and cantor also stood here.

The cemetery, also serving several other communities in the area, was probably first used in 1632 and lies on Judenberg, about two km northeast of the village.

RAVENSBRÜCK

is located about 80 km north of Berlin, off highway 96, close to Fürstenberg (map 2).

* Concentration camp memorial

The SS founded a camp for women here in 1939. The inmates had been arrested for political, racial, religious or other reasons. Between 1939 and 1945 more than 130,000 women and children, from 1941 on also 20,000 men lived and died here. About 800 children were born in the camp, very few survived.

Women also served as SS guards here, and their cruelty was no different from that of their male colleagues. The inmates had to do hard labor for German industry, estate owners nearby and SS-owned companies under the most difficult conditions.

A memorial to the thousands of women who suffered and died here stands on the grounds of the former Ravensbrück concentration camp.

In 1942 the SS doctors began using women as guinea pigs for medical experiments. When the front came closer and closer to the camp in early 1945, about 5,000 old or sick women were killed by poison, gas or shooting, the rest was driven away from the camp on a death march. Tens of thousands of women and children were killed here.

The building used by the former SS staff houses a documentation center dedicated to the events and conditions in this German camp. The concentration camp memorial is open between 8 am and 6 pm from May to September and between 9 am and 5 pm from October to April.

REGENSBURG

(formerly Ratisbon) is located on the Danube about 100 km southeast of Nürnberg or about 110 km north of München on the A 3 and A 93 (map 9, 11).

* Post-war synagogue and community center
* Regensburg museum has 19 gravestones from 16th century and fragments of the Gothic bima from the medieval synagogue
* Cathedral has depictions of Jews in different contexts
* Cemetery from 19th century

It is thought that a community already existed in Regensburg, an old free and imperial city, before 981, inhabiting Germany's first post-Roman Jewish quarter. The community escaped massacre during the First Crusade by receiving baptism in 1096; however, Emperor Henry IV permitted the Regensburg Jews who had been forced to become Christians to return to Judaism the following year.

The Regensburg community was protected by an imperial charter which was renewed by succeeding emperors or kings of Germany until the 14th century. Under this charter, Jews were allowed to trade in gold and silver and other metals as well as engage in moneylending, and were entitled to stand trial against Christians only before judges they accepted.

The wealth and stability of the community allowed it to survive almost unscathed during the Rindfleisch massacres, the Deggendorf host desecration murders, and the Black Death persecutions that destroyed so many other Jewish communities all over Germany.

The 14th and early 15th centuries brought increasing oppression from heavy taxes, restrictions on occupations permitted Jews, debt cancellations, property confiscations, and a ritual murder charge.

Upon the death of their last imperial protector, Emperor Maximilian, in 1519, the community was expelled. Gravestones from the old cemetery were used in construction or taken as trophies to villages in the neighborhood where some stones can still be seen in the walls of churches or town halls.

The synagogue was torn down and a church, the Neupfarrkirche, was built in its place. A few individual Jews were allowed to live in Regensburg from 1669 on but a synagogue could not be built until 1841.

427 Jews lived in Regensburg in 1933; 230 were deported in 1942. The synagogue from 1912 was burned down and the community center was devastated in the 1938 "Reichskristallnacht". A small community was established after 1945 and renovated the old community center. The center now includes a new synagogue as well as memorials to the former synagogue and to the victims of the Nazis. It is located at Am Brixener Hof 2.

The Regensburg museum has 19 gravestones from the cemetery destroyed in 1519 and parts of the Gothic bimah of the medieval synagogue. The museum is located at Dachauplatz 2-4, and is open Tuesday-Saturday 10-4, Sunday 10-1.

The west facade of the Regensburg cathedral shows this dance around the golden calf, together with other scenes from the Pentateuch.

The Regensburg cathedral contains a few depictions of Jews in different contexts.

The Gothic stained glass windows include a few frames showing Jews in medieval pointed hats. Outside, to the left of the main entrance there are three biblical scenes: Jews dancing around the golden calf, Moses receiving the law tablets, and Abraham about to sacrifice Isaac (the angel is telling Abraham to stop the sacrifice, and the ram to be sacrificed in Isaac's stead is caught in a bush). And, on the outside on a column in the south center to the right of the entrance, there is a badly weatherbeaten small Judensau (Jew's sow) sculpture depicting two Jews being suckled by a pig, with another Jew in a pointed hat speaking into the sow's ear.

This kind of medieval statue was once very wide-spread, erected on the outside of churches or town halls or fortification gates to insult and disparage Jews. The Regensburg Judensau is one of the very few examples still to be seen in Germany today.

The early 19th century cemetery is located at Schillerstrasse 29. Entrance is through the Stadtpark. You can reach it through the alley left of the

At the south facade of the Regensburg cathedral you can see this small, weathered Judensau (Jew's Sow): It suckles two Jews, while a third Jew speaks into the sow's ear. During the Middle Ages this defamatory theme was repeated on the outside of many churches.

Schillerstrasse gate. Follow the wall to the left past the taharah house and guardhouse. The cemetery is open at the usual times. This cemetery is remarkable because all the older stones face south instead of the usual east.

RENDSBURG

is located about 110 km north of Hamburg, between the A 7 and highway 77 and on the Baltic-North Sea canal (map 1).

* Former synagogue from 1845 with a small exhibition on the history of Jews in Schleswig-Holstein and a mikveh in the basement
* Cemetery from 1695

Jews began settling in Rendsburg in 1692. By the early 19th century, Rendsburg had one of the largest communities north of the Elbe river with 292 members.

The synagogue, built in 1845, was damaged by an SA bomb on "Reichskristallnacht". The building was then used for smoking fish, and the richly ornamented entrance hall was converted into a garage.

The city bought the former synagogue, now called the Dr. Bamberger House, in the early 1980's, restored it, and set up a small exhibition on the history of the Jews in Schleswig-Holstein in the basement which also includes a mikveh. The exhibition bears the name of the last Rendsburg

The Rendsburg synagogue became a factory for smoked fish after the Jewish community was destroyed. Today it houses the Jewish museum and a cultural center.

parnas, or community president, Julius Magnus. After he had been forced to dissolve the Jewish community by the Nazi authorities, and after he and his wife had received their deportation papers, they both committed suicide.

The exhibition includes photographs and documents from many communities in Schleswig-Holstein as well as a few ritual objects. The Dr. Bamberger-Haus is located on Prinzessinstrasse 8-10 and the museum is open Tuesday-Saturday from 11-1 and 3-6; Sunday 2-6.

The cemetery, opened in 1695, is located in Westerrönfeld, south of the Eider river and a little to the east of the exit from the street tunnel under the Eider. The remaining stones are mostly from the 19th and early 20th centuries. Some of the older stones are richly ornamented. The cemetery is open at the usual times.

REXINGEN

is located about 60 km southwest of Stuttgart off highway 14 (map 10).

* Former synagogue from 1838
* Cemetery from 1760

Rexingen was settled by Jews fleeing the Chmelniecki massacres in Poland in 1650. They established a synagogue in 1710 and bought land for a cemetery in 1760. Emancipation in the 19th century allowed them to own and work land as well as be horse

The former prayer room of the Rendsburg synagogue serves as an exhibition hall today. The former women's gallery can be seen at the far end of the room.

214

and cattle dealers, merchants, bakers, butchers, and innkeepers. By the mid-19th century, Jews made up about one third of the population of Rexingen.

Due to emigration and moving to larger towns and cities, the community declined to 262 members by 1933, many of whom emigrated to Palestine in 1938, where a group of 35 Rexingen Jews founded Shavei Zion near Nahariyyah. 126 Rexingen Jews were deported and only three survived the German camps.

During "Reichskristallnacht" the interior of the synagogue, built in 1838 in the Classicist style, was heavily damaged. The building is now a Protestant church.

There is an inscription in Hebrew and German (This is none other than the house of God, and this is the gate of heaven) and a memorial to the victims of the Nazi years over the entrance door. The interior has been changed completely. The former synagogue is located at Freudenstädter Strasse 16.

The cemetery, opened in 1760, is large and located up the side of a hill in a forest on Kirchstrasse. It is signposted. There are several gravestones with the crown of the good name, and some stones are very old. There is a memorial to the victims of the Nazi years in the newer section. The key is available from the mayor's office in Rexingen city hall.

The former Rexingen synagogue is a church today. There is a tablet with a Hebrew inscription over the entrance; the German translation has been added by the Christian community.

RIMBACH

is located about 70 km south of Frankfurt on highway 38 close to highway 460 (map 8, 10).

* Former synagogue from 1840
* Cemetery from 1845

Jews began settling in Rimbach in the early 18th century under the protection of the counts of Erbach. In 1806, the community came under the rule of the rather liberal-minded grand dukes of Hesse. Thereafter, the community grew rapidly. The Jews of Rimbach mostly worked as cattle dealers and merchants.

Around 1774, the community built a school which also served as the synagogue at Brunnengasse 6. However,

215

with the increase in population in the early 19th century, a new synagogue was built in 1840. It was consecrated by Rabbi Seckel Löb Wormser, the Baal Schem from Michelstadt.

The community began declining in the latter half of the 19th century due to emigration and the opportunities offered by larger cities. This decline accelerated in the 1930s due to the rise of anti-Semitism. Ten Rimbach Jews were killed in the German camps.

Although the furniture, books, and ritual objects of the synagogue were destroyed on "Reichskristallnacht" in November 1938, the village priest prevented the destruction of the synagogue itself. The former synagogue was used as a storehouse and bus

The former synagogue of the Rimbach Jews became a Catholic church after the end of the Nazi reign.

garage and was later converted to a Catholic church which replaced the Torah ark with an entrance, changed all the windows and added a steeple.

The church has set up a commemorative plaque as well as an inscription in Hebrew over the door (the beginning of Sh'ma Israel: Hear, O Israel! The Lord our God is one Lord) in memory of Rimbach's Jewish community. The former synagogue is located at Schlossgasse 5 at the corner of Heinzenwiesenweg.

Until 1845, the community buried its dead in Birkenau, a two hour march away. However, in 1845 the community established its own cemetery up the hill on Zotzenbacher Weg. Take the right fork after the last house. Although the cemetery is surrounded by a stone wall, the gate is unlocked and the cemetery has been disturbed repeatedly.

In 1988, the city council published a book on the History of Rimbach Jews in memory of its former Jewish community.

RÖDELSEE

is located about 80 km northwest of Nürnberg, about 5 km east of Kitzingen, between the A 3 and A 7 and highways 8 and 286 (map 8, 9).

* Cemetery from 1563

The synagogue, probably built before 1646, was sold in 1938 and either torn down or completely altered in renovation after 1945. There is no commemorative plaque.

It is thought that part of the large cemetery existed before 1432; however, it is documented as being established in 1563. Over the centuries it served twelve communities in the neighborhood.

The oldest stones date from the 16th century, with inscriptions only in Hebrew and without much ornamentation. Later stones dating from the Renaissance and Baroque periods are richly ornamented with crowns, pitchers, palms, fish, lions, shofars for cantor's graves, bread for farmers, grapes for vintners, and trees as a symbol of life. There is a memorial to the Jewish soldiers who died for their country in WWI and a memorial to the victims of the Nazi years. The cemetery includes a taharah house and is surrounded by a stone wall.

This very impressive cemetery is located to the south of town close to the old road to Iphofen and contains about 2,500 stones. To get there, drive out Alte Iphöfer Strasse and keep left at the fork with the stone cross. Take the first asphalt road to the right. The cemetery is visible from the road. The key is available from city hall or from the cemetery caretaker who lives at Bachgasse 14.

ROTHENBURG OB DER TAUBER

is located about 80 km west of Nürnberg, off the A 7 and on highway 25 (map 8, 9, 10).

* Former Jewish dance hall from around 1400
* 13th and 14th century gravestones, commemorative plaque
* Mikveh from 1409
* Cemetery from late 19th century

Jews began settling in Rothenburg in the late 12th and early 13th centuries.

The huge old cemetery of Rödelsee lies on a low hill overlooking the village.

217

In the mid-13th century, the community became an important center of German Jewish religious life and learning when the spiritual leader of the German Jews, Rabbi Meir ben Baruch, known as the Light of the Exile, settled here. However, with the increase of taxes and other forms of persecution introduced and expanded by Emperor Rudolph of Habsburg in 1286, Rabbi Meir, along with many other Jews throughout the Holy Roman Empire, left his home and tried to make his way to the Holy Land.

Unfortunately, Rabbi Meir was captured by imperial troops and held for a huge ransom for seven years. He refused to allow the ransom to be paid and died in prison; after his death, his corpse was held for an additional 15 years without burial and ransom was demanded from the German Jews. Eventually a Frankfurt Jew, Alexander ben Solomon Wimpfen, paid the ransom. He had only one condition: that upon his own death he would be buried next to Rabbi Meir. His wish was granted. Today both men lie side by side in the Worms cemetery, and their graves are visited often.

Both the Rindfleisch pogroms of the 13th century and the Black Death persecutions of the 14th centuries were particularly severe for the Jews living in Rothenburg. Conflicts between the emperor, local princes, church officials, and municipal authorities for control over Jewish revenues increased in the 15th century and set the stage for the full and final expulsion of all Jews in the area

Jewish gravestones from the 13th and 14th century can be seen opposite the medieval Jewish dancing hall (Judentanzhaus) of Rothenburg.

upon the death of their protector, Emperor Maximilian, in 1519. Jews were not allowed to return to Rothenburg until 1875.

The medieval Jewish dance hall was built around 1400 and changed considerably after the 1519 expulsion. It was restored after WW II damage and can be seen at Judengasse and Galgengasse.

Set into a wall of the garden opposite the dance hall are Jewish gravestones from the 13th and 14th centuries found in the old fortifications as well as a commemorative plaque to Rabbi Meir ben Baruch of Rothenburg.

More 13th and 14th century stones, among them a memorial to the 450 Jews who were martyred by the Rindfleisch mobs in 1298, as well as a small collection of Judaica including 15th century seals and a sabbath lamp may be seen in the very interesting local Reichsstadtmuseum.

The museum is located in the Klosterhof. It is open from April-October, 10-5 and November-March, 1-4. More Jewish gravestones can be seen on several old houses and parts of the fortifications.

A mikveh from 1409 was found in the basement of Judengasse 10. Unfortunately, at the time of this writing, there is no public access.

The late 19th century cemetery was devastated and the stones destroyed during the Nazi years. In 1947, about 40 new stones were made and put on the old graves. The cemetery is located about ten meters off Würzbur-gerstrasse behind a white wall opposite the intersection of Wiesenstrasse and Parkstrasse.

ROTTWEIL

is located about 100 km southwest of Stuttgart, close to the A 81 and on highways 27 and 14 (map 10).

* Prayer room from 1861
* Cemetery from 1850

Jews first settled in Rottweil before 1315, when their quarter and synagogue are first mentioned in a document. The Black Death persecutions in 1348 decimated the community, and all Jews were expelled from Rottweil in 1500.

Only in 1806 could Jews settle in Rottweil again on a regular basis. The community reached its peak in 1880 with about 130 members, then slowly shrank until it numbered 100 in 1933. Most Rottweil Jews left the town in the following years, and at least nine were killed in German camps.

The 19th century community had several prayer rooms in rented premises. In 1861 a large room was adapted for this purpose at Kameralamtsgasse 6. During the "Reichskristallnacht" pogrom the interior was devastated and the furniture burned in front of the building.

During the next years, the room was used as a workshop, a storeroom and a lecture hall for a driving school. In 1979 it was rented by the city for use as a youth center; the young

219

people found some of the original wallpaintings from the prayer room and restored the paintings under the guidance of specialists. Today the room serves as a lecture hall for a driving school again. After contacting Mr. Benk at Kameralamtsgasse 6 the former prayer room can be visited; the Benk office was open Monday to Thursday from 5 to 7 at the time of writing. There is a commemorative plaque on the building.

The Jewish cemetery of Rottweil lies on Hofer Strasse; it was aquired by the Jewish community in 1850. The key is available from city hall.

RÜLZHEIM

is located about 130 km south of Frankfurt and about 100 km northwest of Stuttgart on highway 9 (map 8, 10).

* Former synagogue from 1833
* Cemetery from 1820

At the beginning of the 19th century the German Jews, who had up to then always used the architectural style prevailing in Germany for their synagogues (sometimes with some delays), started looking for their own style. Apart from the growing self-con-

The former Rülzheim synagogue is one of the few to be built in a Neo-Egyptian style.

220

fidence this search may have been caused by the general inability to come up with a new style; instead, architects went back to former styles and adapted them to contemporary uses.

Many architects had tried to give a visual impression of the temple in Jerusalem, and most of these reconstructions looked Egyptian. For a few years, Egyptian-style synagogues were built in Germany, but then historical awareness gained the upper hand; after all, the Egyptian era had not been a good time for the Jews, but a time of slavery and forced labor, and the feast of Passover annually celebrates the end of this era. Finally the Moorish style, reminding the viewer both of the flowering of Jewish culture in Moorish Spain and their descent from the Near East, became the "typically Jewish" style in wide use for 19th century synagogues.

The Rülzheim synagogue, however, was still built in the Egyptian style by August von Voit in 1833. Today, it is one of the very few remaining "Egyptian" synagogues in Germany.

During "Reichskristallnacht" the interior was demolished. After 1945 the Catholic Youth Organization used the building until it was renovated in 1989 and converted to a "site of history and encounter" by the Rülzheim council. The former synagogue is set back from Schultzengasse, a narrow cul-de-sac off Hauptstrasse.

Leaving Rülzheim for Herxheim, there is a cemetery from 1820 on the right hand side of the road, about 250 meters after the railroad crossing. The cemetery lies under a canopy of old trees. It is surrounded by a wooden fence, but the gate is open. The cemetery is well looked after. The oldest stones stand at the farther end of the cemetery. Some show conventional symbols like the Cohen hands raised in benediction, while others display a winged hour glass or a lion for Löw or Leeb or Leib. In the center of the cemetery there is a memorial to the dead of WW I, with a menorah turned upside down. The newer part shows signs of damage. Many stones have been broken and some are missing altogether.

SACHSENHAUSEN

is located about 30 km north of Berlin, just outside Oranienburg, on highway 273 (map 2).

* Concentration camp memorial

In 1933, after the Nazis took over the government, an old brewery building in Oranienburg was used as a concentration camp. In 1936 the camp was moved outside Oranienburg to Sachsenhausen. From 1938 on the camp served as the headquarters of the German concentration camp system and as a training site for camp management.

Until its liberation in 1945, 200,000 human beings were imprisoned here under terrible conditions. Many of the inmates were forced to work in nearby armament factories or in SS-owned enterprises. About 100,000 people died from hunger, sickness, murder or on a death march towards the Baltic sea in April 1945.

From 1945 to 1950 the camp was used as a prison camp by the Soviet military administration for the eastern part of occupied Germany. First about 50,000 Nazis, but soon also social democrats and other opponents of the emerging German Democratic Republic dictatorship were imprisoned here. Many died or were killed and were buried in mass graves in the surrounding forests.

Today, there is a memorial to the victims of the former camp and a museum with exhibits about its history.

Besides the exhibition that was already displayed in GDR-times, there are two new exhibitions, one about Jews in Sachsenhausen and an "Encyclopedia of Anti-Judaism" as well as an exhibition about the use of the camp for forgeries. There is also a large library and archive.

The camp memorial is open Tuesday to Sunday from 8 to 6 from April to September and from 8 to 4.30 from October to March.

SAFFIG

is located about 80 km southeast of Köln and 10 km south of Andernach, near the A 61 (map 4, 8).

* Former synagogue from 1858
* Cemetery between Saffig and Miesenheim

When the counts of Leyen became lords of Saffig in the 16th century, they looked for additional revenue from their possession and allowed Jews to settle there in exchange for the usual fees and extra taxes.

For a long time the Saffig Jews must have had rather hard lives, since the only professions open to them were peddling and cattle dealing. This situation changed temporarily when the Rhineland was annexed to France under Napoleon and the Jews were granted equal rights; however, the French were defeated, the Rhineland became a part of Prussia and the new rights were lost again. The Saffig Jews were given the same rights as their

The former Saffig synagogue was built in a Neo-Romanesque style, with a gable inspired by Gothic architecture. It stands in a side street.

Christian neighbors only after the German Empire was founded in 1871. At that time there were about 70 Jews in Saffig. However, since Jews could now move to larger towns and cities with better opportunities, the Saffig community started to decline. After WWI it often became very hard to get the necessary ten men together for sabbath services; the last Bar Mitzvah in Saffig was celebrated in 1923.

After the Nazis rose to power most of the younger Saffig Jews emigrated, the older ones hesitated to leave their home country. At least six Jews from Saffig were killed in German camps. The synagogue built in 1858 was badly damaged, but not destroyed on "Reichskristallnacht". After 1945, the building was used as a tool shed. In 1984 the former synagogue was de-clared an historic monument, and a year later a group of concerned citizens started the renovation of the building. It had been built from the local volcanic stone in a simple neo-Romanesque style. There is a round window with a Star of David and an inscription in Hebrew (This is the gate of the Eternal, and the just enter) over the door. The photograph does not show this since it was taken before the renovation in 1991. The ceiling shows the blue night sky with the golden stars again, and the women's gallery was also reconstructed.

The former synagogue is located at Klöppelsberg 12 and can be visited after the key is obtained from Mrs. Windheuser at von-der-Leyenstrasse 26, or from Mr. Rogatz at Andernacher Strasse 40, or from Mr. Bäuerle at Am Wasserwerk 8.

A small cemetery with about 80 stones, on the road to Miesenheim served the Jewish communities of Saffig, Miesenheim and Plaidt.

SALZGITTER

is located about 50 km southeast of Hannover on the A 39 (map 3).

* Cemeteries and memorials

Salzgitter was the site of the Hermann Göring iron and steel works in which an estimated 100,000 labor slaves, including Jews, from all over Europe were forced to work. It is not known how many thousands died here. The

There is an obelisk commemorating the Jewish labor slaves buried here, alongside other victims from most European countries. The inscriptions are in English, German and Hebrew.

memorial cemetery is located in the suburb of Lebenstedt/Jammertal on Peiner Strasse and Neissestrasse.

There are several memorials in the cemetery for the Jews, political prisoners, POWs, and other labor slaves from Austria, Belgium, Bulgaria, Czechoslovakia, England, France, Germany, Greece, Hungary, Italy, the Netherlands, Poland, Romania, Spain, USSR, and Yugoslavia, as well as a memorial to all the unknown dead. Unfortunately, there are no proper parking facilities and visitors have to park on the side of a rather busy road.

SCHLÜCHTERN

is located about 80 km northeast of Frankfurt, on highway 40 in the valley of the Kinzig river (map 5, 6, 8, 9).

* Former synagogue from 1898
* Bergwinkelmuseum has a collection of Judaica
* Cemetery from 1926, memorial to a cemetery founded before 1235 and destroyed by the Nazis

Jews had been living in Schlüchtern almost continuously from the 12th century to 1942. The oldest known Memorbuch (a book giving particulars of burials, e. g. the names, dates of

224

The imposing Neo-Romanesque former synagogue of Schlüchtern houses the library and a lecture hall today.

death and dates of burials) of the Schlüchtern Jews starts before 1235; the copy from 1694 that was preserved, however, no longer contained the burial dates any more but only the names of the dead.

The first entry that can be dated refers to the burial of 34 victims of a blood libel in Fulda in 1235.

The name of Süsskind of Trimberg, a Jewish Minnesänger who died in Schlüchtern around 1300, is also preserved in this book.

The community was very small for much of the seven centuries that it existed. It increased considerably only in the late 18th and 19th centuries, finally numbering almost 400 (about 10 % of the population) in 1907. As often happened in Germany at that time, this relatively large community also declined, to about 100 in 1938 and 26 in 1941. Almost all of the Jews remaining in Schlüchtern then were deported in 1942 and killed in the Nazi camps.

A half-timbered synagogue from before 1670 standing in a backyard became too cramped towards the end of the 19th century, and a grand new

225

synagogue was built in 1898 in the neo-Romanesque style usual for city synagogues then. The old synagogue was sold, then used as a storeroom and torn down in the 1970's. The new synagogue was not burned down because of the persistence of a fire brigade officer, but still devastated in the 1938 "Reichskristallnacht" (when the ancient burial books were destroyed, too).

The building was used as a storeroom during the war, restored for use by a DP community in 1945, and, after most of the members of the DP community left Germany, used as a textile factory until 1970 when it was bought by the city. It serves as a library, popular education site and cultural center today. The impressive building stands on the corner of Grabenstrasse and Weitzelstrasse and has a commemorative plaque.

The Bergwinkelmuseum on Schloss-Strasse 15 has a small collection of Judaica, including the surviving paroketh from the old Schlüchtern synagogue.

A cemetery from before 1235 (the one the Memorbuch mentioned above refers to) was almost completely destroyed by the Nazis. It is located on Breitenbacher Strasse opposite number 4 and has a memorial to 122 victims of the Nazi persecutions from Schlüchtern and neighboring communities. A new cemetery from 1926 is on Fuldaer Strasse.

The former Schnaittach synagogue will become part of a regional Jewish museum based in Fürth.

SCHNAITTACH

is located about 30 km northeast of Nürnberg, on the A 9 (map 9).

* Former synagogue from 1570 and a museum collection of Judaica
* Cemeteries

Although Jews were probably living in Schnaittach much earlier, the town only gained importance as a Jewish settlement when Jews expelled from other parts of Bavaria and Franconia in the 16th century moved to Schnaittach.

The Ganerben of Rothenberg (a co-operative of Franconian noblemen) permitted Jews with sufficient funds to live in Schnaittach under their protection. A synagogue may have been built in 1529 and was enlarged or maybe rebuilt in 1570. A stone plaque survives from this period.

Throughout the 18th century, when Jews were banned from the rest of Bavaria, the Jews in Schnaittach, which had been newly acquired by the dukes of Bavaria, still received letters of protection in intervals of between three and 15 years in return for the payment of fees. By the middle of the 19th century, Jews made up about 20 % of the population of Schnaittach. However, the community then declined, numbering only seven households by the 1930s.

The former rabbi's house and synagogue buildings now house the local museum, or Heimatmuseum, of Schnaittach. It includes an ark, a women's gallery with ornate iron lattice, separate doors for men and women, and part of an inscription in Hebrew over the ark.

Outside, there is a red stone with the letters for the year 330 (1570 CE) in Hebrew. In addition to the synagogue furnishings, the museum owns a collection of Judaica, including Torah scrolls and other ritual objects reputedly saved by SA men. The museum is located at Museumgasse 14-16. However, the museum is being remodelled to house part of the Central Franconian Jewish museum; the museum will open again in 1996 or 1997 and will show exhibits relating to Jewish feasts, the role of the synagogue and the life and circumstances of rural Jewish communities in the area.

The gravestones in the second oldest Jewish cemetery of Schnaittach are unusually massive.

There are three Jewish cemeteries lying close together in Schnaittach. The most recent cemetery, used from the 1890's until 1952, is down the road from the Christian cemetery at Krankenhausweg 12. A memorial to 36 Jewish gravestones destroyed by the Nazis stands here. There is a resident caretaker living in the cemetery's guardhouse.

About 20 meters down the road is the entrance to an older cemetery, from 1834, which contains about 200 large and unusually massive gravestones with Hebrew inscriptions. Due to their extraordinary thickness, none of the stones have been broken, although they are sinking into the ground and the inscriptions are weatherbeaten. These stones come from the oldest cemetery and were taken to their current location after the 1938 desecrations.

The third cemetery, which dates back to 1537, is about 20 meters down the right hand fork of the road, and on its right-hand side. It served as a burial ground for some of the Jewish communities in the area, and until 1607 Jews from Fürth were also buried here. Only one newer stone, inscribed in Hebrew, is left, the older stones were moved to the newer cemetery mentioned above after 1938. In 1993 a memorial to the desecrated cemetery was erected here. All three cemeteries are open at the usual times.

SCHÖNEBECK

is located about 150 km southwest of Berlin and about 150 km north of Erfurt, on the Elbe river and on highway 246a (map 2, 3, 5).

* Former synagogue from 1877
* Cemetery from before 1873

The former Schönebeck synagogue is a church of the Baptist community today.

Jews are first documented in Schöne-beck already in the 10th century. The first documents about a Jewish com-munity, however, have survived from 1372. The community numbered about 100 at the end of the 19th century and then declined rapidly to about 20 in 1932.

In 1877 the community built a new Moorish-style synagogue at what is now Strasse der Republik 43; its pre-decessor had been destroyed by a flood. During the 1938 "Reichskristall-nacht" the interior was devastated, the building itself survived. First it was used as a storehouse, then as an office, a museum, a furniture store and a gym.

In 1983 the building was aquired by the Baptist community and converted to a church. The cupola is crowned by a cross surrounded by four Stars of David, and the basement windows also show Stars of David. The church is called "Schalom-House", and a plaque remembers the former use of the building.

A mid-19th century cemetery lies on Dorotheenstrasse, close to Welsleber Brücke. Only nine stones remain here, the cemetery has been dese-crated repeatedly.

SCHWÄBISCH HALL

is located approximately 80 km north-east of Stuttgart, on highways 14 and 19 (map 8, 9, 10).

* Hällisch-Fränkisches Museum in-cludes a wooden synagogue interior painted in 1738 by Sussmann, a 19th century sukkah, and a Judaica collection
* Former synagogue from 1893
* Synagogue Defeated in St. Michael church
* Jewish cemetery from the early 19th century

The local Hällisch-Fränkisches Museum was still being rebuilt in 1994. After the work is finished, it is planned to exhibit the wooden interior of a synagogue painted by the 18th century synagogue artist Eliezer Sussmann who is known for his colorful painted wooden synagogues throughout Bavaria and Franconia.

This synagogue interior, painted in 1738, which comes from the village of Unterlimpurg, now a suburb of Schwä-bisch Hall, is the only surviving work of Sussmann in Germany today. (His most famous work, the Horb syna-gogue, is on permanent loan to the

This painting of the Synagogue Defeated can be found on the high altar of the church of St. Michael in Schwäbisch Hall. As usual, she is blindfolded and her spear is broken.

A brick cupola is all that can be seen above ground of the Schwedt mikveh.

Israel museum in Jerusalem.) There will also be a 19th century sukkah, a wedding canopy, and a small collection of Judaica on display.

The museum is located at Untere Herrengasse 6. Although the museum was already partly reopened in 1988, there were delays in finishing the rest and the synagogue, sukkah, and Judaica collection will not be ready until 1996 or 1997.

Opening hours at the time of this writing are Tuesday-Sunday 10-5; Wednesday 10-8.

The 1893 synagogue at Obere Herrengasse 8 was devastated on "Reichskristallnacht" in November 1938. The building itself still exists and has a commemorative plaque.

The grandiose St. Michael's church was founded in 1156 but not finished until 1718. It includes Romanesque, Gothic, and Renaissance architectural styles and stands in a commanding position over the main marketplace. Inside, there are depictions of the Church Triumphant and the Synagogue Defeated on top of the main altar. To the left of the main altar is a Gothic "sacrament house" with statues of Jesajah, Salomon, David, and an unidentified prophet.

A memorial to the Jewish victims of the Nazi years can be seen in the Jewish cemetery on Steinbacher Strasse, close to the village of Steinbach. This cemetery dates from the early 19th century. The Hessental concentration camp has a memorial on the camp wall to Jewish and other slave labor victims of the Nazi years.

SCHWEDT

is located about 100 km northwest of Berlin, on highway 2 and the Oder river (map 2).

* Ritual bath
* Former synagogue and school from 1788
* 17th century cemetery
* Commemorative plaque for the destroyed synagogue

In 1673 the first Jewish family settled in Schwedt. 37 families lived here in 1812, while the community had 173 members a hundred years later. In 1788 the community bought a building at what is now Jüdenstrasse 15 and converted it to a synagogue; after 1862 the building was used as a school. It still stands and is being used for offices. It may in the future house an annex of the city museum dealing with the history of the Jews in the region.

In 1862 the Jewish community built a new synagogue at Louis-Harlan-Strasse 1, close to Berlinerstrasse. This synagogue was devastated during "Reichskristallnacht", the building was later destroyed in the war. There is a commemorative plaque next to the former entrance gate.

A few years after the synagogue was completed, a ritual bath was built next to the synagogue. The small brick cupola of the ritual bath can be seen in a garden in Gartenstrasse opposite Karlsplatz. Visits are possible only after contacting Dr. Libert at the Stadt-museum (city museum) in Schwedt.

The Schwedt Jewish cemetery was started in the 17th century. It is located on Helbigstrasse on the corner of Schulweg, surrounded by a wall and well-maintained. This cemetery can also be visited after contacting Dr. Libert at the Stadtmuseum.

SCHWERIN

is located about 130 km east of Hamburg, on highways 104 and 106 (map 1, 2).

* Rabbi's house from 1840
* Community center
* Cemetery from 1717
* Memorial for synagogue destroyed in 1938

Most sites that remind one about Schwerin's Jewish past are situated close together in the center. In Grosser Moor 12 the former rabbi's house still stands. Around the corner, at Schlachterstrasse 3-5, there are two houses that once served as the Jewish school and ritual bath, and after 1945 housed the community center, Jewish organizations, a memorial room and the prayer room. In the backyard of these houses there is a memorial stone to the synagogue that stood here from 1819 until 1938, when it was first devastated on "Reichskristall-nacht" and then torn down at the expense of the Jewish community.

The land for the Jewish cemetery of Schwerin was bought in 1717 and lies on Am Heidensee, a side street of Bornhöved-Strasse. A road splits the cemetery in two, the smaller part still has some 19th and 20th century stones; other stones that were brought here from the larger part that was razed by the Nazis form three semi-circles. There is a memorial to the destroyed cemetery in the center, and two memorials to the Schwerin Jews killed in German camps stand at its sides. The larger part has no remaining stones, but there is a taharah house that also serves as a residence for the caretaker.

The former residence of the rabbi of the Schwerin Jews lies close to the center of the old city.

SOBERNHEIM

is located about 90 km southwest of Frankfurt on highway 41 (map 8).

* Former synagogue from 1859
* Late 18th century cemetery

The Sobernheim synagogue was built in 1859 and devastated during "Reichskristallnacht". Today the building serves as a storehouse for a supermarket. There is still a Hebrew inscription over the entrance gate which is visible in the small shed attached to the west facade of the former synagogue. During business hours it is possible to visit the former synagogue after applying to the storehouse keeper. There is a small commemorative plaque.

The cemetery of Sobernheim was started in the late 18th century. The large cemetery that served several communities in the area lies on Domberg.

Fork lifts transport cases of soft drinks through the doors of the former Sobernheim synagogue.

SONTRA

is located approximately 50 km southeast of Kassel, close to highway 27 (map 5, 6).

* Former synagogue from 1721
* School from early 20th century
* Two cemeteries

Jews are mentioned in Sontra as early as 1367. However, it was only in 1539 that a few Jewish families permanently settled here after Count Philipp of Hesse granted letters of protection to Jews wanting to settle in Sontra, subject, of course, to payment of certain fees and compliance to his newly issued regulations governing what they could or could not do.

In the mid-17th century, the community was augmented by Jews expelled from the larger cities in the area and the population stabilized at around 70 until the community was granted civil rights in 1821.

Up to then, in addition to paying the fees and taxes their Christian neighbors paid, they also paid entrance fees, annual renewal fees and exit fees as well as fees for maintaining the count's mint, fees for the count's annual hunt, and burial fees.

There were the usual tensions between Jewish and Christian bakers and butchers, as documented by the fines the Jews had to pay for working on Sundays and selling without a license. Other fines had to be paid for riding a horse on Good Friday and similar misdemeanors. For the most part, however, the Jewish and Christian communities lived together in peace. In 1861, a local gymnastics club was founded (which elsewhere was very German, very anti-foreign, very anti-Catholic, and extremely anti-Jewish) - in Sontra the gymnastics club elected a Jew for president. And even in the 1930s, the local Nazi leader is supposed to have regularly attended his weekly card group despite the fact that it was partly Jewish.

Nevertheless, all this did not change the fate of the Sontra Jews - several Jewish apartments were destroyed during "Reichskristallnacht" in 1938. Of the 76 Jews living in Sontra in 1933, at least 19 were killed in German camps.

In 1721, the Jewish community built a school which was later converted into a synagogue since it was forbidden to build new synagogues. The synagogue, which was not destroyed in 1938, has been converted into a private home and is located at Fuldaer Strasse 10.

A small and simple mikveh has recently been uncovered nearby at Niederstadt 1, but is also part of a private home and may not be visited. A new school was built at the beginning of the 20th century at Schulgasse 2. This building has also survived the Nazi years and is now a private home.

A cemetery was opened in 1710 and enlarged in 1859 on Quesselberg which is just above the Heinrich-Schneider-Stadion. To get there, either go through the sport grounds past the clubhouse, up the very steep forest path, and turn right at the level path; or go to the opposite end of Pestalozzi-strasse and take the forest path to the right after about 300 meters. The cemetery is on the side of a very steep hill and has about 150 stones. The cemetery is locked but you may get the key from city hall.

A second cemetery was opened in 1921 on what is now part of the school grounds. This easily accessible cemetery was almost completely destroyed by the Nazis. Only seven stones remain.

SPEYER

is located on the Rhine about 110 km south of Frankfurt, between A 61 and highway 9 (map 8, 10).

* 12th century mikveh
* Small exhibition of Judaica in Historisches Museum der Pfalz
* Late 19th century cemetery

Jewish presence in Speyer is documented in the early 11th century. In 1084, large numbers of Jews seeking refuge from persecution in Mainz were invited to settle in Speyer by Bishop Rüdiger who stated in the privilege he gave the new community that this act would "increase the honor of the town a thousand fold."

The bishop granted the Jews rights and privileges such as unrestricted trade, judgment by a Jewish judge, the archisynagogos (also called the Jew's bishop) in disputes between Jews, freedom from duties or tolls upon entering or leaving the city, the right to sell ritually unclean meat to Christians as well as the right to hire Christian servants. These rights were eventually expanded by Emperor Henry IV in 1090.

In 1096 camp followers of the crusaders led by Emicho of Leiningen killed several members of the Speyer community, but the mass murders that occured in other Rhenish towns were avoided due to the bishop's efforts to protect his Jews.

While the next hundred years were difficult, the Speyer community still prospered and became important as a center for Torah study producing many great scholars. The communities of Speyer, Worms and Mainz formed an alliance known as the "Shum" (named after the Hebrew initials of the three towns) which was considered an authority in religious matters all over Germany. All of this was destroyed by the Black Death persecutions in 1349.

Jews settled in Speyer again a few years after this pogrom; however, the new community never regained the position its predecessor had enjoyed before its destruction in 1349. Throughout the 14th and 15th centuries, the Speyer Jews were expelled repeatedly. During periods when their presence was tolerated, they suffered under severe restrictions as to what they could and could not do. In 1534 the Jews were again expelled from Speyer and until the 19th century only a few individual families lived in Speyer.

It was not until 1820 that a new community was founded. In the early 1930's, as a result of the increase of anti-Semitism, Jews from Speyer began to move to larger cities and to emigrate, thus substantially reducing the Jewish population. Of the 77 Jews living in Speyer in 1939, 51 were deported to Gurs in 1940. All but fifteen were killed in the German camps where they were taken in 1942. No community exists today.

A synagogue was first built in 1096, destroyed by the mob following the crusaders, rebuilt and destroyed again in 1195. In 1534 it was abandoned along with the women's synagogue which had been built next to it in 1354. In 1899, the larger part of the ruined buildings was torn down, the west walls were incorporated into a newly built house. Only the east walls and two Romanesque windows remain today of the old synagogues. The outlines of the niche for the Torah ark can still be detected in its weathered stones.

The entrance to the early 12th century Romanesque mikveh lies beneath a small entrance building in a garden east of the synagogue wall. A memorial plaque to the victims of the Nazi years is in the wall opposite the mikveh entrance.

The entrance, formerly at ground level, is now reached by walking down a newly constructed flight of stairs. Once inside, however, the present turns into the medieval past. You continue down into the waiting room with its stone benches polished by centuries of use, down to its little balcony with round arches overlooking the bath, and down until you reach the bath at a depth of ten meters.

The mikveh is located a few blocks from the Romanesque cathedral off Maximilianstrasse on Judenbadgasse, which can be reached through Kleine Pfaffengasse and Judengasse. It is thought that the builders of the cathedral also built the mikveh. As you walk towards the cathedral on Maximilianstrasse, you will see a small sign "Judenbad" on the right-hand side of the street with an arrow directing you to the mikveh. The mikveh is open April-October 10-12 and 2-5. During the winter months, you can get the key by contacting the Verkehrsamt (Tourist Office), Maximilianstrasse 11, in advance of your visit. A guided tour is offered by the Historisches Museum der Pfalz as well as by the Verkehrsamt (tourist office) Speyer and the Verkehrsverband (tourist association) Speyer.

Living water still flows slowly through the basin of the ancient mikveh of Speyer.

Romanesque windows look down upon the basin of the ritual bath in Speyer.

The Historisches Museum der Pfalz shows a permanent exhibition about the medieval Jewish history of the town, among other things Jewish gravestones from the 12th to the 15th centuries, two small Romanesque windows from the early 12th century synagogue, a model of the 12th century mikveh, the front of an 18th century Torah ark from Alsenz (where the synagogue building still stands), the Lingenfeld treasure hidden by a Jew in 1349, objects found in the remains of the medieval Jewry, and about 40 ritual objects.

Guided tours in English are available and include the synagogue ruins and mikveh. The museum is located on Domplatz and is open Tuesday to Sunday from 10 to 6, Wednesday to 8.

A late 19th century Jewish cemetery was established as part of the city cemetery on Auestrasse and Wormser Landstrasse. Follow the path to the left after the entrance.

Another cemetery dating from the early 19th century was destroyed in 1940.

A memorial to the synagogue destroyed in the 1938 "Reichskristallnacht" is in the back of a department store on Heydenreich Strasse.

STADTALLENDORF

is located about 90 km southwest of Kassel, about 80 km north of Frankfurt, on highway 454 (map 4, 5, 6).

* Former synagogue from before 1850
* Cemetery

* Münchmühle Slave Labor Camp memorial

The half-timbered former synagogue from before 1850 at Mittelstrasse 16 is now a private home. Only the two doors - on the ground floor for the men, halfway up to the first floor for the women - are reminiscent of its former use.

A cemetery about 200 meters up Läuserweg on the left hand side includes a memorial, established in 1985, to the victims of the Nazi years. There is also a memorial to 123 Russian POW's buried here.

Outside of town, the former Münchmühle slave labor camp, which was an outpost of the infamous Buchenwald camp, has a memorial, establish-

The small Staudernheim synagogue has been used as a garage and will become a cultural center.

236

ed in 1988, to a thousand Jewish women from Hungary who were forced to work in the Allendorf ammunition factory. The memorial is set in what remains of the camp kitchen and washroom and is surrounded by high barbed wire fences. You can get there by taking highway 454 west from the Stadtallendorf exit and turning off where it is signposted "Gedenkstätte Münchmühle".

STAUDERNHEIM

is located about 90 km southwest of Frankfurt, off highway 41 (map 8).

* Former synagogue from 1896
* Late 19th century cemetery

Jews first settled in Staudernheim around 1700. There were about 85 Jews in Staudernheim around the middle of the 19th century, then the community declined to 21 in 1933. At least eight Staudernheim Jews were killed in German camps, one died in 1934 after having been attacked by a Nazi mob.

The small community built a neo-Romanesque synagogue at Am Wolfsgang 3. After a few years the Staudernheim community did not have the ten men necessary for service and the synagogue was used on special occasions only. During "Reichskristallnacht" the synagogue was devastated and the building was sold to the village administration in 1943. After 1945 the former synagogue was given back to the Jewish community of Bad Kreuznach, which sold it to the village again - this time without any pressure and at a realistic price. Finally the building was sold to a private person who used it as a storeroom and a garage. In 1994 an association for the creation of a museum which had been founded in 1989 bought the building to renovate it and convert it to a Jewish museum and a cultural center. At the time of this writing, the building still stands empty. The Hebrew inscriptions over the gable and over the entrance are still there, but the facade has been partly destroyed by the addition of a driveway. The small cemetery of Staudernheim was started before 1880.

STERNBERG

is located about 160 km east of Hamburg, on highways 104 and 192 (map 1, 2).

* Objects from a 1492 host desecration trial
* Former cemetery from 1824

Jews settled in the dukedom of Mecklenburg from about 1250 on. The small Sternberg community was accused of a host desecration in 1492, the year when Columbus arrived in America and the year that is usually meant to have marked the end of the dark Middle Ages and the beginning of the enlightened Modern Era. After what can best be described as a show trial, 27 Jews from Sternberg were burned alive on Judenberg outside the town.

All Jews were expelled from Mecklenburg as a result of this verdict. The fact that the dukes of Mecklenburg got rid of their main creditors with this trial may or may not have influenced their judgment.

In 1492, Jews from Sternberg were accused of having desecrated hosts on this table. The woodcarving below shows them being burned on the stake.

The magnificent Gothic Stadtkirche displays the table where the Sternberg Jews are supposed to have desecrated the hosts as well as a wooden sculpture depicting the burning of the Jews.

Today these relics, housed in a side chapel to the right of the entrance, are surrounded by a small exhibition about the roots of Christianity in Judaism.

To the left of the main altar Moses, David, Abraham and John the Baptist are depicted as representatives of Judaism and precursors of Christianity opposite Martin Luther.

The Stadtkirche is open for service on Sundays at ten. The key can be borrowed at the parsonage to the south of the church Monday to Friday, 10 to 3.

238

A Jewish community was founded again in the late 18th century. In 1824 this community was given a plot for a cemetery at the foot of the Judenberg where its precursors had been burned in 1492.

This cemetery was destroyed during the Nazi years. Today a memorial stone stands in its stead.

STOMMELN

(part of Pulheim) is located about 20 km northwest of Köln, on highway 59 (map 4).

* Former synagogue from 1882
* Cemetery from late 19th century

The small synagogue, built in 1882, was sold before 1938. Its new owner,

The former Stommeln synagogue stands in a backyard, survived the Nazi years as a barn and serves as an exhibition hall today.

a farmer, used it as a barn. The city of Pulheim has bought the building, restored it and now uses it as a community and memorial center. The former synagogue is in the backyard of Hauptstrasse 85 in Stommeln and includes the wooden women's gallery and Torah ark niche. To visit the former synagogue, contact the culture department of city hall in Pulheim, which lies about 5 km in the direction of Köln on highway 59. Their office hours are Monday-Thursday 8-5, Friday 8-12 at the time of this writing.

The late 19th century Stommeln cemetery is located on Nagelschmiedstrasse opposite No. 15.

The Straubing synagogue was not built until 1907, notwithstanding its very conservative Neo-Romanesque style.

To get there, take the narrow footpath up Mühlenweg off highway 59 leading through the village. However, only a few stones remain in the small, well-kept cemetery which is surrounded by modern family homes.

STRAUBING

is located about 120 km northeast of München and about 140 km southeast of Nürnberg, on the Danube and between highway 8 and highway 20 (map 9, 11).

* Synagogue from 1907
* Cemetery from 1923
* Memorials

Evidence exists that Jews were living in Straubing in the 13th and 14th centuries, but the community was massacred in 1338 as a result of a host desecration libel in nearby Deggendorf.

A new community was established in the late 14th century; however, all Jews in the duchy of Straubing-Bavaria were expelled in 1439 and little mention occurs thereafter until emancipation in Bavaria in 1872.

The community which was founded after emancipation built an impressive neo-Romanesque synagogue in 1907 and opened a cemetery in 1923. Fifty Straubing Jews were killed in German camps, almost one hundred were exiled. In 1945, 700 death march survivors lived in Straubing, and almost a hundred settled there to form the post-war community.

Although devastated in the 1938 "Reichskristallnacht", the synagogue was not destroyed. It was restored in 1945 and thoroughly renovated in 1988. The synagogue complex includes a community center and a mikveh, as well as memorials to the Jewish victims of the Nazi years.

There is a large plaque on the gable of the roof with an inscription in Hebrew and a Star of David below. It is located at Wittelsbacherstrasse 2. There is also a memorial at Rosengasse 22 made from a rabbi's gravestone.

SULZBACH-ROSENBERG

is located about 60 km east of Nürnberg on highways 14 and 85 (map 9).

* Former synagogue from 1824
* Cemetery from 1668

The medieval Jewish community of Sulzbach was decimated in the 1337 Deggendorf host desecration massacres and then wiped out in the 1349 Black Plague persecutions.

Only about 300 years later a new community was founded in Sulzbach. The community of "protected Jews" was enlarged by Jews expelled from Austria in 1670. The situation of the community improved considerably after a liberalization of the ordinances governing Jewish rights and duties in 1685. In 1687, the community converted a house to a synagogue and in 1737 a proper synagogue was built.

This synagogue burned down in 1822, together with a large part of the town, and a new stately late Baroque building was built in 1824. At this time 65 Jewish families with about 330 members lived in Sulzbach. In 1835 a Jewish school that would exist for almost a hundred years was opened, and a Jewish hospital was built in the same year. Due to emigration and a move to larger cities, the Jewish population of Sulzbach declined from 1850 on, and only eight Jews were left in Sulzbach in 1933. The last Jews left Sulzbach in 1936.

Sulzbach became prominent in large parts of Europe after a printshop was founded here in 1669. Until 1851, when it closed down, many Jewish religious books were printed here, most of the time under the management of the Fränkel-Arnstein family. In particular, a mahsor, or prayer book, published again and again from 1699

Little remains of the late Baroque style of the former Sulzbach synagogue.

on, became the standard work all over southern Germany.

In 1934 the town of Sulzbach "rented" the synagogue and converted it to a local museum. In 1936 the town bought the building for an extremely low 1,000 Reichsmark. Today the former synagogue at Synagogenstrasse 9 serves as a storeroom and residence. The facade has been changed, but the arched windows on the ground floor and the original entrance door still exist. There is a plaque commemorating the former use of the building.

The cemetery from 1668 lies to the southeast of town, on the path that continues after Schiessstätte, at the edge of a forest. During fighting in 1945 parts of the cemetery were destroyed, but many old stones remain.

SULZBURG

is located about 230 km southwest of Stuttgart, east of A 5 and highway 3, between Staufen and Müllheim, at the edge of the Black Forest (map 10).

* Former synagogue from 1823 and exhibitions on Jewish themes
* Cemetery from 1550

Although the community is thought to be much older, first mention of Jews living here dates from 1537. At that time, Jews were allowed to own houses, which was rather unusual for the period. The Sulzburg Jews received limited citzenship in 1808 and full civil rights in 1862.

In 1864, Jews made up a third of Sulzburg's population which was then about 1,300. They were occupied

The former Sulzburg synagogue was restored by a very active group of concerned citizens and today serves as a venue for cultural events with a Jewish theme.

primarily as wine and cattle dealers, bakers, artisans, and innkeepers.

When restrictions against Jews living in cities were lifted after the middle of the 19th century, the community started to decline. By 1940, only 30 Jews remained and most of them were deported to Gurs. Many later died in German death camps.

The synagogue was built in 1823 and is quite a beautiful structure with its arched and circular windows, the law tablets over the portico and two columns to its sides. The interior is neo-Baroque with elaborate capitals atop its columns and stars on the vaulted, dark blue ceiling. It was desecrated in the 1938 "Reichskristallnacht", but not destroyed. Freiburg University used it as a book storehouse for a while but it was later sold and used for different purposes until the city bought it in 1977 and restored it. The city, with the support of a very active group of citizens, currently uses it for exhibitions on Jewish themes; it may become a museum of Markgraf life at a time when Jews and Christians lived peacefully together.

A mikveh to the side of the synagogue has not yet been renovated. The synagogue is on Mühlbachgasse which is also the street where the former Jewish school and community center, now apartment buildings, were located. The key to the former synagogue is available from city hall. A very active group of citizens helps the city organize readings and exhibitions.

The Jewish cemetery of Sulzburg was established around 1550. It is located in a Black Forest valley east of town. The tall, dark trees of the forest shade the old cemetery which lies on a steep hillside. Stairs lead up from the gate with its gilded Stars of David through the terraced cemetery. The gravestones, many of which are very old, are made from local stone with rounded tops and beautiful Hebrew lettering. German lettering is on some of the 19th century stones as well. The cemetery includes a memorial to the Sulzburg victims of the Nazis and lists their names.

To get there, follow the "Campingplatz" signs pointing east on Hauptstrasse and Badstrasse. As you drive out of town, you will see the Schwarzwald-Gasthof (Black Forest Inn) on the left and a bridge and the entrance to a camping ground on the right. The entrance to the cemetery is straight through the middle of the camping ground.

TRIER

is located 200 km west of Frankfurt or 180 km south of Köln, close to the border with Luxemburg and on the A1 and highways 51, 52, and 268 (map 8).

* The Rheinische Landesmuseum has medieval Jewish gravestones and a small collection of Judaica
* Houses in medieval Jewry
* City archives collection of documents on Trier Jews
* Karl Marx museum
* Dom- und Diözesanmuseum displays 13th century statue of Synagogue Defeated
* Cemeteries

Archaeological finds in this ancient Roman city establish the presence of Jews here as early as the 4th or 5th century C.E. through the discovery of a clay lamp and lead seals with menorah patterns. Written documents describing the death of Archbishop Eberhard, who tried to force baptism on the Jews, establish that a Jewish community of some size existed in 1066. The archbishop is reported to have died at the altar as he was blessing the baptismal water for the forced baptism of the Jewish community. Accusations of witchcraft (involving a baptized wax effigy of the archbishop) were levied at the Jews as a result of this sudden death.

In 1096, Trier Jews were forced to choose between suicide, baptism, or death at the hands of camp followers of the crusaders. The new converts, however, were given permission to return to their fathers' religion the following year.

The community prospered throughout the 13th century, and its members were occupied primarily as merchants, moneylenders, apothecaries, and doctors. In return for the payment of high taxes to the archbishop, the "Jew's bishop" or parnas received one of the archbishop's coats each year as a symbol of the protection the archbishop provided. In addition to these taxes, the Jews had to pay an annual minting surtax of 12.5 %, which amounted to about four kilos of silver, as well as twelve kilos of pepper, a luxury good worth its weight in gold at the time.

The beginning of the 14th century held continued promise for Trier's Jews as some of them were entrusted with the administration of Archbishop Balduin's finances. By this time the community numbered 50 families with about 300 individuals. The community owned two synagogues, a community center, a mikveh, and a cemetery, and the Jews of Trier could own the houses they lived in. This community ended with the Black Death persecutions in 1349. Only a few Jews lived in Trier after this date, but they were also expelled in 1418.

A few Jews were allowed to return to Trier in the 16th century. The Thirty Years War and the invasion by the French in the 17th century were difficult for Jews and Christians alike. Conditions improved somewhat in the 18th century although there was increased poverty. The community enjoyed a brief period of full civil rights with the arrival of troops of the new French republic in the late 18th century, but these rights were taken away again after Napoleon's defeat. It wasn't until 1871 that the Jews in Trier enjoyed the full rights of citizenship. Of the 800 Jews living in Trier in 1933, almost 400 went into exile. The rest were deported and most of them were killed in German camps.

Very little remains today to tell the story of Trier's long Jewish past. One of the reminders, however, is the wide-spread name of Dreyfuss, which is derived from the French word for Trier, Treves.

A lamp and some lead seals with pictures of menorahs from Roman times are on exhibit in the Rheinische Landesmuseum. There you will also find medieval Jewish gravestones and a small collection of religious and secular objects. The museum is located at Weimarer Allee 1 and is open Monday-Friday 9:30-4; Saturday 9:30-2; Sunday 9-1.

Some old houses still stand in the medieval Jewry. Although Christians have been living in them for more than 600 years now, medieval Jews once lived in the houses on Judengasse, Stockstrasse, Stockplatz, and Jacobsgasse.

A gate to the medieval Jewry is preserved at the corner of Judengasse and Hauptmarkt. Judengasse 2, from 1311, is thought to be the oldest house once belonging to Jews in Germany today. It is located at the left immediately behind the gate.

The city archives at Weberbach 25 maintain a collection of documents about the history of Jews in Trier, including the persecution of the Trier Jews by the Nazis, on microfilm. The library is open Monday-Friday 10-1 and 2-5.

A memorial marks the site where the synagogue, from 1859, once stood. It was damaged in the 1938 "Reichskristallnacht", ruined by bombs in 1944 and torn down in 1949. The memorial is located on Metzelstrasse and Zuckerbergstrasse facing An der alten Synagogue.

A new synagogue, from 1957, is located on Kaiserstrasse/Hindenburgstrasse. A memorial plaque to the Jewish soldiers who died for Germany in WWI was salvaged from the ruins of the Zuckerberg synagogue and can be seen here.

Trier's most famous son, Karl Marx, was born in 1818 in a house at Brückenstrasse 10. His father, a lawyer from an old rabbinical family, became a Protestant shortly after his son's birth in order to secure his career. The house where Marx was born has been converted to a museum. Opening hours are Monday 1-6, Tuesday-Sunday 10-1 and 3-6.

The very rich and very grand Dom- und Diözesanmuseum (Cathedral- and Bishop's museum) displays 13th century stone statues of the Synagogue Defeated and the Church Triumphant taken from the west facade of Our Lady's Church (where copies stand now). The museum is open Monday-Saturday 9-1 and 2-5, Sunday and holidays 1-5.

A Jewish cemetery at Weidegasse 11 on the corner of Gilbertstrasse dates from the mid-17th century and was

This Roman clay lamp from Trier, showing a seven-armed candelabrum, is the oldest witness of Jewish presence in what is Germany today.

used until 1922. The cemetery is surrounded by a high wall and is locked. You may get the key from Mr. Voremberg (telephone 33 295).

A new Jewish cemetery was consecrated in 1920 and is located within the new city cemetery, to the right of the entrance, on Herzogenbuscherstrasse. There are two memorials to the Jews of Trier who died at the hands of the Nazis.

TÜCHERSFELD

is located about 60 km northeast of Nürnberg, on highway 470 (map 9).

* Former synagogue from 18th century
* Small exhibition of Judaica in the Fränkische Schweiz Museum

The unique rock formations and low mountains in this remote area have gained it a reputation of being the Fränkische Schweiz (Franconian Switzerland). Located off the main highways and byways of the more populated areas of Germany, poor Jewish communities here lived alongside their equally poor Christian neighbors in relative peace for many centuries untroubled by the persecutions and expulsions occurring in other German areas.

It is thought that local barons invited Jews to settle here sometime in the 13th and 14th centuries after they had been expelled from larger towns. None of these early communities, however, survived for very long. It was not until about 1700 that new communities were founded which lasted about 200 years. Most of the poor Jewish communities in the area ceased to exist around 1900 after migration to larger cities with better living conditions and improved pos-

In the 18th century the small rural Jewish community of Tüchersfeld established its synagogue in the former castle. Today the synagogue is part of the Museum of the Fränkische Schweiz.

246

sibilities had become possible following emancipation.

The last Tüchersfeld community was founded around 1715. In 1758, after a fire destroyed their synagogue and their houses in the village, the Jewish community of Tüchersfeld was given permission to settle in the abandoned and half ruined lower castle on top of a large rock formation which looks out over the valley below. One of the rooms of this structure was adapted as a synagogue.

Originally the room the Tüchersfeld Jews used as their new synagogue had a flat ceiling, but later the community paid 50 florins to add four glazed windows and a vaulted ceiling. The community ceased to exist in 1872 due to emigration and the move to the larger cities common at the time. The community had buried its dead in the Pretzfeld cemetery nearby (see under Pretzfeld in this guide).

Known as the Judenhof (or Jewish manor), the very picturesque complex has been restored and now houses a museum known as the Fränkische Schweiz Museum containing an assortment of farm implements, local cottage industry tools and products, furniture, and a bake house, as well as the simple 18th century synagogue. The women's annex contains a small exhibit on the Jewish religion consisting of photographs and a few 18th and 19th century ritual objects.

The museum is open Tuesday to Sunday from 10-5 during the summer (April to October) and Sunday from 1:30 to 3:30 during the winter. The museum has published a very interesting and precise guide to its Judaica collection and the history of the Tüchersfeld community (in German).

The former mikveh, by the river bank, was destroyed when the highway was enlarged.

ULM

is located about 100 km southeast of Stuttgart or 150 km west of München, on the Danube and between the A 8 and A 7 (map 10, 11).

* Memorials
* Cemeteries
* Exhibition about the history of Ulm Jews
* Oberer Kuhberg Fortress concentration camp memorial and documentation center

Documents about the payment of taxes provide the first evidence of a Jewish community in Ulm in the middle of the 13th century. There are also some gravestones dating from 1243 to 1491 in storage at the Münsterbauhütte (minster construction workshop). The community was valued by the municipal council because of its revenue contributions and the council unsuccessfully sought to protect it during the Black Death persecutions in 1349. The community was almost completely destroyed in this pogrom, but the few survivors were able to resettle soon afterwards and their synagogue, cemetery, and dance hall were returned to them by the council.

Although the community enjoyed some stability towards the end of the

Dedicated to commemorate the German Jews and the Holocaust: The Israel window over the entrance of the Ulm Minster.

14th century, the 15th century brought restrictions and heavy taxes and by the end of the century the community was expelled. A new community was only established in the 19th century (Albert Einstein, whose parents had moved to Ulm from Buchau, was born here in 1879), but declined rapidly in the 1930's as anti-Semitism increased. More than one hundred Ulm Jews died in German camps.

In 1877, when the minster celebrated its 500th anniversary, the Jewish community donated a statue of the prophet Jeremiah. After 1945, the Christian community donated a very large stained glass window memorial to the fate of German Jews over the entrance door of the minster, including a menorah and a star of David.

A copy of the 13th century Jewish gravestone which was used for the dedication relief of the minster in 1377 can be seen at the Bridal Door of the minster. The stone itself is now in the Ulm Museum at Marktplatz 6. Another such stone is part of the second floor outside wall of an old house nearby at Rabengasse 7.

There is a small commemorative plaque to the synagogue from 1873 which was destroyed in 1938 in an alley over a garage door behind the savings bank at Neue Strasse 66. On Weinhof there is a memorial to the "Reichskristallnacht" pogrom, the destruction of the synagogue and the sufferings of the Jews.

The cemetery from 1852 is now a park. There are only three 19th century stones remaining. It is located on Frauenstrasse opposite no. 93. The stones are standing at the far end near the church. There is a 1987 memorial to the destroyed cemetery.

A second cemetery, from 1897, is part of the city cemetery. It contains a memorial to the Jewish soldiers who died in WWI and many memorial stones to those who were killed during the Nazi years. This cemetery is located at Stuttgarterstrasse 164. Both cemeteries are open.

The Ulm archives show an exhibition on the history of the Jews in Ulm in its annex at Basteistrasse 46. The exhibition can be visited after contacting the city archives at 0731/161 4201 or 161 4262.

The Oberer Kuhberg fortress, which was a concentration camp from 1933-35, is a documentation center today. Guided tours may be arranged through the Ulmer Volkshochschule at Kornhausplatz 5, or through DGB Neu-Ulm at Paulstrasse 10, or through Ernst Rohleder, Sebastian-Fischer Weg 22. Mr. Rohleder was a prisoner at the camp.

UNNA

is located about 100 km northeast of Köln, between A 1 and A 44 and on highways 1 and 233 (map 3, 4, 5).

* Former synagogue from 1851
* Former Jewish old-age home from 1905
* Hellweg Museum has a small collection of Judaica
* Cemetery from 1854

249

Jews lived in Unna from 1304 until 1943. However, the community always remained small; in 1812, there were only 12 Jewish families in Unna. The former synagogue at Klosterstrasse 43 has undergone many changes since it was built as a Gothic monastery chapel in 1468. It was rebuilt after a fire in the 17th century and then used by the Catholic community from the days of the Reformation until 1848. It was converted to a synagogue in 1851 and used until it was devastated in the1938 "Reichskristallnacht". In 1957, it was rebuilt and is now a print shop. There is a commemorative plaque in the alley behind the building where an arched window remains.

On Mühlenstrasse the Jewish old-age home for Westphalia was built in 1905; today the building serves as a Catholic old-age home. There is a commemorative plaque to the home and its inhabitants who were killed in German camps.

The Hellweg Museum exhibits a small collection of Judaica, consisting mostly of ritual objects. The collection includes part of a Torah scroll, a purim rattle, seder plates, a kiddush cup, the lid of an etrog box showing a sukkoth scene, a misrach picture with human figures and a lion forming the letters of the word misrach (= east), and a shochet knife.

The museum is located at Burgstrasse 8 and is open Tuesday-Friday 10-12:30 and 3-5, Saturday 11-1, and Sunday 11-1 and 3-5.

The Jewish cemetery from 1854 is located on Massener Strasse/Beetho-venring. A memorial stone to the Jews of Unna was erected in 1985 outside the cemetery around the corner on Beethovenring, later two more memorials for the victims of the Nazis, both the Unna Jews and the inhabitants of the old-age home mentioned above, were added. The key is available from Mr. Meyer at Massener Strasse 57.

UNTER-ALTERTHEIM

is a small town about 125 km north-west of Nürnberg, or about 100 km southeast of Frankfurt, and 20 km southwest of Würzburg, between the A 3 and the A 81 (map 8, 9).

* Former synagogue from 1841

There is a synagogue from 1841 at Brunnenstrasse 13, a few feet from Ringstrasse, which is now being used as a storehouse for firewood. The interior was destroyed on "Reichs-

The former Unter-Altertheim synagogue is a woodshed today.

250

kristallnacht" in November 1938, but the exterior of the building remains almost unchanged, with its typical saddle roof and the arched windows.

After 1938, the building was taken over by the local council, then handed over to a cooperative, and finally sold to a farmer.

The building is slowly decaying, since hardly any repairs have been made. The current entrance door was constructed by the cooperative when it used the building as a storehouse for fertilizer. The small ramp is from the same period. The original main entrance was on the north side of the building. There is no commemorative plaque, but the building is often visited. The former ritual bath was filled in and destroyed.

URSPRINGEN

is located about 100 km southeast of Frankfurt and about 130 km northwest of Nürnberg, between the towns of Karlstadt and Markt-Heidenfeld (map 8, 9).

* Former synagogue from 1803

The former synagogue is located on Judengasse, a narrow cul-de-sac off Hauptstrasse. The building was devastated during "Reichskristallnacht" in November 1938. After that, it was used as a barn and a shed. The large door in the north wall is a consequence of this use.

The building has been restored in recent years and is a venue for cultur-

The former Urspringen synagogue has been used as a barn; the bronze door today shows the stations of suffering endured by the Urspringen Jews.

al events today. The barn door in the north wall was not bricked up again, but a bronze door was made to fit it; this door shows the itinerary of the 42 Jews from Urspringen who were deported to Belzec in 1942. There is a well-preserved chuppah stone in the east wall, and high arched windows in the south.

The former synagogue can be visited every Sunday between 3 and 5 from the beginning of May until the end of September. At other times a visit can be arranged by calling the local number 385.

VEITSHÖCHHEIM

is located on the Main river about 110 km southeast of Frankfurt, and about 120 km northwest of Nürnberg on highway 27 (map 8, 9).

* Synagogue from 1730
* Jewish Cultural Museum with exhibition of Jewish life in Veitshöchheim from the 16th to the 20th century
* Ritual bath from 1826

Jews settled in Veitshöchheim in 1644 for the first time. By the mid-19th century, there were about 160 Jews living in Veitshöchheim. In 1936, there were only thirty left. Between ten and twenty Jews from Veitshöchheim were killed in German camps.

The synagogue from 1730 was used as a synagogue until 1937 and sold to the city for the bargain price of 200 Reichsmark in early 1938; therefore, it was not damaged in the November 1938 "Reichskristallnacht" pogrom.

However, the wonderful Baroque interior and furnishings were destroyed when the floor of the prayer room was raised to street level. The building was used as a fire brigade depot and a storeroom.

During a recent renovation, parts of the broken remains of the stone Baroque furnishings, wall paintings and a genisah that had been used for almost 200 years were found.

The renovated building is being used as a synagogue again, but also serves as a part of the Veitshöchheim Jewish Cultural Museum. The mikveh in the north-eastern part of the building, next to the teacher's apartment, has been restored as well.

The prayer room, where the men of the community assembled, lies a few steps below street level again; this was either a way of achieving a high room when the height of the building itself was restricted by local regulations, or

The restored Veitshöchheim synagogue displays an unusual structure, with teacher apartment and mikveh incorporated to the north of the prayer room.

252

The Baroque Veitshöchheim bimah still shows traces of having been smashed and used to raise the floor level of the prayer room when it was being used as a fire brigade garage.

253

an architectural expression of the psalm "Out of the depths have I called unto thee, oh Lord". The tiny women's gallery can be reached through a side door to the left of the main entrance and over a staircase. The Baroque bima is octagonal and sits in the middle of the room, as can be expected in a conservative local community. The painted frame of the Torah shrine is also Baroque, the windows have stained glass, and a Mogen David adorns the window over the ark. The synagogue is located at Mühlgasse 6.

Today, the synagogue is part of the Jewish Cultural Museum of Veits-höchheim, consisting of the synagogue, the teacher's apartment and mikveh, and a formerly Jewish house next to the synagogue.

The complex houses an exhibition established in 1994, which includes the contents of the genisah found in the attic. The genisah contained books from the 16th to the 20th century, private letters and 40 mappahs. The mikveh from 1826 and a sukkah (in the attic of the synagogue) are also shown. The entrance to the museum is at Thüngersheimer Strasse 17. The museum is open Thursday from 3 to 6 and Sunday from 2 to 5.

The small ritual bath is located in the northeastern corner of the synagogue building.

VIERNHEIM

is located about 80 km south of Frankfurt, between the A 5, A 6, and A 659 (map 8, 10).

* Heimatmuseum has a collection of Judaica

Jews are first recorded in Viernheim in 1609, although it is thought that the community is much older. In 1927, there were 100 Jews living here out of a population of 10,800. Twenty-one Viernheim Jews were killed in the concentration camps.

There is a memorial to the synagogue from 1828, which was destroyed in the 1938 "Reichskristallnacht" pogrom, on the corner of Karl Marx Strasse and Hügelstrasse.

This memorial for the destroyed Jewish community of Volkmarsen and its cemetery was put together from fragments of old gravestones.

The Heimatmuseum (local museum) has a collection of ritual and household objects on exhibit as well as photographs and documents pertaining to the life and fate of the Jews from Viernheim. The collection includes prayer shawls, skull caps, candlesticks, spice boxes, books, chanukah lamps and seder plates. The museum is located at Berliner Ring 28 and is open on Sunday 2-5 (closed during school vacations.) Guided tours during the week can be arranged by telephoning 701 261 or 701 315.

VOLKMARSEN

is located about 40 km northwest of Kassel, off the A 44 on the Twiste river (map 4, 5, 6).

* Former synagogue from early 19th century
* Memorial for Jewish cemetery destroyed during the Third Reich

A very fine memorial to the Jews of Volkmarsen has been established in their former cemetery. During the Nazi years, the cemetery was razed and the stones broken up for use as roadbuilding material. After 1945, some remaining fragments were used to construct a stele, commemorating the Jewish victims of the Nazis. The surrounding low wall was also put together from broken gravestones. The fragments show parts of inscriptions in Hebrew as well as gravestone symbols of Cohen hands, decorative scrollwork, and some names and dates in a stone collage.

The early 19th century half-timbered synagogue building, typical for the rural synagogues of Hesse, has survived and is now a private home. It is located in the backyard of Baustrasse 11.

The building in front may have been the Jewish school once, but it has been changed a lot. If you walk around to Popenteich 13, you can see the half-timbered unrestored but altered former synagogue in the backyard.

WEIDEN

is located about 100 km northeast of Nürnberg, off A 93 and on highways 15, 22 and 470 (map 9).

* Synagogue
* Cemetery from 1900

The synagogue, at Ringstrasse 17, was devastated, but not burned down by the SA during the November 1938 "Reichskristallnacht" pogrom. In 1948, the building was handed over to survivors of the Flossenbürg camp then living in Weiden. Many members of this post-war community emigrated in the 1950's, but the community has since stabilized.

The cemetery, from 1900, is on Sperlingstrasse.

WEISENHEIM AM BERG

is located about 100 km southwest of Frankfurt off highway 271 (map 8, 10).

* Former synagogue from 1832

Jews have been living in Weisenheim since the 18th century. In 1788 a prayer room in a private house is mentioned. In 1832 the tiny community built a small synagogue in the Protestant Baroque style with some help from two neighbouring communities. Like most other rural communities, the Weisenheim community dwindled after the middle of the 19th century due to emigration and moving to larger cities with better opportunities; in 1909 the synagogue had to be sold to a cabinetmaker, who used the building as a barn. In 1983 the building was declared an architectural monument. In 1989 it was renovated and in 1990 it was opened as a cultural center. A local group of citizens was active both in the renovation process and in the programming of the cultural center.

The small building of the former synagogue stands in a cul-de-sac off mainstreet. The address is Hauptstrasse 28, and it is signposted. The Hebrew inscription over the entrance is preserved (This gate of the Lord,

One of the smallest former synagogues in Germany is located in Weisenheim; it serves as a cultural center today.

256

into which the righteous shall enter). There is an exhibition of some ritual objects found in the genisah in the women's gallery. The former synagogue can be visited by calling Ms. Müller (06353/2950) or Ms. Hauser (06353/8838) afternoons or evenings.

WENKHEIM

is located about 110 km southeast of Frankfurt, 130 km west of Nürnberg, between the A 3 and highway 27 (map 8, 9).

* Former synagogue from 1841
* Cemetery from 17th century

The synagogue complex, built in 1841 from local stone, not only housed the synagogue, but also a school, the mikveh and the teacher's apartment. It has a few neo-Baroque style elements,

but otherwise blends in with the other buildings from the period. It was devastated during the 1938 "Reichskristallnacht", then converted to apartments by the city council. The prayer room itself remained practically unchanged.

The building is located at the corner of Breite Strasse and Bachstrasse; it will be renovated and used as a memorial and cultural center. The Jewish cemetery of Wenkheim is from the 17th century.

WIESENFELD

is located about 100 km east of Frankfurt and 140 km northwest of Nürnberg, off highway 27 and northwest of Karlstadt (map 8, 9).

* Former synagogue from 1863

The former Wenkheim synagogue serves as a residence today.

* Former synagogue from 1836 in nearby Laudenbach

* Cemetery from 1665 in nearby Laudenbach

The former Wiesenfeld synagogue is a tall and self-confident building erected from reddish sandstone. It was devastated in the November 1938 "Reichskristallnacht" pogrom and served as a barn until 1994. From 1994 on it underwent renovation and will be a concert hall for the Wiesenfeld choir. At the time of this writing neither completion date nor possibilities for visiting the former synagogue are known.

The former synagogue building stands on the corner of Schätzleingasse, Erlenbacher Strasse and Schlossmannsgasse. In 1995 the niche for the ark, parts of the women's gallery and wall paintings were still visible. The gable in the east of the building shows the Hebrew letters for (5)622,

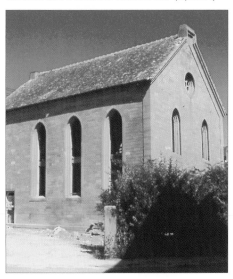

This tall, prominent former synagogue will become the Wiesenfeld concert hall.

which corresponds to 1862.

In nearby Laudenbach there is a former synagogue from 1836. This building is much smaller and does not stand out like the Wiesenfeld synagogue. It serves as a shed today and has been left to deteriorate, there are no plans for renovation. The building is located at the end of Bandwörthstrasse, close to Mühlbacher Strasse 19.

The Laudenbach cemetery is old, large and well-maintained. It is located in the forest above the village; it served many communities in the area. There is also a taharah house in the cemetery.

To get to the cemetery, turn right immediately after the church of Laudenbach (coming from Karlstadt) and follow the signs to Schützenhaus. Beware - after about 100m there is a very sharp curve to the right, and the sign is behind the curve. After reaching the Schützenhaus, continue on the road for a short distance, and the cemetery will appear at the right-hand side, behind a low stone wall. There are guided tours of the cemetery every second Sunday of the month between 1:30 and 3:30, and visits at other times can be arranged by calling 09353-8638.

WITTENBERG

is located 120 km southwest of Berlin, on the Elbe and on B187 (map 2, 7).

* Medieval "Judensau" (Jewish Sow), memorial

Wittenberg is known as the town where Martin Luther nailed his 95 theses to the church door in 1517, thereby expressing the desires for religious reform that he shared with many of his contemporaries. This reform movement within the Catholic church led to a schism and Protestantism developed. It also led to countless wars devastating and ripping apart the heart of Europe for centuries.

Wittenberg is also one of the very few towns in Germany to still possess one of the remaining monuments of medieval Jew baiting. On the southeast corner of the Stadtkirche, where Luther preached, you can still see the "Judensau" from 1305. During the Middle Ages, the display of the "Judensau" on the outside of churches and other public buildings was very common. The only purpose of these sculptures or paintings was the public humiliation of Jews and their religion. Most of these depictions have disappeared, but a few remain in Germany.

The Judensau served to demonstrate Christian contempt for the stubborn and inveterate Jews. Most often a sow is shown suckling Jews, sometimes a Jew rides the sow, talks into its ear or looks under its tail. It is generally known that the pig is considered unclean by the Jews; in the "Judensau" the sow represents the Torah, the holy book of the Jews and their spiritual nourishment.

The Wittenberg Judensau looks towards the east. A rabbi looks under the tail of the sow, other Jews drink

The "Judensau" (Jew's sow) on the facade of the Wittenberg city church has been witness to the irrational hatred of the church towards Jews for almost 700 years.

from its teats. The altogether senseless inscription "Rabini Shem-ha-mphoras" is partly a transmogrification of the Hebrew expression "shem ha-meforasch", the immeasurable name of god.

In 1988, the 50th anniversary of the "Reichskristallnacht", there was a lively debate about the fate of the Wittenberg Judensau. Finally it was decided not to remove the sculpture and hide it away in some museum depot, but to leave it in place, restore it and complete it with a memorial.

The memorial is located on the sidewalk at the foot of the church and also recognizes the centuries of church hostility against the Jews which to some degree contributed to the murder of six million Jews by the Nazis. The bronze plaque in the pavement shows a cross dividing a square area into four parts. These four squares are partly raised by fermenting, swelling matter below.

The German text around the cross reads:

> The proper name of god,
> the maligned Schem-ha-mphoras,
> which was held holy by the Jews
> long before the Christians
> died in six million Jews
> under the sign of a cross.

The Hebrew inscription is the beginning of the 130th psalm: Out of the depths have I cried unto thee, O Lord. The tension between the Wittenberg Judensau and the memorial for millions of dead and their faith at its feet encompasses much of the thousand years of German-Jewish history, much of the relations between German Christians and German Jews.

In 1988 the Wittenberg "Judensau" was not removed, but instead received a counterweight in this memorial reminding us that Jews were murdered in German camps "under the sign of a cross".

WITTLICH

is located about 130 km south of Köln or 170 km west of Frankfurt, on the A 48 and highways 49 and 50 (map 8).

* Former synagogue from 1910
* Cemetery from 1620

Jews settled in Wittlich after 1300, encouraged by Archbishop Balduin of Trier. The Black Death persecutions of 1349 seem to have spelled death for all members of this first Jewish community.

Wittlich was only resettled by larger numbers of Jews in the 17th century. From then on, Jews and Christians of Wittlich shared wars, poverty, and good times until the arrival of the 1930's.

The synagogue, from 1910, was devastated and damaged but not destroyed in the 1938 "Reichskristallnacht" pogrom because the mayor of Wittlich used police to stop the SA. It was used as a camp for French POW's and then stood empty for 30 years. In 1976, the building was restored and is now a cultural and conference center. The former synagogue was built in a very grand mixture of Art Nouveau and neo-Romanesque style and is quite large.

The interior is characterized by cupolas and arches under the women's gallery as well as by the typical Art Nouveau ornaments of the wall decoration. The former synagogue building serves as a cultural and exhibition center today. The former Torah ark is now outside the building, to the left of the main entrance.

The building is located at Himmeroder Strasse 44. The council of Wittlich has set up large signs "Synagoge" with arrows in several parts of the city to direct visitors.

During exhibitions, the former synagogue can be visited daily from 2-6. There is a memorial plaque for the victims of the persecutions by the Nazis outside.

A cemetery used by several Jewish communities in the area is located a short distance from Wittlich. The cemetery was started in 1620 and used until 1941.

The large and modern former Wittlich synagogue serves as a cultural center today.

261

WÖRLITZ

is located about 120 km southwest of Berlin, on the Elbe river and highway 107 (map 2, 7).

* Former synagogue from the end of the 18th century

The Classicist Wörlitz synagogue is unique in Germany in many ways. The princes of Anhalt-Dessau started building a summer palace in Wörlitz in 1765. The first German park in the English style was designed around this palace. The Wörlitz summer palace was the first Classicist building in Germany. The landscaped islands in the park were named for Rousseau, Herder and Stein, all proponents of the Enlightenment movement. The synagogue of Wörlitz was constructed as part of this overall architectural design. It was built by Friedrich Wilhelm von Erdmannsdorff, the architect of the prince, and paid for by the prince. This stone expression of the Enlightenment and its efforts in integrating the Jews still stands on the bank of the Wörlitz lake, just outside the town of Wörlitz.

Erdmannsdorff did not use a historical synagogue, like the Gothic Worms synagogue, in his design, but instead modelled the new synagogue on the temple of Vesta in Rome. The former synagogue is a circular building with a semicircular women's gallery supported by six Doric columns inside. High in the wall, below the conical roof, twelve round windows admit light to the interior. Below the syna-

The remarkable synagogue of Wörlitz, using pagan temples as its model, was a gift by an enlightened German prince to his Jews.

gogue is the ritual bath with a stove to warm up the "living water" it shares with the Wörlitz lake. The synagogue became known as the Jew's temple (Judentempel). Some maps of the Wörlitz park, however, show it as Vestatempel, or temple of Vesta.

Jews have been living in Wörlitz since 1680. Their first synagogue stood in the market square of the town and was torn down when the Wörlitz town hall was built. To replace this older synagogue, the prince had the synagogue by the lake built.

The new synagogue served the community until 1910, when the Wörlitz community became too small to maintain its synagogue. In 1921 it was sold to the Dessau community, which used it until 1937 and then had to close it down. It was not destroyed in the 1938 "Reichskristallnacht", although furnishings and books were.

In 1988, it was restored and opened again to show the overall policy of tolerance of the Anhalt-Dessau rulers of the late 18th century. It lies at the edge of park and city, at the end of Amtsgasse, and the remarkable view from the island opposite comprises church, park and synagogue.

A Jewish cemetery from 1795 had a taharah house also built by Erdmannsdorff. The cemetery and the taharah house were devastated in 1938, and gravestones were later removed and used as construction material. The cemetery is a garden today, and the taharah house became a residence after 1945.

The synagogue and the cemetery can be visited after applying to the palace administration.

Nearby Gräfenhainichen/Jüdenberg has a memorial from 1988 at the Bomsdorf farm to the pupils and teachers of a Jewish agricultural school who were murdered in German camps. The name Jüdenberg usually indicates the site of an old Jewish settlement or cemetery.

WORMS

is located on the Rhine about 70 km southwest of Frankfurt, off the A 61 and on highway 47 (map 8, 10).

* Restored synagogue complex including 12th century mikveh, museum
* Oldest Jewish cemetery in Europe with stone from 1076
* Two more cemeteries

Known as Little Jerusalem to Central European medieval Jews due to the good conditions it offered Jewish life and Jewish learning, Worms, along with its sister communities in Speyer and Mainz, played an important role as a seat for religious learning in the Middle Ages. Amongst its great teachers, known collectively as the Sages of Worms, were those who instructed Worms' most famous student, Solomon ben Isaac from Troyes, better known later as Rashi.

The community was rich and influential until camp followers of the First Crusade came to Worms in 1096; most Jews sought sanctuary in the bishop's castle, but were overwhelmed and killed by the crusaders or died by their own hands. About 800 Jews died in Worms then. A few members of the community saved their lives by accepting baptism, but returned to Judaism the following year.

During the Second Crusade, the Jewish community fled to fortresses in the area and survived. The protection of the Jews (and the special taxes paying for it) passed from the emperor first to the local ruler, the bishop of Worms, and later to the city council.

In 1349, during the Black Death persecutions, the Jewish community set fire to their houses and perished in the flames in order to avoid being massacred. In 1353, a new community was established. Except for two short interruptions, this community existed until 1942 when the last Jews were deported from Worms. 462 Worms Jews died in German camps; today, there is no Jewish community in Worms.

The first Worms synagogue was built in 1034. A stone tablet, with an inscription of that year as well as its founder's name, can be seen in an outer wall of the rebuilt synagogue next to the doorway. This old synagogue was severely damaged in both the First and Second Crusades, and a new synagogue was built at the end of the 12th century. The new synagogue was built to the east of the old structure, using the old east wall as its west wall. Thereafter, though often suffering partial destruction and frequently restored, the synagogue remained relatively unchanged in principle until its burning on "Reichs-kristallnacht", November 9-10, 1938.

The entrance to the rebuilt Worms synagogue. To the right the dedication inscription from the first Worms synagogue, from 1034, can be seen. The older synagogue lay to the west of the present structure

In the following years, the ruin was torn down. Until then, however, the Worms synagogue had been the oldest continuously used synagogue in the world.

Great care has been taken to rebuild this ancient place of prayer and worship to its former splendor, using, when possible, the stones of the original structure. Although Jews have not returned to Worms in sufficient numbers for a community to be re-established, Jewish members of the American armed forces in the area periodically hold service here, bringing with them their own rabbi.

The men's synagogue is a high vaulted room with two Romanesque columns forming the two-nave room with the bimah in the center. This

The "Men's school" of Worms, rebuilt after its destruction by Nazis and the bombs of WW II

arrangement became typical for Central European synagogues until the beginning of the 19th century. The entrance shows a richly sculpted Romanesque portal, with pillars, capitals and arches; the unfinished ornamentation is not due to restoration, but was left unfinished when the gate was originally built.

Adjoining the men's synagogue is the women's synagogue originally built in 1213 in a late Romanesque style and frequently destroyed, rebuilt, and restored thereafter. It was originally separated from the main building by a wall with five small windows allowing the women to follow the service being conducted next door. Much later the separating wall and windows were removed, leaving two open arches connecting the two rooms of worship. The women's synagogue is supported by a single column, thus being the earliest known example of a one-column structure in Germany.

In the garden behind the synagogue, a flight of stone steps leads down to the entrance of the 12th century Romanesque mikveh. Forty-one spiraling stone steps wind their way down past small dressing rooms, niches for lamps, and a balcony with Romanesque windows looking over the living waters below. This mikveh was in regular use until the 18th century. In the 19th century, however, the mikveh was abandoned and used as part of a sewer system. In 1895, it was cleaned and restored. The mikveh is still used occasionally by Jewish travelers wish-

The Gothic "Women's school" of Worms is the oldest structure resting on one central column known in Germany.

266

Romanesque windows look down at the basin of the Worms mikveh.

ing to perform this ancient purification rite where and as it was performed more than eight centuries ago.

The spirit of the Renaissance pervades the Rashi Yeshiva which lies beyond the west wall of the men's synagogue. The yeshiva, built in 1624, honors the great medieval rabbi who studied in Worms around 1060 and whose commentary of the Talmud is still printed and studied today. Although myth has Rashi teaching from the Rashi chair preserved in the yeshiva, Rashi was but 20 years of age and a student, not a teacher, when he studied in Worms and the chair, although old today, is 600 years younger than the great Rashi. It was saved, as were many other valuable objects and documents, through the efforts of Dr. Friedrich Illert, the head of the City Archives during the Nazi years.

While the Rashi Yeshiva is old, the great Rashi predates it by almost six hundred years.

A Jewish museum building now stands on the Roman and medieval foundations of what was once a yeshiva and later a dance and wedding house, a house built by the Jewish community for celebrations.

The museum contains a collection of secular and ritual objects and documents concerning Worms' thousand years of Jewish life. The exhibition includes a document signed by Charles IV giving the Jews to the council of Worms in 1348, facsimiles of the 15th century Darmstadt haggadah (see Darmstadt), the 15th century London haggadah, the 1272 Worms machsor, and numerous other items of historical interest.

The synagogue complex is located on Synagogenplatz just off Judengasse, a few meters from the Rashi Gate. The museum is open 10-12 and 2-5, Tuesday-Sunday.

The synagogue and mikveh can be visited daily, from May to October 10-12 and 2-5, from November to April 10-12 and 2-4.

The Worms cemetery is the oldest remaining Jewish cemetery in Europe. It served the community continuously for almost 900 years. The oldest existing stone is dated 1076. Almost all the old stones face south instead of the almost universal east.

Many notable Jews are buried here, including Rabbi Meir of Rothenburg, leader of a group of Jews planning to leave Germany for the Promised Land in the 13th century. To prevent the loss of Jewish revenues, the emperor held this great German rabbi hostage from 1286 until Rabbi Meir's death in 1293. Throughout his imprisonment, Rabbi Meir refused to allow ransom to be paid for his freedom and continued to teach through his writings. After his death, even his corpse was left unburied and held for ransom for 14 years until Alexander ben Salomon Wimpfen paid the ransom on the sole condition that he be buried next to Rabbi Meir's grave. Their gravestones, usually covered with pebbles and slips of paper left behind by visitors, can still be seen standing side by side.

The cemetery, unlike the synagogue complex, survived the Nazi regime through the efforts of a non-Jew, Dr. Illert mentioned above. Dr. Illert made a point of showing the cemetery to the SS leader Heinrich Himmler during an inspection visit and thereby gained Himmler's interest in the cemetery's historical value. From then on, Dr. Illert was able to ward off local Nazi attempts to destroy the cemetery by directing their attention to Himmler's interest in the site and suggesting that they better check with the awesome Herr Reichsführer SS and chief of the dreaded Gestapo in Berlin before proceeding. No one ever dared check and the cemetery survived almost without damage. The cemetery is located on Willy-Brandt-Ring near the Andreastor and can be visited daily between 8 and dusk. A very instructive brochure in English about the cemetery is available in the guardhouse.

Groups desiring a guided tour (in English) should make reservations a week in advance by contacting the

It is a miracle: This ancient Jewish cemetery close to the cathedral has weathered the storms of close to a thousand years almost unscathed.

The gravestones of Rabbi Meir of Rothenburg and Alexander ben Salomon Wimpfen, who paid the high ransom for the bones of his revered master, have been standing side by side for almost 700 years.

269

Stadtinformation, Neumarkt 14. The tour includes the synagogue complex as well as the 11th century cemetery.

There is a further cemetery from the 17th century in Herrnsheim, east of local highway (Landesstrasse) 425. A cemetery from 1911 is located next to the city cemetery at Hochheimer Höhe, and a Art Nouveau/Jugendstil taharah house still remains.

At the southern gate of the cathedral you can see a Synagogue Defeated from the 13th century. The statue shows a dejected woman with eyes blindfolded, a broken staff and a lamb, the burnt offering. During the Middle Ages such a statue vis-a-vis the Church Triumphant was very common.

WÜRZBURG

is located on the Main river about 110 km northwest of Nürnberg and about 120 km southeast of Frankfurt between the A 3 and A 7 and on highways 8, 13, 19, and 27 (map 8, 9).

* Mainfränkisches Museum has small collection of Judaica
* Jewish old age home is now a documentation center
* Cemeteries from 1811, 1820 and 1880

Jews are thought to have settled in Würzburg in the 11th century. The Jews suffered greatly during the Second Crusade (1147), the Rindfleisch persecutions (1298), the Armleder pogrom (1336) and the Black Death persecutions (1349). In 1565, the Jews were expelled; some moved to nearby Heidingsfeld, which has since become part of Würzburg, others moved to Veitshöchheim. Heidingsfeld thus became an important religious center and by the early 18th century was the seat of the chief rabbinate for Lower Franconia, for both the Unterländer and Hochstift Jews of the area.

It wasn't until the late 18th century that conditions stabilized sufficiently for the community to re-establish its religious institutions in Würzburg. By the 19th century, these institutions included a Jewish school, a teachers' seminary, yeshivah, and hospital. By the end of the 19th century, the Würzburg community was one of the most important in Bavaria. More than 2,000 Jews lived in Würzburg in 1933; about 1,000 were deported to the German camps in 1941/42, and very few survived.

The Mainfränkisches Museum in Würzburg displays a collection of Judaica. A collection formed in 1913, which included the interior of a Baroque synagogue from Kirchheim, was almost totally destroyed in a 1945 bombing raid. While greatly reduced, the collection still includes a few Torah shields, some displaying the imperial eagle, Torah pointers, besomim boxes, kiddush cups, a purim plate, sabbath lights, seder plates (one of which has a picture of a pessah meal under sabbath lamps), rimonim, etrog box, and chanukah candlesticks (one of which has two "hidden" stags). There is also a well-preserved gravestone from 1326 for the two daughters of a rabbi who died the same day as well as gravestone fragments from about 1350. There is an English guidebook available as well as guided tours through the museum. The museum is located in the Marienberg fortress overlooking Würzburg and is open April-October 10-5, November-March 10-4.

There is a commemorative plaque to the synagogue devastated in the 1938 "Reichskristallnacht" pogrom and destroyed by bombs in 1945 on Domerschulstrasse and a memorial to the Würzburg Jewish victims of the Nazi years in the new synagogue at Valentin-Becker-Strasse 11. On the outer wall of the synagogue law tablets from a destroyed synagogue, a chuppah stone from 1780 from Heidingsfeld and a stone ornament from the destroyed Domerschulstrasse synagogue are displayed.

The Jewish old age home, at the same address, was established in 1930. The Nazis used it as the collecting point for deportations of Würzburg Jews. It is now an old-age home again as well as a documentation center for the local Jewish communities. There is an exhibition of a small collection of Judaica including ritual objects, gravestones from the 12th and 13th centuries, objects found in genisoth and other objects witnessing Jewish life in Lower Franconia from the Middle Ages up to the present day. The center is open from Monday to Thursday 1-5 and Friday 8-12.

In 1864, the "Würzburg Raw" Seligmann Bär Bamberger founded a teachers' seminary at Bibrastrasse 6. The seminary moved to Sandbergstrasse 1 in 1929. Both buildings - one now a monastery, the other a school - still stand and have commemorative plaques.

The cemetery, from 1880, is located on Werner-von-Siemens Strasse. It includes a memorial to Jewish soldiers who died in WWI and a memorial to the Würzburg Jewish victims of the Nazi years around which is a half circle formed of individual memorial stones to some of the victims of concentration camps. There is also a taharah house and guardhouse and a resident caretaker. The cemetery is open and can be visited at the usual times.

The cemetery of the Heidingsfeld Jewish community, from 1810, is located on Hofmannstrasse in Heidingsfeld. The key is available from the house below the cemetery.

A cemetery from around 1820 still exists in Höchberg, just outside Würzburg. Rabbi Seligmann Bär Bamberger is buried here.

VOCABULARY

The following provides explanations of Hebrew or Yiddish words as well as translations for specific German terms used in museum exhibits. Since there are no precise rules for the transcription of Hebrew or Yiddish words, spelling varies in German as well as in English. If you can not find a term right away, please use your imagination and check other possible spellings.

ALMEMOR: (from the Arabic): Lectern where the Torah is read, also called bimah. See under synagogue.

ALMOSENBÜCHSE: German for alms box.

AMUD: Lectern of the cantor.

ARBA MINIM: A bundle of branches (one from a palm, three from myrtle and two from willow) used during the celebration of sukkoth.

ARK: Shrine for keeping the Torah scrolls, usually in a niche in the east wall of a synagogue. See under synagogue.

ARON or ARON HA-KODESH: Ark of the Law. See under ark.

ASHKENAZIM: Hebrew name for Jews whose ancestors originally lived in Germany, and who later moved to Poland, Russia or elsewhere in Central and Eastern Europe. The Biblical country Ashkenaz was idetified with Germany. See also Sephardim.

BAR MIZWA (= son of the commandment): The religious ceremony admitting a boy as an adult member of the religious community. It is usually held on the first Sabbath after the boy's 13th birthday. The boy is then called up to read from the Torah for the first time. From then on he is counted as an adult, responsible for his actions, and he is also included in a minyan, the ten men necessary for a Jewish service.

Since the 19th century, Reform communities have introduced the Bat Mizwa, a corresponding ceremony for girls.

BESAMIM BOX: See under besomim box.

BESCHNEIDUNG: German for circumcision.

BESCHNEIDUNGSBANK: German for circumcision bench. See under circumcision.

BESCHNEIDUNGSBESTECK or BESCHNEIDUNGSGERÄTE: German for circumcision instruments. See under circumcision.

BESOMIMBÜCHSE or BESOMIM-DOSE: German for besomim box.

BESOMIM BOX: An ornamented box containing fragrant spices, used in the home at the end of the sabbath in order to pass some of the "sweet smell of the Sabbath" on into the workweek. The box is often made from gold or silver filigree and may resemble a castle, a tower, a fish or poppyseed.

BIMAH: The platform and desk from which the Torah is read in the synagogue. See under synagogue.

BLOOD LIBEL: See under ritual murder.

B'RIT MILAH: See under circumcision.

CEMETERY: Also called House of Life or House of Eternity in Hebrew, Good Place in Yiddish, Friedhof in German. The cemetery is both an unclean and a venerable place for the Jews. Special cleansing rituals are prescribed after a visit to the cemetery, and Cohanim were not allowed to enter a cemetery at all (which is the reason why Cohen graves are often close to the entrance, so that the families could visit the grave without actually entering the cemetery). Cemeteries can not be visited on a Sabbath or Jewish holiday. On the other hand, the dead must not be disturbed and no grave must ever be used for another purpose, and visits to graves were quite frequent. When Jews were expelled from an area, the loss of the graves of their relatives was particularly painful for the exiles.

Often cemeteries were outside the village or town, if possible on a hill to the east. In most cases there was a wall around the cemetery. Often there would be a taharah house, where the bodies could be prepared for burial and where the mourners could assemble. Sometimes there would also be a guardhouse. In some areas, one cemetery served many communities in the neighborhood, and long distances had to be covered to attend funerals or visit graves.

All that grows in a cemetery is the property of the dead and may not be used for anything; also, flowers are for the living and not for the dead. Small stones are put on the grave or gravestone as a sign of respect. Often Orthodox cemeteries give the impression of being seemingly untended, since the grass is not being cut and the graves are not ornamented with flowers. In older German Jewish cemeteries, burials took place in order of death, with no consideration for family ties, but with special places for rabbis, Cohanim and other outstanding persons as well as for children, suicides and criminals; stones were of about equal size and there were no stone borders, as in death all are equal. Usually the stones face east or south and stand at the head of the grave; in some rare cases the inscription on the stone is in the rear, so anybody reading the inscription would be facing east also.

Horizontal grave plates indicate a Sephardic (Spanish or Portuguese) community; however, in some cemeteries formerly vertical stones have been laid flat in order to make them safer.

In the nineteenth century, under the influence of the Reform movement, family plots and grave borders emerged, the cemetery began to resemble a Christian cemetery, and the orientation of the graves was abandoned.

Some rural and Orthodox communities, however, maintained the old traditions well into the 20th century. Torah scrolls that have been desecrated, damaged or worn out by many years of use are buried like dead community members.

Gravestones have gone through many stylistic changes over the centuries.

Throughout the middle ages, German Ashkenazi gravestones consisted of a medium size upright slab made from locally available stone, undecorated, with the name, short characterization, and date of death carved in Hebrew. The top of the stone was either straight or, rarer, semicircular. (The unevenness of the writing on some old stones is due to the rules forbidding Jews from carving gravestones which were considered unclean. On the other hand, Christian stonemasons, hired for this service, were rarely familiar with Hebrew characters.)

Later, gravestones were decorated with ornamental scrolls or symbols indicating the tribal status of the person (hands raised in benediction for a Cohen, ewer and basin for a Levi), name (stag for Hirsch, lion for Löw or Leib, heart for Herz, ship for Schiff, star for Stern), house-mark (similar to symbols for the name), occupation (bread loaf for farmer, grapes for vintner, scissors for tailor), religious office (circumcision implements for the mohel, shofar for the cantor), reputation (the "crown of the good name"), or symbols of religion (law tabets, lions of Judah, paroketh, columns of the temple). In addition to these vertical stones, sarcophagus-type monuments appear for important persons. Sephardic gravestones are often horizontal grave plates with elaborate decorations and texts in Hebrew and Spanish or Portuguese.

In the 19th century, German writing appears, first in addition to the Hebrew, then almost exlusively except for the abbreviations mentioned below. Also, the two-part gravestone is introduced, a pedestal and a top stone, often made from polished granite or marble not available locally. Gravestones shaped like lecterns with stone books appear. The size of the gravestone became an indication of wealth and family plots were introduced, resulting in the construction of some mausoleum type structures.

Towards the end of the 19th century, most city cemeteries included a Jewish section whose stones resembled Christian gravestones of the same period. Most Jewish stones display a star of David and Hebrew letters at the beginning and at the end of the inscription which translate "Here lies" and "May their soul be part of eternal life", respectively.

There is a chapter "Hebrew Letters and Numbers" further on in this book which will help you to identify and read dates on gravestones.

Men are supposed to cover their heads when entering a cemetery.

CHAIRS OF ELIJAH: Circumcision bench, see under circumcision.

CHALLAH: A special leavened bread which is often braided and strewn with poppy seeds and served on the Sabbath.

CHALLADECKE: Challah cover, an embroidered cloth to cover the challah.

CHAMISHA ASAR B'SHEVAT: The New Year of the Trees, a spring celebration.

CHANUKAH: Eight-day festival of the lights, dedicated to the re-inauguration of the temple in Jerusalem after the Maccabees successfully defeated the Syrians in 165 B.C.E. The Syrians had desecrated the temple. When the Maccabees re-consecrated the temple, the holy oil to be used for the perpetual light was mostly desecrated also, and oil for only one day was left, while the ritual cleansing of oil for this purpose requires eight days. Miraculously, the one-day supply of holy oil lasted eight days. At chanukah, an eight-day feast in November or December, an additional light of the chanukah lamp is lit every evening until all eight lights burn on the last evening of chanukah.

CHANUKAH LAMP: A candlestick or oil lamp with eight lights (and often an additional ninth light, the servant or shamash) used at chanukah. It is most often shaped like a tree or like a bench.

CHANUKAHLAMPE or CHANUKAH-LEUCHTER: German for chanukah lamp.

CHANUKAH MENORAH: See under chanukah lamp.

CHANUKJAH: See under chanukah lamp.

CHASSIDIM: Literally, the Pious. Followers of a religious movement that started in Poland in the 18th century under the influence of the Kabbala and after the disappointments of Messianism. God is not looked for in studying the Torah, but in the power of prayer and in mystical introspection.

CHEVRA KADDISHA: An association to assist the dying and the family of the dead through visits, washing and dressing the body, digging the grave, etc. Participating in the Chevra Kaddisha is held to be especially charitable, since a motive of egoism can be suspected in any charitable act involving the living; the dead and the dying are not in a position to do something for their benefactor in the future.

CHUPPAH: Canopy held over the bride and bridegroom at their wedding in or in front of the synagogue.

CHUPPA-STEIN: German for chuppah stone.

CHUPPAH STONE: Stone with a star of David or similar ornament on the outside of some synagogues, near which weddings were celebrated. Often in the course of the wedding ceremony the bridegroom would dash a glass against this stone in memory of the sufferings of the Jews.

CIRCUMCISION: B'rit mila in Hebrew, traditionally the removal of the foreskin of male babies, usually on their eighth day, to claim them for the Jewish faith. Circumcision is performed by the mohel, often in the synagogue or in its lobby. The circumcision bench was used: The sandek, or godfather, sat in one seat, with the little boy on his lap, while the second seat was reserved for the prophet Elijah.

The circumcision instruments consist of the short, narrow, very sharp and rounded knife, the Y-shaped metal shield to protect the penis, a bowl for the foreskin, a bottle of styptic powder, and a bottle of ointment. These instruments are often depicted on the gravestone of the mohel.

The boy is also named after the ceremony.

When adults are admitted into the Jewish religion or when admission is repeated due to uncertainty of their religious status, circumcision can be replaced by a pricking of the foreskin with a needle.

CIRCUMCISION BENCH: See under circumcision.

CIRCUMCISION INSTRUMENTS: See under circumcision.

COHEN, pl. COHANIM: descendant(s) of Aaron and the priests of the Jewish people. Special privileges and regulations apply to the Cohanim: they play a prominent role in services, for instance, but are prohibited from marrying divorced women or entering cemeteries. Their gravestones often stand at the edge of cemeteries and show their priestly descent symbolized by two hands raised in blessing. The office of rabbi is not connected to the priestly status.

DAVIDSTERN: German for Star of David.

DREIDEL: Also Trendel, a four-sided top with the Hebrew letters nun, gimel, he, and shin which are abbreviations for "a great miracle happened there". It is used for a game played by children during chanukah.

EHEVERTRAG: German for wedding contract.

ELIASBECHER: German for cup of Elijah, see under pesach.

ERUW: The border of the "house", within which you were allowed to move around on the sabbath; the borders of a Jewish community. In some cities wires were stretched across streets to mark the borders; in the country features of the village or the landscape were used. Also called Sabbath Gate.

ETROGBÜCHSE or ETROGDOSE: See under etrog box.

ETROG BOX: The etrog box is often shaped like a fruit and contains the etrog, a citrus fruit used in the Sukkot festival.

EWIGE LAMPE or EWIGES LICHT: German for Ner Tamid, see under synagogue.

FRIEDHOF: German for cemetery.

GEBETSBUCH: German for prayer book.

GEBETSMANTEL or GEBETSSCHAL: German for prayer shawl, or tallit.

GEBETSRIEMEN: German for tefillin.

GEBETSSCHAL: German for prayer shawl.

GEMARAH: See under Talmud.

GENISAH: A place where worn-out or unusable ritual objects and books containing the name of God are kept until they are buried. In Germany, the attic of the synagogue was often used.

GRABSTEIN: German for gravestone.

HAGGADAH: A book, often beautifully illustrated, containing the liturgy for the Seder meal recited during Passover.

HANNUKA: See under chanuka.

HAVDALAH: Prayer recited at the end of Sabbath or other festival distinguishing between the sacred and the profane. Also a ritual at the end of the sabbath, involving special braided havdalah candles and besamim boxes.

HEIRATSVERTRAG: German for wedding contract.

HOCHZEIT: German for wedding.

HOCHZEITSBALDACHIN: German for chuppah.

HOCHZEITSRING: German for wedding ring.

HOCHZEITSSTEIN: German for chuppah stone.

HOCHZEITSURKUNDE or HOCHZEITSVERTRAG: German for ketubah, or wedding contract.

HOLOCAUST: From the Greek, all-consuming fire. Used for the destruction of large parts of the Jewish population of Europe during the reign of the Nazis.

HOST DESECRATION: An accusation repeatedly levelled against Jewish communities since the beginning of the 13th century. According to the Christian faith, the host, a small wafer, turns into the true flesh of Christ when consecrated by a priest. Jews were accused of having desecrated hosts bought or stolen from priests by piercing or burning them. Often such hosts were said to be indestructible and show blood drops. This accusation was repeatedly investigated by papal and imperial courts and declared unfounded.

INTEREST: The gain from a loan with a monetary value. The Torah expressly forbids interest; the medieval church prohibiton of interest refers back to this Jewish law. The gemarah, the law part of the talmud, also forbids interest on money, but allows interest on leased or rented property. The mishnah, however, indicates several evasions of the prohibition on interest. (Actually, when Islamic banks gained some prominence in the 20th century, they had to turn to similar methods of circumvention - interest is prohibited under Islamic law, also.)

Since canonic law made it impossible for Christians to engage in moneylending, this became one of the few possibilities of earning a living for the medieval Jews. Interest was extremely high during most of the Middle Ages, two or three pence interest in the pound per week was not unusual, corresponding to 43,3 and 65 % per year (one pound had 240 pence). Duke Frederick the Quarrelsome even introduced maximum interest of eight pence in the pound per week, or 173 % per year! However, the risk of lending was very high, too. Later interest rates declined.

JARMULKE: Skull cap, see under kippah.

JUDE: German for Jew.

JUDENBAD: German for mikveh.

JUDENSTERN: A yellow badge resembling the Star of David with the inscription "Jude". Jews in Germany and occupied areas were forced to wear this emblem on their outer clothing between 1941 and 1945.

KABBALA: Secret teachings searching to harmonize the infinity of god and the finiteness of creation. According to the kabbala it is impossible to learn anything about god except indirectly, by studying and interpreting his emanations. The kabbala also assumes that any message contains many secret messages which are only unveiled to the initiated; every question, for instance, contains its answer which can be arrived at by re-evaluating and rearranging the elements of the question following certain rules. Needless to say, the fact that letters and numbers are identical in Hebrew added endless possibilities to kabbalistic research.

KAPPORETH: Paroketh, the curtain in front of the ark; see under synagogue.

KETER TORAH: Torah crown, see under Torah.

KETUBAH: A marriage contract which was often handwritten and richly ornamented.

KIDDUSH: The consecration of the Sabbath or other holiday recited over wine by the head of the household.

KIDDUSHBECHER: German for kiddush cup.

KIDDUSH CUP: Cup of wine drunk during prayers consecrating the Sabbath meal or other festival.

KIPPAH: Small flat skull cap worn by religious Jewish men. During all religious acts the head of a man must be covered.

KOSHER: Clean according to Jewish ritual law. The term refers to food,

drink, objects of everyday use, places and humans. The opposite is called trefe - ritually unclean. What follows is just a small and simplified example of a few rules that govern ritual purity:

The meat of animals that chew their cud and part the hoof is kosher if the animal has been slaughtered properly (by a shochet, according to the rules). Most birds are kosher, and so are fish with fins and scales. If, during the preparation of food, milk or its products and meat or its products have come into contact, the food is unclean; this happens even if dishes or pots have been in contact with both milk and meat. Leavened bread is unclean at Passover. Dishes bought from a non-Jew are unclean. A person who came into contact with a corpse, or who has been to a cemetery or a taharah house is unclean. Menstruating women and women after childbirth are unclean. Cemeteries and the houses where a death has occurred are unclean.

In most cases ritual purity can be achieved again by washing and the appropriate prayer. See also under mikveh.

KRISTALLNACHT: see Reichskristallnacht.

LAUBHÜTTE: German for sukkah, a booth.

LAUBHÜTTENFEST: German for the Sukkoth festival.

LEVITES: Descendants of the tribe of Levi, guardians of the temple service in Jerusalem, assistants to the Cohanim. The gravestones show the pitcher and bowl used for washing the priest's hands before service.

LULAV: A sheaf of palm which is part of the Arba Minim together with three twigs of myrtle and two of willow; see under Sukkoth.

MACHSOR: A prayer book containing prayers for festivals and holy days.

MAGEN DAVID: See under Star of David.

MAPPAH: A piece of cloth used for tying a Torah scroll. In Germany, mappahs were often made from the swaddling worn by a baby boy at his circumcision. These were later embroidered and/or painted and then donated to the synagogue on his first birthday. For his bar mitzvah, the boy would read from the Torah that had been tied with the mappah made from his swaddling. See under Torah.

MARANNEN: German for

MARANOS: Spanish and Portuguese Jews who as a matter of form, or necessity, converted to Christianity.

MATZE or MATZES: German/Yiddish for mazza/mazzoth.

MATZENTASCHE: German for mazzoth bag. A cloth bag for mazzoth which was often embroidered.

MAZZOTH: Bread made from un-leavened dough for Pesach (Passover) to commemorate that the Jews left Egypt in such a hurry that they couldn't take leavening with them.

MEGILAT/MEGILLAH SCROLL: Most often refers to the scroll containing the book of Esther which is read on Purim, but the term also includes the scrolls of Ecclesiastes, Songs of Solomon, Ruth, and Lamentations. The Esther scroll has only one staff, not two like the Torah scroll, and is often beautifully illustrated; this is deemed permissible since the name of god does not appear in it.

ME'IL: Torah mantle, see under Torah.

MENORAH: Seven-branched candle-stick used only in the temple in Jerusalem or in non-Orthodox synagogues; from antiquity frequently used as a symbol of the Jewish religion.

MEZUSAH: A small parchment or paper with texts from the fifth book of Moses (6:4-9, 11:13-21) contained in a small capsule made of glass, wood, tin or silver which is fastened to the right-hand doorpost. The word "shaddai" (almighty) can be read through a little window.

MIDRASH or MISRACH: East; a sign indicating the east wall of a dwelling.

MIKVEH: Ritual bath for purification purposes. A bath serving the ritual purification of humans and objects. For instance, Jewish women have to purify themselves after their menstruation, after childbirth and before the wedding, converts to Judaism are immersed, and cooking utensils bought from non-Jews are also ritually cleaned in the mikveh. The main rule for the ritual bath is that "living" water has to be used, meaning that the water must flow by natural means, not being brought by vessels or pipes (at least not more than a certain proportion). When the use of creeks or rivers became unpractical due to harassment or the severity of the climate, shafts were often dug below the ground water level, which often involved considerable effort. The Köln and Frankfurt areas have the oldest and most beautiful remaining mikvoth in Germany. See entries for Andernach, Friedberg, Köln, Offenburg, Speyer, and Worms.

MINYAN: The ten Jewish men necessary for service.

MISHNA: See under talmud.

MISRACH: See under midrash.

MOHEL: A specially trained Jew who performs circumcisions.

NER TAMID: The perpetual light burning in front of the ark, see under synagogue.

OMED: Also amud, the lectern for the cantor in the synagogue.

PARNAS: The elected president (head) of the Jewish community.

PAROKETH: The curtain in front of the ark, see under synagogue.

PASSOVER: See under pesach.

PESACH: Literally, the passing over of the Jewish houses when all the first-born in Egypt were killed; the Jewish festival of freedom, commemorating the flight from Egypt.

Seder is the first evening of the pesach. The seder meal involves many preparations, among other things a complete cleansing of the house to clean it of all traces of leavening or leavened bread. (Since pesach occurs in spring, often around the date of Easter, some people think that the traditional spring cleaning of German houses is an imitation of this old Jewish rite.) Then the seder evening follows with a special ritual in the home. On a special plate symbolic food is placed, including three mazzoth (for the Kohanim, Leviim and Israelim, and to remember that the Jews left Egypt in such a hurry that they could not take any leavening with them), a lamb bone and an egg (for the pessach offering in the temple), a bitter herb (for the bitter years of slavery in Egypt), a mixture made from grated fruit, nuts and wine (for the mortar the Jews had to prepare for the Egyptians), and sweet herbs (for the new life of spring). Dishes of salt water (for the tears shed by the Jews in exile) and glasses of wine for the four blessings are placed before each guest at the table, with an additional cup of wine for the prophet Elijah. The host wears a white vest and a white kippah, symbolizing his willingness to be called up to start another migration after the meal. The meal also serves for the religious instruction of the children; the pesach haggadah is read at the seder table.

POGROM: Russian for devastation. The organized attack of the minority by the majority, often used for attacks on Jewish communities.

PRAYER SHAWL: A rectangular piece of cloth, mostly white with dark stripes along the sides and threads (zizith) at the end. Worn by men over the head or over the neck during prayer.

PURIM: The Jewish festival of deliverance, commemorating how Esther, wife of the Persian king Ahasverus (or Xerxes), saved the Jews from destruction. Haman, a minister at the Persian court, plotted to have all Jews killed because the judge Mordecai, the brother of Esther, would not bow to him. Esther exposed Haman's plans to Ahasverus who had Haman and his sons hanged. Purim, in February, is a festival with Carnival-like traits; the book of Esther is read, and in some parts of Germany the children had the task of being noisy with their purim rattles whenever the name of Haman occurred.

PURIM PLATE: A bowl or plate containing little gifts for the poor or for visiting children at purim.

PURIMRASSEL: German for a rattle used to drown out the name of Haman when the Book of Esther is read at purim.

PURIMTELLER: German for purim plate.

RABBI (= my master): Today the rabbi is the specially trained and ordained religious leader of a synagogue community. In earlier times, a Jew well versed in the Torah and the Talmud who was elected to be the judge (both in religious and secular matters) of a Jewish community.

REICHSKRISTALLNACHT: A popular expression of obscure origin mocking official Nazi pomposity, literally meaning the Reich's night of broken glass. A name used for the pogrom of November 9-10, 1938.

Hershel Grynszpan, son of Polish Jews expelled from Germany a few weeks previously, shot the German diplomat vom Rath in Paris on November 7. Vom Rath died on November 9, and the Nazis used his death as a pretext for a well-orchestrated "spontaneous protest" against Jews, their synagogues and their property. No exact figures were compiled, but the German security service (SD) claimed that 91 Jews were killed, many more wounded, about 30,000 Jews were arrested and taken to concentration camps, about 200 synagogues were set on fire, a hundred more devastated, and many Jewish shops or dwellings were destroyed or devastated.

Grynszpan was arrested by the French police, later fell into the hands of the Gestapo, but was never brought to trial.

RIMONIM (literally: pomegranates, plural of rimon): Ornament for the Torah, usually consisting of a pair of silver or gold tops, often with little bells, for the two wooden sticks that the Torah scroll is wound on.

RITUALMORD: German for ritual murder.

RITUAL MURDER: An accusation levelled against Jewish communities ever since the beginning of the 13th century. According to it, Jews are supposed to use the blood of Christian children or adults to make mazzoth or for other ritual purposes. This accusation has repeatedly been investigated by papal and imperial courts and found unfounded, even absurd. However, the last ritual murder trial in

Central Europe took place in Western Prussia in 1900.

ROSH HASHANAH: Days of judgement, the first two days of the new year and the beginning of the High Holy Days, or Days of Awe. During these days, Jews render their accounts to god, who decides their fates for the coming year. Debts are settled and enemies are reconciled. During service, the shofar, an instrument made from a ram's horn, is blown. Rosh Hashana in most years will be in September.

SABBATH: The seventh day of the week is set aside for rest and study of the Torah. The sabbath starts at sundown on Friday and ends at sundown on Saturday. It includes visits to the synagogue and festive family meals. On sabbath eve, after the men have returned from the synagogue, the sabbath dinner is eaten accompanied by challah, braided white bread with poppyseed. On Saturday morning the synagogue is visited again; service is festive, and the Torah is read. At the end of the sabbath two braided havdalah candles are lit and the besomim box filled with spices is taken around the room so a little bit of the fragrance of the sabbath can be transferred to the coming workweek.

Since all work (with very few and very narrow exceptions, e. g. to avert danger to somebody's life) is forbidden on the sabbath, the practicalities of the day became a rich source for Jewish customs. It was necessary to put Saturday lunch in the oven already on Friday, since cooking or even lighting a fire is forbidden on the sabbath.

Typical Jewish dishes like sholet or kugel, well suited to being kept warm for almost a day, originated this way.

Since carrying things was also work and forbidden, handkerchiefs were sewn to the sleeve, thus becoming part of the clothes and not being carried any more. Since it was also forbidden to leave the house, the borders of the house had to be stretched a little; sabbath gates (eruw) came into existence in many places.

Especially in the country the shabbes goi, a Christian neighbor willing to do the work that simply had to be done, was the norm. However, the neighbor had to know very well what had to be done, since asking for work to be done was equivalent to doing work and was also forbidden accordingly.

SABBATH LAMP: Oil lamp with eight flames, often in the shape of a star, suspended from the ceiling by a chain and lit for sabbath meals.

SABBATLAMPE: German for sabbath lamp.

SANDEK: The godfather who holds the baby boy during circumcision.

SCHABBES: Yiddish for sabbath

SCHÄCHTER: German for shochet, or ritual butcher.

SCHÄCHTMESSER: German for shochet knife.

SCHAMMES: Yiddish, see under shamash.

SCHOFAR: German for shofar.

SEDER: Ritual order of prayers during

282

pesach. For all combinations, see under pesach.

SEDERSCHÜSSEL or SEDERTELLER: German for seder plate. See under pesach.

SEFER: Book, another word for the Torah

SEFER TORAH: Scroll containing the five Books of Moses, written by hand by the sofer following very strict rules.

SEPHARDIM: Jews whose ancestors lived in Spain or Portugal; Jews of the Balkans, Northern Africa or the Near East. The Spanish and Portuguese Jews were forced to convert or expelled at the end of the 15th century. Many went to the Turkish realm or to Italy. The Sephardic Jews of Germany arrived there by fleeing persecution in Spain by first going to the Netherlands, where they enjoyed religious freedom and reverted to Judaism, and then moving on to Northern Germany. The common language of the Sephardim, Ladino, is an old Spanish dialect and, like Yiddish, has survived until today.

SHAMASH (= servant): The sexton who looks after the synagogue and assists the cantor. Also the ninth light of the chanukah lamp used to light the other lights.

SHAVUOTH: The festival of the Torah commemorating the day when the law tablets were given to Moses.

SHOCHET: According to ritual law, animals must be killed with a single cut across the throat with a straight, unblemished knife to make meat kosher and suitable for consumption by Jews. The consumption of blood in any form is prohibited by the Jewish religious laws. If the decisive cutting of the throat is flawed, the meat is ritually unclean and can not be sold to Jews.

The shochet, or ritually trained butcher, is highly respected in the community and often holds additional community offices.

SHOCHET KNIFE: A long, straight, very sharp knife for ritually correct slaughtering of animals.

SHOFAR: Ram's horn, blown as part of the ritual at certain feasts, especially Yom Kippur.

SIDDUR: Book of everyday prayer

SIMCHATH TORAH (= rejoicing in the Torah): The festival two days after the end of sukkoth when the reading of the Torah in the synagogue is completed and started again from the beginning. On that evening, the Torah scrolls are danced around the synagogue; on the next morning, every community member is called to read from the Torah. Simchath Torah takes place in September or early October.

SOFER: Specially trained scribe, one who writes Torah scrolls, Esther scrolls, haggadoth or marriage contracts.

STAR OF DAVID: An ancient symbol of Judaism, consisting of two equilateral triangles combining to form a hexagonal star.

SUKKAH: A temporary hut adorned with green branches and seasonal fruit with an open roof where families had their meals during the festival of Sukkoth.

SUKKOTH: A seven-day celebration of the harvest in memory of the exodus from Egypt when Jews wandered the earth living in booths, two weeks after Rosh Hashanah (the New Year), usually in late September or October. During this time, the family has its meals in the sukkah. Blessings are said over the arba minim, branches of palm, willow and myrtle, as well as the etrog, a citrus fruit. In some areas, the sukkah was erected in the attic of Jewish houses; there would have been a large flap in the roof that could be opened in order to allow the sukkah to stand under the open sky.

SYNAGOGUE: The Greek word synagogue (meaning assembly) first occurs in our area around the year 1,000, but the function of the synagogue as a place of Jewish worship and learning is much older. Synagogues already existed while the temple in Jerusalem still was the center of Jewish religious life; from 70 on, when the temple was destroyed and exile began, the synagogue emerges as the center of community life. However, the synagogue never becomes a surrogate temple, neither architecturally nor functionally - it would actually be easier to draw parallels between most Christian churches and the Jerusalem temple. For a long time, the synagogue was not a sacred room. No priest is needed for service. Wherever ten Jewish men assemble they can hold service.

The Hebrew name for the synagogue is Beth ha-Kenesseth (house of assembly) in Latin it is called Schola, the Yiddish name is Shul.

In Germany, synagogues are usually oriented, in most cases towards the east, sometimes towards the south or south-east, in the general direction of Jerusalem. The prayer room is rectangular in most cases, sometimes square. During the middle ages synagogues had one or two naves, never three like churches. Only in the 19th century did three-naved synagogues emerge in emulation of Protestant churches.

Usually the medieval synagogue would have stood in the center of the Jewish quarter, a stately, self-confident building, larger and taller than the houses surrounding it. The rule was that the synagogue should not be surpassed in height by any of the buildings in the community; wherever that was not possible for whatever reason, the synagogue was made higher by adding a pole to the roof.

Later the synagogue was forced into the backyard. The street front was occupied by the school or the living quarters of the cantor and/or teacher, or by a private house. With few exceptions that was the state of things until the middle of the 19th century. Then the synagogue regains the street front, and its size, position and architecture express the stronger economical and civic position of the Jews in Germany.

How does the interior of a synagogue look? In older synagogues, the floor of the prayer room is often below street level, and a few steps lead down to it. That may be because restrictions imposed by the local construction regulations which would not allow the building to be high enough to allow for an interior of appropriate height; religious reasons may also have played a role, with the architecture mirroring the prayer "Out of the depths have I called unto thee, oh Lord". The Aron ha-Kodesh is placed in the east wall. This shrine, often placed in a niche or apse and ornamented, houses the Torah scrolls of the synagogue behind an embroidered curtain, the parokhet. In front of the ark the ner tamid, the eternal light, is burning, indicating a synagogue still in use by a Jewish community.

During the Middle Ages the bimah or almemor, the lectern from which the Torah is read, was in the center of the room. In conservative communities, especially in rural settlements, the bimah retains that position until today. The community members used to face the bima, not the east wall, sometimes they will also have their backs to the bimah in order to better utilize whatever space and light there is. Towards the end of the 18th century the bimah moves in front of the ark, and the community members face the east wall; the synagogue starts to resemble a church, with bimah and ark instead of the altar.

In Sephardic synagogues the bimah is situated at the west wall of the synagogue, leaving the center of the room empty; we know of no surviving example of this arrangement in Germany.

The lectern of the cantor is often situated next to the ark, sometimes the floor is lowered where the cantor stands as a sign of humility.

Apparently men and women used the prayer room during classical antiquity; However, in the oldest remaining German synagogues the separation of the sexes is already complete, and only men enter the prayer room. Later a space for the women is added which is connected to the main room by a few narrow slots in the wall so the women can follow services. The office of female cantor is known to have existed at that time. Even later women's galleries are added to synagogues that have enough height, or a part of the room is divided off by wooden lattices. Only in the Reform synagogues of the 19th century will men and women share the same prayer room again.

The Jewish religion expressly forbids pictures of humans (or, according to some commentaries, all depictions of natural or supernatural objects). For a long time there are no wallpaintings and no sculptures in German synagogues except for geometric patterns or written religious texts. During the Baroque period some synagogues in southern Germany are painted with biblical motifs by Polish-Jewish painters. Only one of these synagogues remains in Germany, in the Schwäbisch-Hall museum. The private synagogue of the Landauer family in Ellingen, however, has ceiling paintings of Abraham and Isaac that would do honor to many Baroque churches. As a rule, figural ornaments disappear again during the 19th century. The exceptions are the recurring religious motifs most often seen around the ark: The lions of Judah, the crown of the Torah, the star of David and the Menorah (mostly in reform synagogues).

The architectural style of the synagogues follows the prevailing style of the period, often with considerable delay - apparently Jewish communities were especially conservative in their architectural expression. Therefore, you will find Romanesque, Gothic, Baroque, Rococo and Classicist synagogues in Germany. It is not until the 19th century, which was unable to develop its own style and had to imitate the styles of previous periods, that Jewish communities try to develop a Jewish architectural style. From 1830 on neo-Romanesque and a few neo-Gothic synagogues are built; neo-Gothic, however, is soon deemed suitable for churches only. The sparse Protestant Baroque is also imitated for synagogues. A few pseudo-Egyptian synagogues are built, but the style was not successful due to its historical background - the years in Egypt were a time of slavery and hardship for the Jews. The Moorish or neo-Oriental style emerged as the favored architectural style for synagogues. It is well accepted by the Jewish communities as the Jews of Spain and Northern Africa lived in a climate of freedom and tolerance, and Jewish religious and scientific life flourished under Moorish rule. Also, the style allows for non-figural splendor.

After WWI no favourite architectural style for synagogues emerged.

Many German synagogues were badly damaged or destroyed during "Reichskristallnacht", November 9/10, 1938.

Men must cover their heads before entering a synagogue.

TAHARAH HOUSE: A special house where the dead are prepared for burial, and where the community can assemble for burials. Since corpses are considered unclean, the taharah house is either located in the cemetery or, if it is in the settlement, stands apart from other buildings.

TALLIT: See under prayer shawl.

TALMUD (= learning): Two collections of laws, interpretation of laws, and rabbinical discussions about questions of Jewish life after the destruction of its religious and political center.

The Palestinian talmud was codified in the years after the destruction of the second temple by the Romans, it consists of the mishna (repetiton, learning) and the gemerah (interpretation). Mishnah is written in Hebrew, gemarah is written in Aramaic, and both frequently use words from other languages, e.g. Persian or Babylonian.

The Babylonian talmud came into existence in exile, in the rich and important communities living between the Euphrates and the Tigris river, and mostly deals with the discussion and interpretation of the mishnah for the purposes of the exile.

The Sephardic Jews adopted the Babylonian talmud, while the Ashkenazim at first went by the Palestinian talmud; later the Babylonian talmud was accepted by almost all European Jews. This was to be very important during late antiquity and the Middle Ages: since the same laws were accepted by all Jewish communities in the Mediterranean and European regions, trade between them was facilitated.

The German translation of the Babylonian talmud comprises about 10,000 pages. Until printing with moveable letters was developed, the talmud was probably one of the most numerous manuscripts, since every Jewish community had to own at least one. For the pious Jew, the study of the talmud is a life-long task. The most important commentary on the talmud was written by Rashi (Rabbi Salomon ben Isaak) and is about 900 years old (see under Worms).

TASS: Torah shield, see under Torah scroll.

TEFILLIN: The small square wooden capsules containing thin strips of parchment with inscriptions from the Torah fastened to long leather straps. These are tied around the left arm and the forehead during weekday prayers by Jewish men.

TORAH: The law. The teaching. The five books of Moses. The Pentateuch.

TORAH CROWN: Part of the vestment of the Torah scroll. The crown, often made from gold or silver, covers both protruding ends of the staffs.

TORAH MANTLE: Part of the vestment of the Torah scroll. It covers the scroll and is often richly embroidered.

TORAH POINTER: A small staff, often made from silver or ivory, that ends in a hand with an extended index finger. The pointer is used in following the text of the Torah reading since the Torah should not be touched with the bare hand. When not in use, it is hung by a small chain from one of the staffs of the scroll.

TORAH SCROLL: The Torah is written by hand, by a specially trained man called the sofer, on parchment sewn together to form a scroll. The Torah scroll is then wound around one wooden staff and the other end of the scroll is fastened to a second staff. The Torah scroll is then tied with the mappah and dressed with the me'il or Torah mantle. The tass or Torah shield is hung in front and the yad or Torah pointer is hung from one staff. Finally, the kether Torah (Torah crown) or the rimonim cover the protruding upper ends of the two staffs. When the Torah is read, the scroll may not be touched by the bare hand, so the Torah pointer or yad is used to follow the text. The scroll is kept in the ark in a close to vertical position. When a Torah scroll is damaged, desecrated, or too worn out to be read, it is buried in the Jewish cemetery and a stone is placed on its grave.

TORAH SHIELD: Part of the vestment of the Torah scroll. It hangs from a chain, over the mantle, suspended from the two staffs of the scroll. It is often made from gold or silver, and is richly ornamented. The usual ornaments are the crown of the Torah, the lions of Judah, the two columns of the temple, the law tablets, the menorah, the shewbread table, the ark, or stags symbolizing the Jewish people being hounded by the Gentiles. An exchangeable tablet shows the name of the day.

TORAHHELM: German for rimon(im).

TORAHKRONE: German for Torah crown.

TORAHMANTEL: German for Torah mantle.

TORAHROLLE: German for Torah scroll.

TORAHSCHILD: German for Torah shield.

TORAHSCHREIN: German for ark.

TORAHVORHANG: German for parokhet.

TORAHWIMPEL: German for mappah.

TORAHZEIGER: German for Torah pointer, or yad.

TRAURING: German for wedding ring.

TRAUSTEIN: German for chuppah stone.

TREFE: Ritually unclean. See also kosher.

TRENDEL: German-Jewish for dreidel.

WEDDING CONTRACT: See under ketubah.

YAD: See under Torah pointer.

YESHIVAH: Academy for the study of the Torah and talmud.

YOM KIPPUR: The Day of Atonement, the last of the ten High Holy Days that the Jewish year starts with and the great fast day of the year. On this day, the judgement of god will be received by the heart. Fasting sets the frame of mind.

288

HEBREW LETTERS AND NUMBERS

Reading the Date on a Jewish Gravestone

All European alphabets as well as all Indian and Arabic alphabets are derived from an early form of the Hebrew alphabet. This was formed more than 3500 years ago, probably under Egyptian influence, and later taken over and adapted by the Greeks, who passed it on to the Romans and later to the Slavs to form the Latin and Cyrillic alphabets, respectively.

The shape of letters has changed considerably in these newer alphabets, additional letters were introduced and texts were written from left to right, not from right to left as in Hebrew, but the general order of letters has remained more or less the same. Even the word alphabet is indirectly derived from the names of the first two letters of the Hebrew alphabet, Aleph and Beth, which were slightly altered to Alpha and Beta in Greek.

Hebrew was (and still is) written from right to left. Originally, it had 22 consonants, but no vowels. Much later, vowels were indicated by a system of dots or lines below or above the preceding consonant. The lack of vowels and the frequent use of words from other languages makes reading texts written in Hebrew very hard, and in many cases the meaning of a text is open to speculation.

Below is a list of Hebrew letters, their names and their approximate transcription. Please remember that this is a current form of the alphabet and that age, local usage or ornamentation may make a text hard to transcribe.

aleph	א	Not spoken	
beth	ב	b	
vet	ב	v	(modern)
gimel	ג	g	
daleth	ד	d	
he	ה	h	
vav	ו	v	
zayin	ז	s	
cheth	ח	ch	
teth	ט	t	
yod	י	i	
kaph	ך כ	k	
lamed	ל	l	
mem	ם מ	m	
nun	ן נ	n	
samekh	ס	ss	
ayin	ע	not spoken	
peh	ף פ	p	
sadhe	ץ צ	z	
koph	ק	k	
resh	ר	r	
shin	שׁ	sh	
sin	שׂ	ss	(modern)
tav	ת	t	

(When we show two Hebrew letters, the second form (the one to the left) is used when the letter occurs at the end of a word.)

Hebrew originally had no special symbols for numbers; instead, letters were used. When letters are used for numbers, numbers are also written from right to left.

Since this way of writing numbers was developed before the Indians invented the zero, there is no symbol for zero.

The 22 letters of the Hebrew alphabet correspond to our numbers 1-9, 10-90 and 100-400. 500-900 are written in combinations of hundreds. Thousands are either omitted (especially in dates), or the letters for 1-9 are used with a qualifier, often two dots before or above the letter.

To make things a little more complicated, 15 and 16 are not written in the obvious way, i.e. 10 + 5 (jh) and 10 + 6 (jv), since that might be interpreted as an abbreviation of the name of god . Instead, 9 + 6 (tv) and 9 + 7 (tz) are used.

Often, but not always, the use of a letter as a number is indicated by a dot or dash over the letter. Thus, when you see an inscription on a gravestone and notice dots or dashes over one character, or a group of two characters with the first (from the right) character a yod or a mem, the day of the month is given and the year soon follows (to the left, remember!). Groups of three or more, especially if the character at the right is a tav, are probably the year. Below is a list of numbers we hope will be helpful for deciphering dates on gravestones.

The Jewish calendar starts about 3760 years before the Christian calendar. A rather complicated calculation is necessary to arrive at the exact corresponding Christian date from a Jewish date, or vice versa. For our purposes, a simple subtraction or addition should do, even if it may be one year off.

To arrive at the Christian calendar year, subtract 3760 from the Jewish calendar year; to arrive at the Jewish calendar year, add 3760 to the Christian calendar year. If the thousands have been omitted in the Jewish date, add 1240 to the Jewish calendar year.

For those who do not like calculating, here is a table of years in steps of ten. Please keep in mind that the figure for the thousand will have been omitted in most cases. For instance, a year 592 might be inscribed in a gravestone; this means 5592 and corresponds to 1832 C.E.

1 א	11 אי	10 י	100 ק
2 ב	12 בי	20 כ	200 ר
3 ג	13 גי	30 ל	300 ש
4 ד	14 די	40 מ	400 ת
5 ה	15 טו	50 נ	
6 ו	16 טז	60 ס	
7 ז	17 יז	70 ע	
8 אח	18 יח	80 פ	
9 ט	19 יט	90 צ	
10 י			

4860	1100	4960	1200	5060	1300
4870	1110	4970	1210	5070	1310
4880	1120	4980	1220	5080	1320
4890	1130	4990	1230	5090	1330
4900	1140	5000	1240	5100	1340
4910	1150	5010	1250	5110	1350
4920	1160	5020	1260	5120	1360
4930	1170	5030	1270	5130	1370
4940	1180	5040	1280	5140	1380
4950	1190	5050	1290	5150	1390
5160	1400	5260	1500	5360	1600
5170	1410	5270	1510	5370	1610
5180	1420	5280	1520	5380	1620
5190	1430	5290	1530	5390	1630
5200	1440	5300	1540	5400	1640

5210	1450	5310	1550	5410	1650
5220	1460	5320	1560	5420	1660
5230	1470	5330	1570	5430	1670
5240	1480	5340	1580	5440	1680
5250	1490	5350	1590	5450	1690

5460	1700	5560	1800	5660	1900
5470	1710	5570	1810	5670	1910
5480	1720	5580	1820	5680	1920
5490	1730	5590	1830	5690	1930
5500	1740	5600	1840	5700	1940
5510	1750	5610	1850	5710	1950
5520	1760	5620	1860	5720	1960
5530	1770	5630	1870	5730	1970
5540	1780	5640	1880	5740	1980
5550	1790	5650	1890	5750	1990

For readers who do not get confused easily, a few words about the Jewish calendar:

As mentioned above, the actual year may be one (Christian) year earlier or one (Jewish) year later than the date calculated by our simplified method or the date in the table, depending on the month and day of the event. The reason for this is that the Jewish New Year occurs in fall, in September or early October; therefore, the first three months of the Jewish year, Tishri, Marheshvan and Kislev, will certainly be in the preceding common year, while common dates from the second half of October, November and December will certainly be in the following Jewish year. Dates in Tebeth, the fourth month, or in September or early October are uncertain and depend on the year.

The flexibility of the Jewish year has its source in the combination of a lunar and a solar year, which has to be very variable in length (between 353 and 385 days), while the Common year is rather fixed at either 365 or 366 days.

MAPS

Map 1	Hamburg Region
Map 2	Berlin Region
Map 3	Hannover Region
Map 4	Köln Region
Map 5	Kassel Region
Map 6	Erfurt Region
Map 7	Dresden Region
Map 8	Frankfurt Region
Map 9	Nürnberg Region
Map 10	Stuttgart Region
Map 11	München Region

Some Remarks on our Maps

The following maps are meant to give an approximate overview over the relative position of the sites mentioned in our guide. They are definitely not meant to be a replacement for a very good map of Germany that will be necessary to find many of the smaller sites in our guide.

In order to improve orientation, only the main cities, the sites mentioned in our guide and sketchy motorways are drawn in our maps. The maps do not reproduce distances with any measure of exactness; however, the approximate scale is 1 : 1.500,000, or 1 cm for 15 km or 1 inch for 25 miles.

Distances mentioned in the guide represent the shortest distances by road, distances by motorway will be longer in most cases.

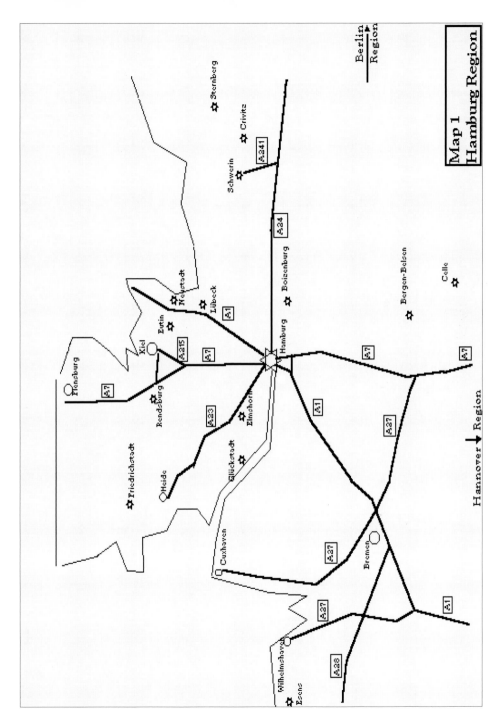

Map 1
Hamburg Region

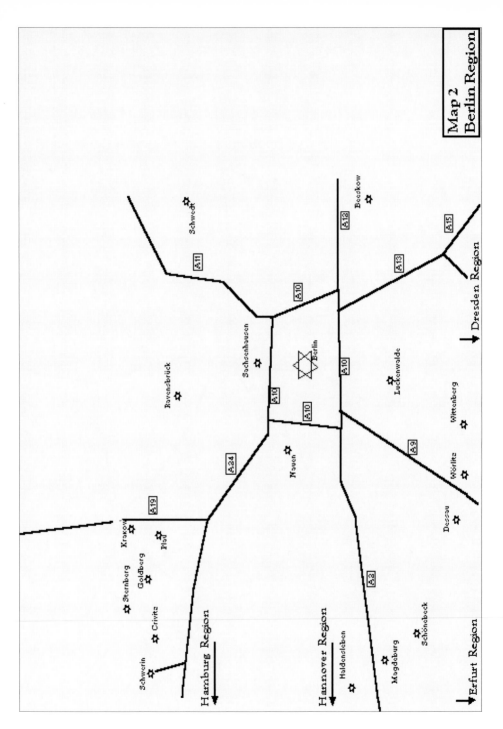

Map 2
Berlin Region

294

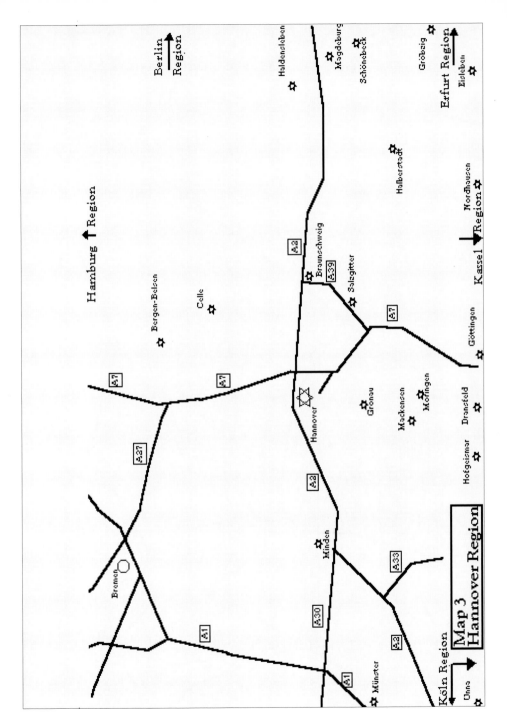

295

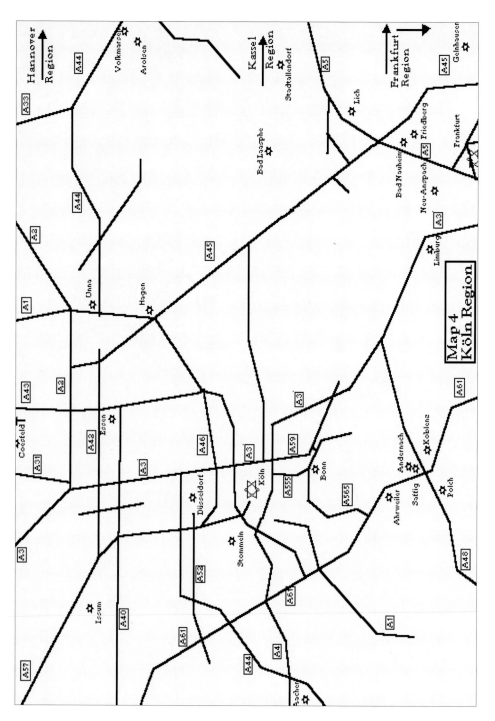

Map 4
Köln Region

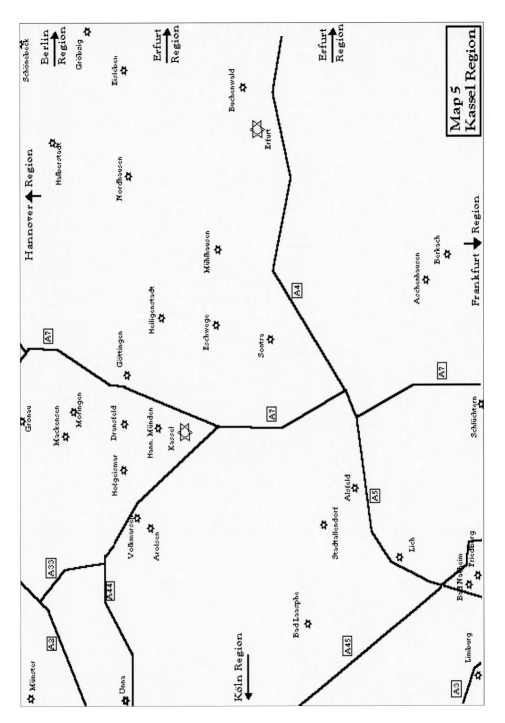

Map 5
Kassel Region

297

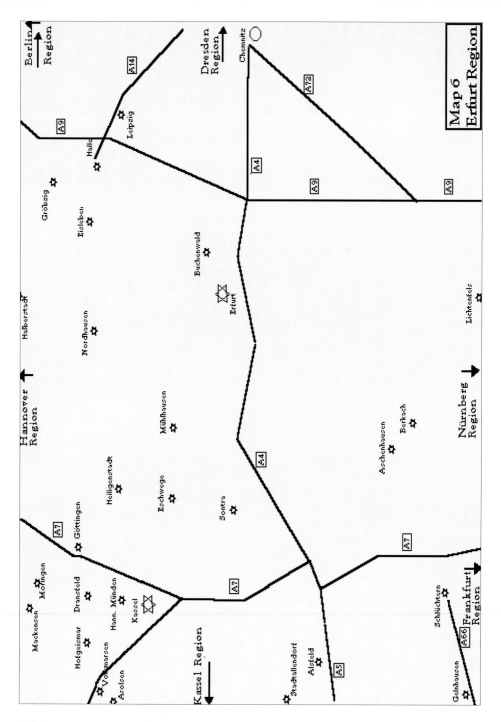

Map 6
Erfurt Region

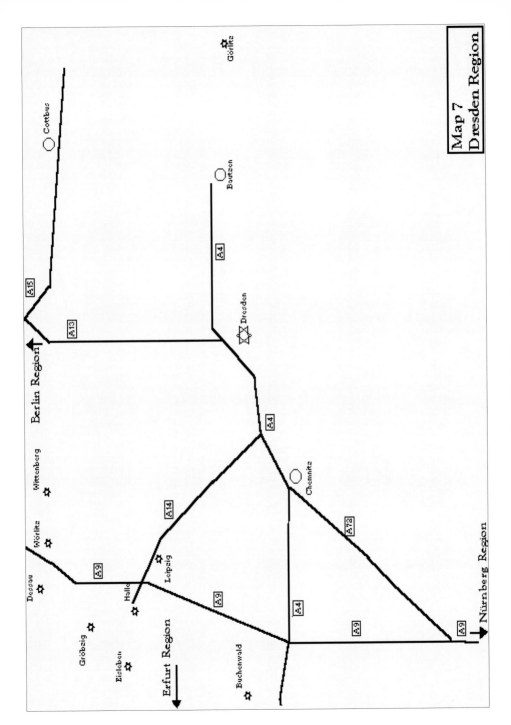

Map 7
Dresden Region

299

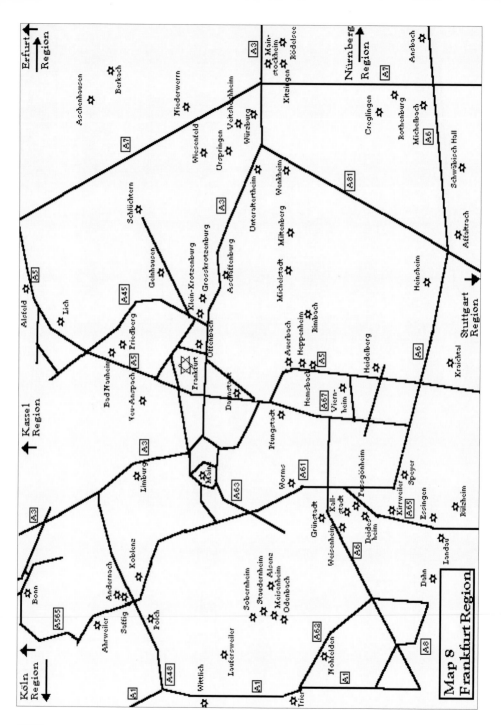

Map 8
Frankfurt Region

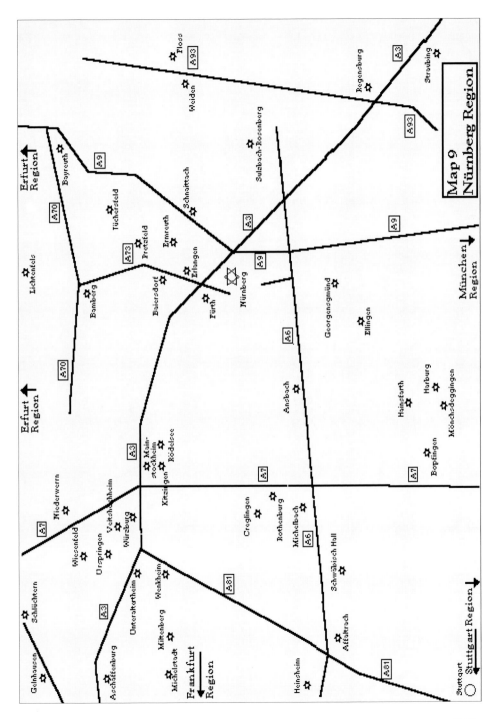

Map 9
Nürnberg Region

Floss

A93

Regensburg

A3

Straubing

Weiden

Erfurt Region

Bayreuth

A9

Sulzbach-Rosenberg

A93

A70

Tüchersfeld

Schnaittach

A9

Lichtenfels

A73

Pretzfeld

Ernreuth

A3

München Region

Bamberg

Baiersdorf

Erlangen

A9

Erfurt Region

Fürth

Nürnberg

Georgensgmünd

A70

Ellingen

A6

Harburg

Hainsfarth

Ansbach

Mönchsdeggingen

Main-stockheim

Bödelsee

Wiederwern

A3

Kitzingen

A7

Bopfingen

A7

Wiesenfeld

Volkabhach

Creglingen

Rothenburg

Michelbach

A6

Schwäbisch Hall

Schlüchtern

Urspringen

Würzburg

Wenkheim

A81

Gelnhausen

A3

Unteraltertheim

Mittenberg

Affaltrach

Aschaffenburg

Michelstadt

Heinsheim

Frankfurt Region

Stuttgart

Stuttgart Region

301

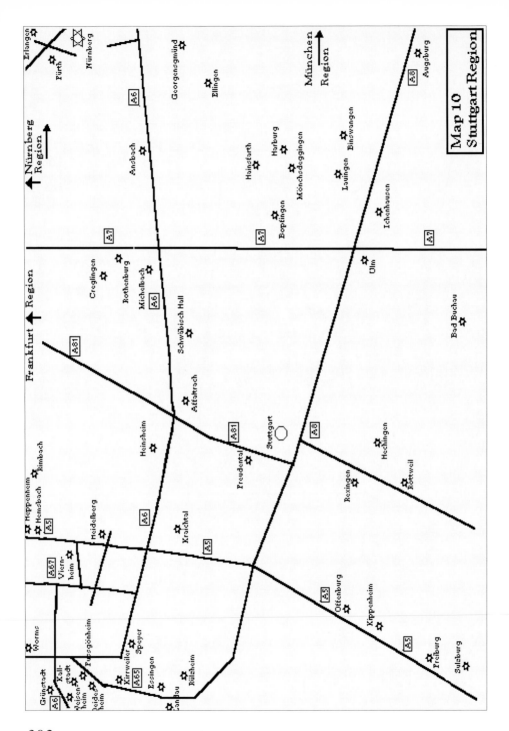

Map 10
Stuttgart Region

302

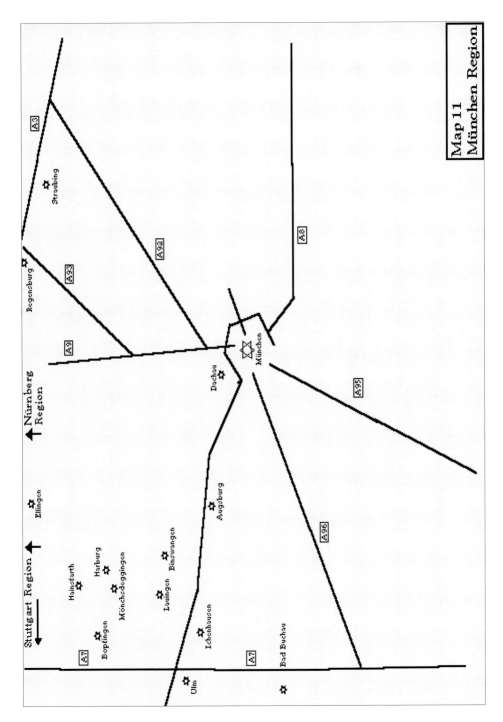

INDEX

310

Photo Credits:
Page 245: Rheinisches Landesmuseum, Trier

All other photos: The authors